# Professional Ethics

# putyourknowledgeintopractice

- Written specifically for students on the Bar Professional Training Course

- Expert author teams include barristers and BPTC tutors

- Clear, authoritative guides to legal practice and procedure

**Advocacy**
**Company Law in Practice**
**Conference Skills**
**Criminal Litigation and Sentencing**
**Drafting**
**Employment Law in Practice**
**Evidence**
**Family Law in Practice**
**Opinion Writing and Case Preparation**
**Professional Ethics**
**Remedies**

 **Online Resource Centre**

www.oxfordtextbooks.co.uk/orc/barmanuals/

The Bar Manuals are also supported by an Online Resource Centre with further materials and updates to selected manuals.

The Bar Manuals are published by Oxford University Press in conjunction with The City Law School

**The City Law School**
CITY UNIVERSITY LONDON

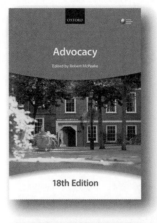

Advocacy
Edited by Robert McPeake
18th Edition

Conference Skills
Edited by Marcus Soanes
18th Edition

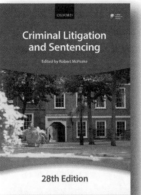

Criminal Litigation and Sentencing
Edited by Robert McPeake
28th Edition

Drafting
Edited by David Emmet
18th Edition

Evidence
Edited by Romilly Edge and Alexander Mills
18th Edition

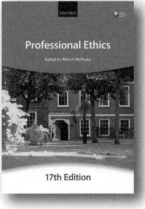

Professional Ethics
Edited by Robert McPeake
17th Edition

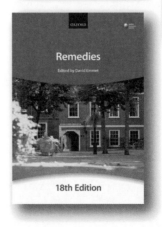

Remedies
Edited by David Emmet
18th Edition

# Professional Ethics

**Authors**

Nigel Duncan, Professor of Legal Education, The City Law School
Oliver Hanmer, Director of Supervision, Bar Standards Board
Robert McPeake, Barrister, Principal Lecturer, The City Law School

**Editor**

Robert McPeake, Barrister, Principal Lecturer, The City Law School

**Series Editor**

Julie Browne, Barrister, Senior Lecturer, The City Law School

# OXFORD

UNIVERSITY PRESS

Great Clarendon Street, Oxford, OX2 6DP,
United Kingdom

Oxford University Press is a department of the University of Oxford.
It furthers the University's objective of excellence in research, scholarship,
and education by publishing worldwide. Oxford is a registered trade mark of
Oxford University Press in the UK and in certain other countries

Fourteenth edition 2009
Fifteenth edition 2010
Sixteenth edition 2014

Impression: 1

Published in the United States of America by Oxford University Press
198 Madison Avenue, New York, NY 10016, United States of America

British Library Cataloguing in Publication Data

Data available

ISBN 978–0–19–876597–4

Printed in Great Britain by
Bell & Bain Ltd., Glasgow

# FOREWORD

These manuals have been written by a combination of practitioners and members of staff of the City Law School (formerly the Inns of Court School of Law), and are designed primarily to support training on the Bar Professional Training Course (BPTC), wherever it is taught. They provide an extremely useful resource to assist in acquiring the skills and knowledge that practising barristers need. They are updated regularly and are supported by an Online Resource Centre, which can be used by readers to keep up to date throughout the academic year.

This series of manuals exemplifies the practical and professional approach that is central to the BPTC. I congratulate the authors on the excellent standard of the manuals and I am grateful to Oxford University Press for their ongoing and enthusiastic support.

*Peter Hungerford-Welch*
*Professor of Legal Education*
*The City Law School*
*City University London*
*2016*

# PREFACE

Since 2010, students joining the Bar Professional Training Course have sat a separate assessment in Professional Ethics. The Bar Standards Board was concerned that this topic should play a more prominent role in the training of barristers and the use of a separate assessment reflects that. The Professional Ethics module will prepare you for your career with the rigour that is required in an age of high public scrutiny and expectation.

The barristers' Code of Conduct, while it remains the primary reference point, is no longer sufficient to indicate the far-reaching ethical considerations that should inform a barrister's working life. Ethics denotes a much wider scope for the values that underpin the profession. The Code itself underwent a drastic rewriting as it entered its ninth edition, coming into effect in January 2014. The Code is an integral part of a new Handbook, the entirety of which needs to be considered and absorbed by barristers. There are now outcomes, rules, and guidance set down throughout the Handbook, not simply in the Code of Conduct itself.

This is a time of great change for the Bar and for the way it is regulated. The Legal Services Act 2007 has led to new ways of working for solicitors and barristers with the introduction of multidisciplinary teams known as Legal Disciplinary Practices (LDPs). Barristers will be regulated under the terms of the new Handbook but may also find themselves in situations where they also need to comply with other professional codes, most obviously that issued by the Solicitors Regulation Authority. The increasing public prominence of both the Bar Council and the Bar Standards Board, through their websites and other publications, indicates a concern to demonstrate transparency and public accountability in a profession that has often been criticised in the past. Many of those criticisms are unjustified. But if the Bar is to be proof against all challenges, the highest ethical standards are required. A proper approach to ethics in a specialist area can only arise through thorough knowledge and an understanding of the relevant sources.

The aim of this manual is to give you the necessary grounding. By studying the manual and by putting to use what you have read in the exercises and discussions that take place throughout the BPTC, you should be in a position to make an informed decision on any ethical problem that arises in the course of your practice. There will always be areas of uncertainty, though. If ethics were easy, the world would be a different place. But with thoughtful application of what you learn, you will be in a position to choose the best of a number of possible options and be able to justify your choice.

As a barrister you will have weighty responsibilities. You have a duty to the court and a duty to your client. You also have a duty to the public at large to help maintain confidence in the legal profession. Problems most commonly arise when these duties appear to conflict. Decisions on professional ethics can be difficult. They will be even more difficult when you are dealing with real clients. So make the most of this year of preparation. Maintaining professional ethics and working to professional standards are central to everything you will do in practice.

*Robert McPeake*
*Barrister,*
*Principal Lecturer,*
*The City Law School,*
*City University London*

# ACKNOWLEDGEMENTS

Grateful acknowledgement is made to the publishers of copyright material which appears in this book, namely the Bar Standards Board, <http://www.barstandardsboard.org.uk>, for kind permission to reproduce sections from *The Bar Standards Board Handbook* second edition (as at September 2015), including Sections A, B, C, and D of the Code of Conduct of the Bar for England and Wales (ninth edition), Scope of Practice, Bar Training Rules, and the CPD rules; and the Bar Standard Board Code Guidance, available at <https://www.barstandardsboard.org.uk/regulatory-requirements/bsb-handbook/code-guidance/.>.

# GUIDE TO USING THIS BOOK

The Bar Manuals series includes a range of tools and features to aid your learning. This guide will outline the approach to using this book, and help you to make the most out of each of the features within.

## Practical based approach

The authors have taken a practical based approach to Professional Ethics at the Bar. This manual uses realistic examples of ethical dilemmas that may confront a barrister.

## The code and beyond

The manual looks beyond the Code to consider related issues such as the scope of practice in a more liberal legal profession. There is also coverage of the requirements placed on barristers under the Proceeds of Crime Act 2002.

## Core texts

The barristers' Code of Conduct, and other essential content from the BSB Handbook, are included in an Appendix to this manual. Where content in the Handbook has not yet been approved by the Legal Services Board, it is scored through to indicate this status.

## Online Resource Centre updates

The barristers' Code of Conduct and supplementary guidance can change rapidly. For information on these guidance documents and other materials relating to manuals in this series please visit the Online Resource Centre at <http://www.oxfordtextbooks.co.uk/orc/barmanuals/>, or refer directly to the Bar Standards Board website at <http://www.barstandards.board.org.uk>.

# OUTLINE CONTENTS

# DETAILED CONTENTS

# Introduction

## 1.1  A time of change

In a previous edition of this manual, we wrote that

> you are hoping to join this profession at a time of change. The courts, for example, are no longer the exclusive adversarial platforms of barristers, but are now open to solicitor advocates, in-house solicitors, and the employed Bar. In the course of your career you may find yourself working closely with non-lawyers in a 'Legal Disciplinary Practice', a new form of business structure permitted by the Legal Services Act 2007. You may act as a mediator or arbitrator, in addition to your court practice. Furthermore, the nature of your work is likely to change rapidly, with an increasing emphasis on the interpretation of regulations and the defining of quality standards. In these changing times, there is nothing more important to practise at the Bar than maintaining the highest standards with respect to the way in which barristers conduct themselves, and the regard in which they are held by their peers, judges they appear before, their instructing solicitor, and members of the public with whom they come into contact during their professional lives.

Those words still hold good today, some six years later. Of course, in addition to being well-thought of by others, the barrister should demonstrate that he or she holds those others in high regard as well. It has also become clearer that we should add *colleagues* to the list of others to whom we should pay regard, as more barristers enter the world of work in legal disciplinary practices ('LDPs'). It is possible that a barrister will be working as a manager in an LDP, perhaps with other barristers and solicitors around but also perhaps managing, or being managed by, someone who is not qualified as a lawyer—for example, an accountant. We should also reflect on the fact that there will not always be an instructing solicitor, someone to support the barrister and provide such a valuable link with, and sometimes a buffer against, the lay client. These days, many barristers are engaging in direct or public access work, where there is no instructing solicitor to act as an intermediary. These relationships raise many new challenges, to which the barrister needs to be alert.

These changing times are also reflected in other ways, sometimes rather contentiously. The Bar Standards Board ('BSB') has moved, in partnership with the Solicitors Regulation Authority and the Institute of Legal Executives, to establish the Quality Assurance Scheme for Advocates or 'QASA'. This is intended to create a benchmarking scheme to ensure that advocates, from whatever branch of the legal services sector, have attained a specific level of competence for the work they are undertaking. It is being rolled out initially for those in criminal practice. It is fair to say that opinion has been divided amongst the legal professionals affected, and that there has been opposition and even legal challenge in the courts (see *R (on the application of Lumsdon and others) v Legal Services Board* [2015] UKSC 41). At the same time, members of the profession have taken the unprecedented step of refusing 'returned' work and not attending court, in protest about cuts to public funding. Scenes of barristers standing outside Crown Courts, bewigged and somewhat embarrassed, have appeared on national news channels.

So, the profession is not able to stand still. The environment in which we work is changing, quite fundamentally, in many ways. Public scrutiny and our accountability are increasingly significant. Barristers certainly need to find their 'sea legs', potentially working with other professionals and finding that they are expected to adhere to other sets of ethical behaviours, sometimes as well as or instead of their own code. The need for new entrants to the profession to begin their careers with a solid ethical foundation is probably more important now than ever before.

## 1.2   A new Code of Conduct

In 2013, the BSB introduced the ninth edition of the Code of Conduct. The most recently amended edition came into effect in September 2015. This ninth edition is radically different from earlier iterations of the Code; according to the then-Chair of the BSB, Baroness Deech,

> superfluous rules have been stripped away and others modernised. The Handbook's approach is less prescriptive, with more focus and guidance on what the outcome of a rule should be, rather than attempting to define how a barrister should act in every situation.

The BSB wanted to move from the previous rule-focused scheme to a more contemporary outcomes-focused one. The approach taken for supervision is 'risk-based', according to Baroness Deech. This is intended to assist in preventing misconduct in the first place, and to avoid any recurrence of less serious non-compliance. At the same time, it is intended to ensure that action to enforce the Code is 'reserved for the most serious cases of non-compliance'—specifically those cases where there are 'considerable consequences for the client and the public interest'.

The new Code is part of a new BSB Handbook. The overall structure of the Handbook is to split the content into six parts. Part 1 introduces the new Handbook, whilst Part 2 is the Code of Conduct. Part 3 addresses the scope of practice and the role and functions of the BSB in terms of authorising and licensing entities to provide legal services. Part 4 sets out the Qualification Rules, Part 5 is the Enforcement Regulations, and Part 6 gives the definitions. The Handbook is available as a PDF from the BSB website and can also be downloaded in a searchable format to smart phones and tablets, from <http://handbook.barstandardsboard.org.uk>. The Code of Conduct and other relevant extracts from the BSB Handbook are set out as an Appendix in this manual, as it stood on 2 September 2015.You may see that some of the content of the Handbook is 'scored through'. The explanation for this is that this content deals with alternative business structures and at the time of the Handbook's publication it had not been approved by the Legal Services Board (the 'super regulator' which oversees the BSB and the Solicitors Regulation Authority).

The Code of Conduct contains five components—the Core Duties (see **1.3**), outcomes, rules, guidance, and regulations. According to the BSB, the core duties apply to all barristers, and sometimes to others; compliance with these duties is mandatory. The outcomes are descriptive and supply the thinking behind the rules, why a rule is necessary. They should assist with understanding the rules and the guidance. Compliance with the outcomes is not mandatory but, when a breach of the rules is being considered, the relevant outcomes will be taken into account. Rules are there to supplement the core duties, where it is felt that specific rules are required. The Introduction to the Handbook makes it clear that the Conduct Rules (those relating to the Code of Conduct in Part 2) are not intended to be exhaustive, so that in any specific situation where no Conduct Rule applies, one should still refer to the Core Duties. Even where there is a specific Conduct Rule that applies, compliance with that may not be sufficient—as the Introduction states 'compliance with the Rules alone will not necessarily be sufficient to comply with the Core Duties' (I6.3.a). Guidance, as its title implies, is there to assist in interpreting the rules, not least through giving examples of the behaviour that is expected (but is not mandatory). However, the guidance in the Handbook is not exhaustive; other documents are published from time to time which supplement the Handbook. Regulations provide the enforcement framework where professional misconduct is alleged or suspected; they are found in Part 5 of the Handbook. See further I6 in the Handbook.

The Code (and Handbook) uses a particular tripartite reference system for its content. For example:

> **rC4**   Your duty to act in the best interests of each client is subject to your duty to the court.

The first indicator shows the nature of the statement. So, outcomes appear as 'o', always in lower case; rules (and regulations) appear as 'r'; and guidance is shown as 'g'. The next indicator shows the relevant section within the Handbook, so the Code of Conduct is in Part 2 but its indicator is 'C', always in upper case. Similarly, the indicator for Part 1 'Introduction' is 'I';

for Part 3 'Scope of practice' it is 'S'; Part 4 'Qualification Rules' uses 'Q'; and Part 5 'Enforcement' uses 'E'. The third and final indicator is always a number and runs sequentially through each part of the Handbook. So, to return to our example, 'rC4', we can see that this is a rule; it is in Part 2 'The Code of Conduct', and it is the fourth rule in that part.

## 1.3    The ten Core Duties

The first thing to note about the new Code is that it lays down ten 'Core Duties' for every barrister to attend to. Specifically, these apply to all BSB regulated persons, except where the Code provides otherwise. A 'BSB regulated person' includes all barristers, including unregistered barristers, and registered European lawyers; an 'unregistered barrister' is someone who has been called to the Bar by an Inn of Court and has not ceased to be a member of the Bar but does not hold a practising certificate (see Part 6 of the Handbook).

The core duties are:

CD1    You must observe your duty to the court in the administration of justice [CD1].

CD2    You must act in the best interests of each client [CD2].

CD3    You must act with honesty and integrity [CD3].

CD4    You must maintain your independence [CD4].

CD5    You must not behave in a way which is likely to diminish the trust and confidence which the public places in you or in the profession [CD5].

CD6    You must keep the affairs of each client confidential [CD6].

CD7    You must provide a competent standard of work and service to each client [CD7].

CD8    You must not discriminate unlawfully against any person [CD8].

CD9    You must be open and co-operative with your regulators [CD9].

CD10    You must take reasonable steps to manage your practice, or carry out your role within your practice, competently and in such a way as to achieve compliance with your legal and regulatory obligations [CD10].

The Code makes it clear that whilst the ten are not presented in order of precedence, nevertheless there will be circumstances where one core duty does take priority. In fact, CD1 overrides any other core duty where they are inconsistent (gC1).

A BSB regulated person may face disciplinary proceedings where the BSB considers that (a) that person has breached one or more of the core duties and (b) such proceedings are in accordance with the Code's enforcement policy.

## 1.4    The new Code and the Bar Professional Training Course

This manual is designed to support students through their time on the Bar Professional Training Course ('BPTC') and specifically to help them to prepare for the assessment that they will undertake on Professional Ethics.

The assessment in Professional Ethics is an assessment set centrally by the BSB, through its Central Examinations Board. In early 2016, the BSB announced that the format of the assessment, for 2016–17 onwards, would be in the form of six short answer questions. The current syllabus for 2015–16 is set out below. For this manual, the focus is mainly on the areas indicated in the syllabus, but there is also some coverage given to other areas where it is hoped that this will assist student comprehension of the topic. The current syllabus for the BSB indicates the following content for teaching and assessment purposes:

**Handbook Part 1  Introduction**

sections A–D

A: General

In addition to these sections in the Handbook, other BSB guidance documents may be included, following advice from the Central Examination Board of the BSB. Currently, these include the following:

- Guidance for unregistered barristers (barristers without practising certificates)—supplying legal services and holding out
- Guidance for barristers supervising immigration advisers
- Public access guidance for barristers
- Cab rank rule guidance
- First tier complaints handling
- Guidance on referral and marketing arrangements for barristers permitted by the BSB
- Confidentiality guidance
- Guidance on self-employed practice
- Guidance on reporting serious misconduct of others
- Media comment guidance
- Guidance on insurance and limitation of liability
- Guidance on clash of hearing dates (Listings)
- Guidance for pupils and newly-qualified barristers
- Guidance for barristers—conducting litigation.

Other assessable documentation which originates outside the BSB and is in the current syllabus includes:

- the Code for Crown Prosecutors, 7th edition, January 2013
- the Farquharson Guidelines—the Role and Responsibilities of the Prosecution Advocate
- the anti-money-laundering framework in outline only (the Money Laundering Regulations, the Guidance to the Regulations and the Prevention of Crime Act 2002).

## 1.5  Structure of the manual

The manual is organised to reflect the structure of the Code of Conduct. Specifically, we have taken the five sets of 'conduct rules' as our template. Thus, we have chapters on:

- you and the court (**chapter 2**)
- behaving ethically (**chapter 3**)
- you and your client (**chapter 4**)
- you and your regulator (**chapter 5**)
- you and your practice (**chapter 6**).

This should allow us to concentrate on the Code. However, other parts of the Handbook are also important and assessable and these will be picked up in **chapter 7** onwards, looking at the scope of practice, practising certificates, Qualification Rules, and continuing professional development. As indicated earlier, several substantial sections of the BSB Handbook are *not* on the current syllabus for the BPTC Professional Ethics module. These parts (and Part 6 of the Handbook, on definitions) will be referred to as appropriate throughout the manual.

# 2

# You and the court

## 2.1 Making sure that the legal system works properly

There are five outcomes for this section of the Code of Conduct. The aim is essentially to provide a guarantee that the public interest is served by having a robust legal system, not one that is affected by lawyers seeking partisan benefit or advantage. The outcomes seek both substantive justice and the appearance of justice in the legal system. So, oC2 requires 'the proper administration of justice' to be served whilst oC5 insists that the public must be enabled to have 'confidence in the administration of justice and in those who serve it'. The advocates who appear before the court owe duties to the court but the system cannot function properly unless the lay client and anyone who is professionally connected to the litigation also abide by their obligations; an example of this might be the disclosure obligations in civil litigation, where lay clients sometimes struggle to see the benefit to themselves of disclosing to their opponent relevant but damaging evidence. Outcome oC4 makes the point that both the advocates in court and others who are conducting litigation owe duties to the court and there will be occasions when these duties will override duties owed to the lay client. It is important that both advocates and clients clearly understand the scope of those duties and what situations may give rise to a client's interests being effectively set aside.

Probably the key outcome is oC1—that the court can trust the information that is given to it, whether by someone conducting litigation (perhaps through filing documents at court) or by an advocate at court. In a sense, this harks back to long-standing duties owed by barristers not to mislead the court (and see rC3.1) and not to devise evidence but this outcome is rather wider than that. Finally, oC3 recognises that the interests of lay clients are of course to be protected but only to the extent that this is compatible with the core duties and with oC1 and oC2; see also rC4. In other words, the interests of any individual client are subservient to justice and the wider public interest in the proper administration of justice. This reflects Core Duty 1 and its primacy over all other provisions, outlined in gC1.1.

The requirement not to be partisan is reflected in rC3 which states that you are to 'act with independence in the interests of justice'. This will include being independent of any pressure being placed upon you by a client, by anyone else involved in conducting the litigation, or by any third party. This obligation can be hard for clients to understand, not least because they are often paying for your services and feel that your interests should coincide with theirs; that you should be arguing to win for them, not striving for justice. It is rather an abstract concept and it may be helpful to look at some of the more specific rules and guidance on this point.

## 2.2 Independence in the interests of justice

As an advocate, you will be privy to certain information—some of it (typically factual and specific to this case) will have come from the client and some of it (typically legal and normative) you will have acquired independently of the client. When factual information is presented to the court by an advocate, often the court will have to take on trust that the information is genuine as it has no way of testing the veracity.

The court may ask itself has counsel just said something 'on instructions'—that is, based on information that has come from the client or a witness but which has not been presented to the court as evidence? Or has counsel just made something up? Of course, clients and witnesses may well make up evidence and allegations from time to time and the advocate has to trust them not to do so, to an extent. The system breaks down without the element of trust.

Is the law conclusively in one side's favour in a court hearing? Do both parties' advocates know the same cases and statutes? Suppose one party's advocate is more up to date on the relevant law than the advocate acting for the other party? We might say that this is as it should be, the more up-to-date advocate is better informed and should be able to take advantage of his more accurate legal knowledge. That is certainly how his client would see things. But suppose his more accurate legal knowledge tells him about an authority that damages his arguments and makes it more likely that the *opponent* will succeed? Then, the instinct of the lay client may be to keep it quiet—if the opposition advocate doesn't know about this authority, that's his and his client's problem and they should both take the consequences. The difficulty with this is of course that the court should stand impartial and seek to make the correct decision, both in law and fact. Although it is typically the position in an adversarial system that the parties decide what evidence to present to the court, the advocate cannot knowingly present false evidence nor withhold material evidence (at least it would have to be disclosed to the opponent before the hearing). Neither of these steps would promote a factually correct decision. Similarly, it is not a requirement that the advocates present every single case and statutory principle that they can find on the point under argument; apart from anything else, there would be replication and time would be wasted. So the advocates will winnow out the marginal, the old, and the less persuasive legal authorities before they come to court but what they cannot do is knowingly present a false legal argument. The argument would be false if there is an authority which contradicts or undermines their argument. This is not an insistence that the advocate must know every single case and piece of legislation relevant to the argument—we do not seek perfection! But it does mean that if the advocate actually knows of an authority that damages his argument, he must bring it to the court's attention and not set it aside.

## 2.3 The advocate must not mislead the court

### 2.3.1 The advocate's knowledge and belief

This is a clear example of the requirement of professional independence, that one's representation of a party and his interests is overridden by the interests of justice. Rule rC3 makes it clear that the advocate must not mislead the court, knowingly or recklessly, or attempt to do so (see also rC9.1 for a broader example of the duty not to mislead). One example of this is the obligation to 'take reasonable steps to ensure that the court has before it all relevant decisions and legislative provisions' (rC3.4). Thus, we seek to maximise the chance of a legally sound and just decision from the court. Also, the advocate must not make submissions to the court or any other sort of statement which he knows are untrue or misleading. If his client instructs him to do this, he must refuse. This could cover both legal and factual points. More plainly fact-based is the requirement not to ask a witness questions which suggest facts that the advocate knows, or is instructed by his client, to be false or misleading (rC6.1). This is most obviously demonstrated in cross-examination, where the advocate is putting his client's case to an opposing witness. Suppose the witness testifies that she sent an email to the barrister's client but she is unable to produce evidence of the email in court; there is just her oral testimony as to its existence and content. If the cross-examiner has previously been told privately by his client that he did receive such an email from the witness but he deleted it, then the cross-examiner cannot ask questions of the witness which suggest that no such email existed or was ever sent by her to the client.

It is important not to confuse knowledge with belief. The guidance under these rules (gC6) makes it clear that the advocate does not need to turn detective or pretend to be omniscient; you do not have to believe that what your client tells you in his instructions is factually true. Suppose your client tells you that it isn't him on the CCTV footage, you may view it and feel very strongly that it definitely looks very much like him and his appearance is so unusual that you cannot imagine it could have been anyone else. Nevertheless, you must present his case based on his instructions, not on your intuition or belief. Of course, if the client says 'Look at me there on the CCTV! Of course, I'm going to tell the court that it's not me, see what I can get away with', you cannot call him as a witness to say that it does not show him—you *know* it would be a lie. So, your knowledge is important but your belief is irrelevant here. That should be clear. Where things become a little grey is when we introduce the idea of *recklessness*. This crops up in various areas of substantive law, most obviously criminal law. Here, though, it is applied to the advocate, not to the client. Rule rC3.1 says that the advocate must not mislead the court knowingly or recklessly. Guidance gC4 expands on this—recklessness means 'being indifferent to the truth, not caring whether something is true or false'. One might be tempted to say that this imposes certain additional obligations on the advocate—to turn detective, to cross-examine one's client, to establish 'the truth', regardless of the client's interests in the outcome of the case. If the advocate is to 'care' whether something that he is responsible for putting before the court is true or not, shouldn't he test it? Do some investigating? Play devil's advocate? The simple answer, it is suggested, is 'no' to all of the above. What it ought to mean is that the advocate has to keep his wits about him and not let things pass into evidence which, if he had been paying attention, he would have spotted and addressed. This is the sort of thing that is much more of a danger inside the courtroom than outside. In the heat of the moment, the cut and thrust, the need for the advocate to be concentrating on so many things, you can just lose focus on something, the witness says something in the witness box and then it's gone in as evidence, possibly without you even realising its significance. So we would suggest that this is really what the obligation not to be reckless means in effect—pay attention! If you do not, then at least you should try to rectify matters if you realise later what has happened. Guidance gC4 makes it clear that these obligations run throughout the lifespan of the case. If you discover later that you have unwittingly misled the court, you have to correct the position; failure to do so would mean that you are now knowingly misleading the court. This may mean making a statement to the court, withdrawing a particular claim or assertion, perhaps recalling a witness for further questioning to correct a point.

### 2.3.2 Respecting client confidentiality whilst not misleading the court

The advocate has a fundamental obligation to respect the confidentiality of information imparted by the client or gathered whilst working for the client; see Core Duty 6. This information may also be covered by legal professional privilege (see the *Evidence* manual); where it is privileged, it will be exempt from the usual disclosure obligations. However, here the confidentiality requirement may come into conflict with the obligation not to mislead the court. Remember that the obligation not to mislead the court falls within Core Duty 1, and that takes precedence over any other Core Duty. It is quite easy to envisage a situation where your client gives you information which is relevant to the litigation but which they do not wish to disclose to anyone else, certainly not the opponent or the court. This information may come in the form of verbal instructions or perhaps a document or a copy of an email. There are four possible situations here:

1. The information is not protected by legal professional privilege and must be disclosed to the opponent as usual; the client agrees to the disclosure; or

2. The information is not protected by legal professional privilege and must be disclosed to the opponent as usual; the client refuses to agree to the disclosure; or

3. The information is protected by legal professional privilege and need not be disclosed to the opponent; and there is no danger of the court being misled by reason of the information being withheld; or

4. The information is protected by legal professional privilege and so need not be disclosed to the opponent but there is a risk that the court may be misled if the information is withheld.

In situations 1 and 3, there is no problem, this shows the system running as it is designed to. In situation 2, the disclosure regime is malfunctioning. In situation 4, there is no issue with the disclosure regime but there is nevertheless a problem in that incorrect factual information may be given to the court.

### 2.3.2.1   Non-disclosure of a document

The most obvious example of situation 2 is where your client has a document which predates the proceedings and is perhaps an email between claimant and defendant evidencing a business deal, or a copy of an invoice, the content of which is prejudicial to his case. Therefore, he does not want it to be disclosed. Under rC3.5, the advocate must ensure that his 'ability to act independently is not compromised'. His duty to the court takes priority and so the advocate must advise the client to disclose the document. If the client refuses permission, the advocate cannot reconcile his conflicting duties and is in a dilemma.

### 2.3.2.2   Non-disclosure of guilt

Probably the most obvious example of situation 4 is the criminal case where the accused tells his advocate that he is guilty of the crime but wants to plead not guilty. How is the advocate to handle this in court?

### 2.3.2.3   Solutions

These are tricky situations—so what is the solution? First, the advocate should not breach the client's confidentiality. It is not acceptable for the advocate to take it upon himself to make an unsanctioned disclosure. So, if your client refuses to allow the document to be disclosed, you should not disclose it (gC13). Likewise, if your client insists on pleading not guilty, you should not go into court and inform the court that he has told you that he committed the crime (gC9.1). Thereafter, the solutions diverge somewhat.

If the client refuses to disclose the document, the advocate has no alternative but to withdraw from the case (gC13); the conflict between the obligations is irreconcilable. This is straightforward.

If the client insists on pleading not guilty, the defence can put the prosecution to proof. The burden of proof is on the prosecution and the defence advocate can legitimately test the reliability of the prosecution evidence through cross-examination, and then make a closing argument that the burden of proof has not been discharged. In this way, the defence advocate is not advancing an alternative explanation which he knows (because of his client's instructions) to be false. Thus, the advocate is not actively presenting false information or a false hypothesis to the court but merely challenging the information and hypothesis offered by the prosecution (gC9.2). However, if the defence advocate were to call evidence, or suggest through cross-examination, that the accused had not committed the offence, then this would be actively misleading the court and constitute a breach of Core Duty 1 (gC10). This distinction can be difficult to justify.

It becomes more difficult if we look at rC6. This says that the advocate must not make a submission which, on his instructions, he knows to be false. Applying that to our situation, the defence advocate *can* make a closing speech that challenges the prosecution evidence but he *cannot* explicitly assert that the accused is innocent, because he knows this to be untrue. Rule rC6 also says that the advocate must not present evidence which he knows to be, or is instructed is, untrue; the rule goes on—'unless you make clear to the court the true position as known by or instructed to you'. This seems to suggest a positive obligation on the advocate to breach the client's confidentiality. It is submitted that this is not a correct interpretation of the rule. In effect, as you cannot breach the confidentiality, the rule is really saying that you simply cannot present that false evidence to the court. This interpretation is supported by gC11 which states that where there is a risk of the court being misled if confidential information is not disclosed, the advocate should seek the client's permission to disclose it. If that permission is not given, then the advocate must cease to act for the client and withdraw from the case. Guidance gC11 explicitly states that, in this position, when you withdraw 'you must not reveal the information to the court'.

### 2.3.2.4 Non-disclosure of criminal record

Another example of the fourth situation occurs, again, in a criminal setting. Suppose that you are representing the defendant. The evidence disclosed by the prosecution to you and to the court indicates that there are no previous convictions recorded against the defendant. But suppose that your client tells you that the prosecution has got it wrong, and he does have a previous conviction? Guidance gC12 addresses this in the context of a sentencing hearing. Clearly, the defendant's criminal record *could* be relevant to determination of the sentence at the hearing. So if the court is unaware of the true position, it may impose the wrong sentence; it will have been misled. Conversely, if any offender is a man of good character—has no criminal record—then this will be a strong mitigating factor for the defence advocate to rely upon in the plea in mitigation. So the defendant in our example will be motivated to keep the court in the dark about the truth. The guidance distinguishes two situations, with the distinction turning on the presence or absence of a mandatory sentence.

The first situation arises where a mandatory sentence should be imposed if the court knew the true position; for example, where the defendant *in fact* has two previous convictions for domestic burglary and now awaits sentence on his third, so he should receive a mandatory minimum sentence of three years' imprisonment. If this defendant refuses to allow his advocate to disclose the true position, the court will inevitably fail to pass the sentence which the law requires it to pass. The advocate must advise the defendant that if he refuses to sanction disclosure of the true position to the court, then the advocate has no choice but must withdraw from the case.

The second situation is where no mandatory sentence is in play. If this defendant refuses to allow disclosure of his true record, the advocate can continue to act for him but will be limited in what he can say on the defendant's behalf. The advocate must not mislead the court and so cannot assert that the defendant is of good character. This powerful potential mitigating factor will be lost, as it should be here. The advocate needs to advise the client that if the court asks him a direct question—for example, 'Is it correct, Mr Green, that your client has never been in any trouble with the courts before?'—then he cannot mislead the court and so, if the defendant were not to permit this question to be answered truthfully, the advocate would have no choice but must withdraw at that point. What this tends to produce is a tactical discussion between advocate and client before the hearing begins and where, having advised the client of these various scenarios, the advocate asks the client whether or not the true position may be disclosed. If the client agrees to disclosure, the ethical dilemma is removed. In fact, disclosure might be beneficial to the client: the true position may emerge anyway during or even after the hearing and the correct sentence would then be imposed, so why not get some credit for being frank? Candour can be a mitigating factor too.

## 2.4 The advocate must not abuse his role

This requirement is specifically stated in rC3.2 and expanded upon in rC7.1–4.

### 2.4.1 Insulting people

It would be an abuse of one's role to make a statement or ask a question *merely* with the aim of insulting, humiliating, or annoying a witness (or any other person). If you have a different aim but your question or statement may have the incidental effect of insulting, etc, you will not be prohibited from asking it.

One example might be taken from the criminal prosecution of the Grillo sisters, Elisabetta and Francesca, in 2013. The two women had been personal assistants employed by Charles Saatchi and Nigella Lawson, to assist with the family and in particular Ms Lawson and the children. In December 2013, they were tried in the Crown Court on a charge of fraud, having spent over £650,000 on credit cards belonging to Lawson and Saatchi. Their defence was that Nigella Lawson had agreed to their spending. This would seem rather unbelievable at first blush, so they supplied a motive for her to agree with their spending, namely that they had agreed in return not to inform her husband about her cocaine consumption. Clearly then, in order to run that defence, it would be necessary for the defence advocate to cross-examine Nigella Lawson on her drug consumption. The result of that was that when Ms Lawson was called as a prosecution witness, she was subjected to lengthy cross-examination about her personal life, her relationship with Charles Saatchi, her previous marriage to John Diamond, and her consumption of illegal drugs, an experience that she subsequently described as 'deeply disturbing' and one that had 'maliciously vilified' her (according to BBC News, 20 December 2013). We should note that the trial judge did not prevent this line of cross-examination; indeed, it was essential to the sisters' defence. They were acquitted but even if they had not been, this would still have been a central and highly relevant line of questioning to put to this witness *notwithstanding* that it left her distressed, facing a possible police investigation, and with an embargo on entering the USA due to her admissions of drug-taking.

### 2.4.2  Making a serious allegation against someone

This is closely connected to the preceding obligation. An advocate must not make a serious allegation against any person (not only someone who is a witness in the proceedings), or, in particular, suggest that someone else is guilty of the crime with which the advocate's client is charged, unless that allegation is relevant either to the client's case or a witness's credibility. In addition, there must be reasonable grounds to support the allegation, although usually it will be sufficient to have instructions from the client that the allegations are true. Finally, if the allegations concern someone who is not a party to the proceedings, the advocate should not name them in open court unless it is reasonably necessary to do so. That is no doubt because they are not present or represented in the proceedings and so are unable to defend themselves or protect their reputation.

### 2.4.3  Putting your case

rC7.2 makes it clear that the advocate will not be allowed to make a serious allegation about a witness whom the advocate has had the chance to cross-examine unless he gave that witness the chance to answer the allegation during cross-examination. This is commonly known as the duty to 'put your case'. Again, one can see that this is connected to the preceding two points: it is by definition a serious allegation and so it needs to be both relevant to the client's case and based on reasonable grounds (rC7.3); further, if it satisfies those requirements, it may be insulting or annoying but it will be a topic which is necessary to address in the proceedings (rC7.1). So, what does this specific rule add?

There are two key points here. First, if you want to make a serious allegation against someone who is appearing as a witness in the proceedings, you must give them the chance to give their account of the allegation. They may accept the allegation but offer an innocent explanation for it, or they may deny it, or they may just agree with it. The point here is that the advocate has to give them the chance to respond to the allegation. This is partly a matter of fairness but it is also a matter of allowing the court to hear both sides on the point, the better to make an informed decision. Secondly, if the advocate fails to 'put the case' and to give the witness a chance to respond, then the advocate will not be allowed to rely on that allegation. Thus, the point will be barred and any argument that is based upon the allegation cannot be made in the proceedings. This can be quite damaging to one's case, of course. If need be, and if it is possible to do so, one might ask for the witness to be recalled to the witness box so that the point can be addressed properly. In effect, the advocate would be asking for permission to reopen cross-examination and so, if permission is granted, the advocate who called the witness should be allowed a further opportunity to re-examine on any matters arising from the new questioning. The judge may decide not to recall the witness, though, and if so the point is lost. If the judge does allow the witness to be recalled, the cross-examiner may find himself liable for wasted costs, flowing from the original failure. The obligation to put your case to material witnesses in cross-examination is so fundamental that a failure to do so is almost certainly an innocent oversight, rather than a deliberate attempt to dodge the matter.

### 2.4.4  Personal opinions

This is fairly straightforward. The advocate is simply required to present the evidence in accordance with his instructions from the client (subject to not misleading the court, of course). The law is whatever court judgments and statutes say it is. No one is concerned with the advocate's belief in the evidence, as noted earlier. Nor is it relevant whether the advocate agrees with the legal principles being advanced in the proceedings. The law is the law and one can argue about its scope, its applicability, and its interpretation but no one is interested in the advocate's opinion of whether it is good or bad law. So, rC7.4 states that the advocate must not put forward his *personal* opinion of the facts or the law *unless* the court invites him to do so or he is required to do so by law.

# Behaving ethically

## 3.1 Introduction

The outcomes here build upon those seen in **chapter 2**. Once again, we see the emphasis on the need to ensure the proper administration of justice, whilst the best interests of the client are reiterated. In addition, this time we must ensure access to justice, so this section looks at how that is to be achieved. Those who are regulated by the BSB must maintain the standards of honesty, integrity, and independence which run throughout these provisions (see CD3 and 4). In order to maintain these standards, it is necessary to understand them; to assist the advocate, it is important that the client understands these obligations as well (oC9). Finally, regulated persons must ensure that they do not engage in unlawful discrimination themselves and they should also take steps to avoid discrimination occurring in their practices. So, for example, they need to look at chambers' policies and procedures and make sure that these are non-discriminatory (see CD8).

## 3.2 Honesty, integrity, and independence

These three requirements are established directly by the Core Duties. Rule rC8 goes further and states that an advocate must not do anything that could be seen by a member of the public as undermining these professional standards (and see CD5). So, the appearance of honesty is just as important as actually behaving honestly. Indeed, so important are these standards that gC14 advises us that the advocate's duty to act in the best interests of the client is sub-servient not only to CD1 (duty to the court) but also to CD3 and 4 (see rC16, in section C3 'You and your client').

As one might expect, there are several more specific rules to assist the advocate. In order to act with honesty and integrity, the advocate must not:

- knowingly or recklessly mislead *anyone* or attempt to do so (cf rC3.1—not mislead the court)
- draft a statement of case, witness statement, affidavit or any other document which contains:
  - any statement of fact which is unsupported by his client or by his instructions
  - any contention which he does not consider to be properly arguable
  - any allegation of fraud, unless the advocate has (i) clear instructions from the client to make this allegation and (ii) reasonably credible material to establish an arguable case of fraud
  - any statement of fact which is not what he reasonably believes the witness would say if giving evidence orally (when drafting witness statements or affidavits)
- encourage a witness to give evidence which is misleading or untruthful (cf rC6.2—not call an untruthful witness)
- rehearse, practise, or coach a witness on the evidence that they will give
- communicate about the case with any witness (including the client) whilst they are giving their evidence, unless the opponent or court gives permission to do so

- make or offer any payment to any witness which is contingent on the evidence they will give or the outcome of the case
- propose or accept any fee arrangement which is illegal (see rC9).

## 3.3 Money, gifts, and the advocate

Plainly, a number of the don'ts set out in **3.2** relate to money and it is easy to see how one's independence might be affected or at least be reasonably seen to be affected by dealings with money, or its equivalent. So, the guidance here indicates that the barrister must not offer or give a commission or a referral fee to a client or professional client or an intermediary, regardless of the amount involved (and see rC10; but note that an *employed* barrister may pay or receive a referral fee where permitted by his employer or approved regulator). The barrister should also avoid giving them gifts, other than items of modest value, or lending them money; and should not accept any money from them unless it is payment for professional services or reimbursement of expenses. If the barrister is offered a gift, and this does sometimes happen, he should assess the size of the gift and the circumstances in which it is being offered, and consider how acceptance would appear to others bearing in mind the need to be independent and have integrity. If the circumstances are such that it might lead others to question his independence, the gift should be politely declined. The gift may be offered by a current client, a former client or a prospective client and arguably the decision whether or not to accept may be partly dependent on which of these categories applies. Of course, the gift may be offered by a professional client or someone else with whom the barrister has a professional connection or who wishes to have such a connection with the barrister; as the circumstances shift, so may the proper decision on acceptance or refusal.

It sometimes happens that at the conclusion of a successful case, the client offers to treat his lawyers to a slap-up meal. In many instances, that may mean at best a curry at the local Indian; on rare occasions, it may mean an opportunity to indulge in fine dining. In both instances the same principles apply—whether one is being entertained in this way, or offering it to another, how might it appear to an outsider? If it could reasonably be seen as compromising the barrister's independence, it should not take place.

The author cannot recall ever being offered a meal by a client but he was once offered a lift to the nearest Tube station in his client's car, a very throaty Renault 5 Sport. The Tube station was about 200 yards from the court, the court was next to the police station and the client had just been disqualified from driving, so prudence (and a desire not to break the law by allowing oneself to be carried in a vehicle driven by a disqualified driver) would indicate a polite refusal, perhaps the need to stretch one's legs, get some fresh air, and so forth.

The guidance suggests that these sorts of dilemmas are perhaps more pertinent to the self-employed barrister (gC21).

## 3.4 Other ways to compromise your independence and integrity

Engaging in criminal conduct is an obvious way to fall foul of CD3 (acting with honesty and integrity) and CD5 (behaving in a way likely to diminish public confidence in himself or in the profession). Minor criminal offences are unlikely to count here; this term is defined in Part 6 as including (a) fixed-penalty offences in the United Kingdom, (b) offences anywhere which are dealt with in a substantially similar way as a fixed-penalty offence, or (c) an offence whose main ingredient is the unlawful parking of a motor vehicle. As can be seen then, these are very minor crimes indeed (see also gC28).

Engaging in seriously offensive or discreditable conduct towards third parties is likely to damage one's integrity (gC25.4). Behaving dishonestly will necessarily affect one's commitment to honesty. Unlawfully victimising someone or harassing them is likely to be seen as not acting with integrity or diminishing public confidence and trust. Abusing one's professional position is wrong; an example of how this might be done is to fall foul of the 'do you know who I am?' syndrome. So, using chambers notepaper to write to the man who services your partner's car, to complain about the cost of the new tyres, might be seen as an abuse. If you are dealing with someone in your professional capacity, then of course they need to know what that capacity is. If you are dealing with someone in your personal capacity, you should not try to intimidate them by referring to your profession. You may well have legal knowledge that they don't, and of course you can use that. But what you mustn't do is try to bully people because 'I'm a barrister, I'll have you know.'

Apart from criminal behaviour and the 'abuse' situation identified above, usually the BSB is not interested in a barrister's personal or private life unless it might diminish the trust placed by the public in the barrister or the profession as a whole (see CD5).

## 3.5 Media comment

Since 2013, the BSB's position is that barristers have freedom of expression so that 'the starting point is that barristers are free to make comments to or in the media'. This freedom is nevertheless constrained by various considerations: first, the need to act in the client's best interests; secondly, the need to preserve one's professional independence and integrity; thirdly, the need to not conduct oneself in such a way as to diminish public trust and confidence in the individual barrister or the profession; finally, the need to preserve the confidentiality of the client unless given permission to make a particular disclosure. All of these elements are present in the Code of Conduct.

The Code reiterates that practising barristers are under no prohibition from expressing a personal opinion in the media relating to any current or future proceedings in which they are briefed. It is submitted that this must also apply to commenting on their past cases. The point is made though that practising barristers must still ensure that any comment they make does not, and is not seen as, undermining their professional independence. Furthermore, comments should not bring the profession, or a fellow barrister, into disrepute. The Handbook refers the reader to the guidance document; this can be found at <https://www.barstandardsboard.org.uk/regulatory-requirements/bsb-handbook/code-guidance/>. Important points to take from that guidance include the need for each barrister to weigh up the nature and type of proceedings involved, the stage that has been reached, and the need to ensure that any comment could not prejudice the administration of justice. The barrister should also consider whether any comment might require the client's consent because of issues around confidentiality or professional privilege. As the guidance says, an ill-judged comment could cause unintended harm to the client's interests. Finally, the barrister should remember that although he is now generally free to comment to the media, he is under no obligation to do so and could not be criticised for declining an invitation to comment. If the barrister is instructed by the client to make a statement to the media on the client's behalf, this is quite a different situation but the barrister still should probably bear in mind all of the factors identified above.

## 3.6 Referral fees

As noted earlier, referral fees are generally unacceptable for BSB regulated persons. This is stated plainly in rC10—you must not pay or receive referral fees. *Referral fee* is defined in Part 6 as 'any payment or other consideration made in return for the referral of professional instructions by an intermediary'. In another era, this might have been described as 'touting for business' or 'you scratch my back and I'll scratch yours'. Anyway, it is forbidden and gC29 makes it clear that getting involved with such payments is inconsistent with the barrister's obligations under Core Duties 2, 3, 4, and possibly 5!

If that is not enough, the legal position should deter the barrister from any meddling with referral fees. If the case is publicly funded, then the standard terms of the Legal Aid Agency's contract expressly prohibit a contract holder from paying or receiving a referral fee; the lay client's knowledge of and/or consent to the payment of the fee is irrelevant. In any case, however it is being funded, a referral fee to which the lay client has not consented may constitute a bribe and would thus be a criminal offence under the Bribery Act 2010—clearly not something the barrister should be involved with. Finally, if the case involves a claim for damages in a personal injury or fatality matter, then referral fees and inducements are prohibited by LASPO 2012, s 56 (see also Criminal Justice and Courts Act 2015, s 58).

There are exceptions though. Payment for the provision of a particular service, for example clerks' fees, are not referral fees. This would also cover payments for advertising and publicity, where they are payable regardless of whether any work is generated for the barrister as a result. However, where a payment is linked to, or conditional upon, or will vary in amount according to, the receipt of instructions—these usually *are* referral fees and prohibited. Applying those criteria, we can see that clerks' fees are an exceptional arrangement. The amendment to gC31.3, made in April 2015, states that the fact that a fee varies with the amount of work received does not necessarily make it a referral fee, so long as it is a genuine payment for a marketing service and the person who provides that service is not directing work to one lawyer rather than another, according to who is paying him more. See gC29–32; also the BSB guidance on referral fees—accessible at <https://www.barstandardsboard.org.uk/regulatory-requirements/bsb-handbook/code-guidance/>, 'Guidance on referral and marketing arrangements for barristers permitted by the BSB'. This guidance also addresses the position where a barrister is employed in a non-authorised body and the approved regulator or the employer permits payments which would otherwise fall foul of rC10. Essentially, the barrister may make or receive such payments but only in his capacity as an employed barrister in a non-authorised body and in a manner approved by the regulator or the employer.

## 3.7  Giving an undertaking

This is relatively straightforward. When a barrister gives an undertaking in the course of conducting litigation, then he must comply with it either by an agreed deadline or else within a reasonable period of time (rC11). He should also have adequate insurance cover for any liability he may incur as a result of giving the undertaking. In other words, an undertaking is a serious matter, not to be given lightly, and with potentially damaging consequences if it is not adhered to.

## 3.8  Non-discrimination

Of course, Core Duty 8 prohibits unlawful discrimination. Rule rC12 unpacks this to make it clear. The barrister must not discriminate unlawfully against, victimise or harass any other person on grounds of:

- race
- colour
- ethnic or national origin
- nationality
- citizenship
- sex
- gender re-assignment
- sexual orientation
- marital or civil partnership status
- disability

- age
- religion or belief
- pregnancy and maternity.

The Handbook guidance gC34 refers the reader to supporting information on the BSB Handbook Equality Rules; these are available at <https://www.barstandardsboard.org.uk/about-bar-standards-board/equality-and-diversity/equality-and-diversity-rules-of-the-bsb-handbook/>. Reference is also made to rule rC110, in section D1.2 of Part 2. This section deals with equality and diversity. Briefly, rC110 requires the barrister to take reasonable steps to ensure that his chambers have a written policy statement on equality and diversity accompanied by a written implementation plan and that numerous specific requirements are complied with in chambers. These include: the use of fair and objective criteria in recruitment and selection processes (clearly relevant to pupillage and tenancies as well as the appointment or dismissal of chambers' employees), the appointment of (at least) one equality and diversity officer, fair access to work (including the fair distribution of work opportunities amongst pupils and members of chambers), policies on parental leave and flexible working, and a written anti-harassment policy.

It is important not to confuse these rules, which are about non-discrimination in its usual sense, with rule rC28. This rule is titled 'Requirement not to discriminate' but it does not address non-discrimination on the protected characteristics. Its aim is a broader one—to provide that a barrister must not withhold his services from a prospective client where his reason for doing so is either:

(a) that the client is objectionable to him or to a section of the public or

(b) that the conduct, opinion, or beliefs of the prospective client are unacceptable to him or to a section of the public or

(c) is based on the source of any financial support which is being given to the client in connection with the proceedings.

## 3.9  Foreign work

As defined in Part 6 of the Handbook, *Foreign work* means legal services (of whatever nature) which relate to court or other legal proceedings which are taking place (or are contemplated to do so) outside England and Wales. It also covers legal services related to any matter, or contemplated matter, which is not subject to the law of England and Wales, where there are no such proceedings. *Legal services* include providing legal advice, representation, and drafting or settling any statement of case, witness statement, or other legal document. See Part 6.

The Handbook at rC13 requires a barrister who undertakes foreign work to abide by any applicable rule of conduct which is laid down either by the law or by any national or local Bar of the place where the work is to be performed and the place where any proceedings or matters to which the work relates are taking place, unless any such rule is inconsistent with anything required by the Core Duties.

For example, barrister George provides legal advice in Athens to a client who is being sued in Delaware, USA. George must comply with Greek legal requirements on lawyers' conduct and the professional requirements of the Greek Bar and the Athens Bar. George must also comply with the equivalent obligations under USA federal provisions and the Delaware state Bar. Unlikely as it is that anything here will be incompatible with the BSB Core Duties, in the event of a conflict George must abide by the Core Duties.

If George had got this work as the result of soliciting work outside of England and Wales, then he should take care to do it in ways that would not be prohibited for members of the local Bar where the soliciting took place. The onus is on George to inform himself about the relevant conduct rules. See gC35.

# 4

# You and your client

## 4.1 Introduction

This is a fundamentally important section of the Handbook and the Code of Conduct. The relationship between barrister and client lies at the core of what we do and how we do it. It is of course reflected in Core Duty 2—'you must act in the best interests of each client'. As we have seen already in earlier chapters, this Core Duty is subservient to others, not least the duty owed to the court, but also the need to act with honesty and integrity, and to maintain your independence. This relationship is made explicit in rC16. The balance between these core duties is a thread running throughout Part 2, section C3. Probably, from the client's perspective, the 'bottom line' here is to be found in the two outcomes oC10 and 11: clients must receive a competent standard of work and service, and their best interests must be protected and promoted by those who act for them.

## 4.2 Personal responsibility

Any practising barrister is personally responsible for his own conduct (how he behaves towards others as well as how he conducts his life) and for his professional work. It matters not whether he is a self-employed barrister in chambers or is acting in an employed capacity. This does not mean that particular tasks cannot be delegated or outsourced but the barrister remains personally responsible for the work done. Similarly, the barrister is responsible for the service provided to the client by others who represent him, such as his clerks. Making any necessary adjustments, these principles apply equally to pupils and registered European lawyers. See further rC20 and guidance gC64–68.

## 4.3 Duty to act in the best interests of your client

### 4.3.1 Introduction

As noted earlier, the obligation to act in your client's best interests comes in Core Duty 2. One aspect of this is the obligation to promote fearlessly and by all proper and lawful means the best interests of the client (rC15.1). This obligation has been carried straight over from the previous edition of the Code of Conduct. As well as applying CD2, it also picks up CD4 as the duty to be independent could include resisting external pressures to advise or act in a particular way that contradicts what you perceive to be in the client's best interests. We should also note that the duty under CD2 is to act in the *best* interests of the client, thus there may be some need to consider and prioritise competing interests of the client; it is also slightly paternalistic in that the barrister may justifiably substitute his own opinion for the client's opinion about what is in the client's best interests.

The need to be independent and free from pressure in order to do the best by the client is also shown by rC15.2–4. Here, we see that the barrister must put the client's best interests above his own and regardless of any consequences which may befall him or anyone else. The barrister is not to allow anyone—for example, a professional client or an employer—to limit his own discretion as to how best to serve the client's interests. If the barrister can see that he is likely to be compromised in his representation of a *prospective* client because of instructions he has received from other current or former clients (often related to his knowledge of confidential information, see **4.5**), he must not accept the new instructions—he cannot operate with limitations (rC21.1). These rules put the barrister into a very powerful yet responsible and isolated position vis-à-vis the client once he has accepted the instructions. The need to act in a client's best interests is perhaps heightened when the barrister represents a vulnerable client; it may even be that additional expertise is required (oC14).

According to the Handbook, it is always in the client's best interests to be informed about *who* is working on their case, *what* they are doing, and *how* they will be doing it (rC19 and gC53). The barrister must explain clearly to the client the nature and scope of the legal services he will be providing and the terms on which those services will be provided. The client must get a clear statement that the barrister is entitled to provide those services. It must be clear who will do the work on the case and the basis on which the work will be charged. Care needs to be taken on this point where any work is done by a pupil or a 'devil' (gC59). 'Devilling' describes an arrangement whereby one member of chambers arranges for some of his work to be undertaken by a fellow member (his 'devil') on the basis that he will pay the fellow member for the work, and he will remain responsible to the client for that work as if he had done it himself. A pupil must be careful not to hold himself out to other people as if he were a member of chambers or permit himself to appear as such, for example, in the information publicly displayed at the entrance to chambers. Clients must not be misled over a pupil's status (gC62). Finally, a client or prospective client must not be misled about the extent of any insurance cover in case of professional negligence by the barrister.

It is possible that a client may be misled about some of these matters by the appearance of a chambers' 'brand', perhaps when paying a visit to chambers' premises or looking on the chambers' website. The Handbook suggests that this is a particular concern where 'unsophisticated lay clients' are dealing directly with 'a set of chambers' (gC56). So, there needs to be special care taken by a set of chambers whose members undertake public access work. There may be a large pool of such clients and the potential for confusion may not be limited to situations where the client is a public access client (see **chapter 7**). In any event, the possibility of being misled can be reduced if the chambers (or the individual barrister) explains that the members of chambers are not responsible for each others' work but are self-employed individuals. A similar problem can arise through advertising, so care needs to be taken there too. The Handbook advises that special care should be taken about comparative advertising as this 'may often be regarded as misleading' (gC57).

### 4.3.2 Conflicts of interest

There are several relationships which *could* give rise to a conflict of interest, or at least the risk of one. There could be a conflict between the client's interest and

- the interests of the barrister
- the interests of another client of the barrister—whether past, present, or prospective
- the interests of the professional client, if there is one
- the interests of anyone else.

That the barrister's interests are subservient to those of the client can be seen, for example, in oC16, which states that a barrister must not accept, refuse, or return instructions where this would have an adverse effect on the administration of justice, access to justice, or the best interests of the client. Further, rC17 requires the barrister to consider whether the client's best interests are served by having different legal representation (that is, someone other than this barrister) and, if the barrister considers this to be so, he must advise the client of this opinion. This applies where the barrister considers that he should be replaced by another (perhaps more senior, more junior, or just one with different expertise)—an obvious example of putting the client first. It also applies where the barrister thinks that the client needs to be represented by more lawyers, or fewer, or by different solicitors. The latter may arise where the barrister thinks that the solicitor has been professionally negligent. Where this occurs, the barrister must tell the client about this; this is an example of giving primacy to the client's interests over those of the professional client (gC51). There is a particular example of this point when handling public access work: the barrister must consider whether the client should instruct a solicitor, either as well as the barrister or instead of the barrister. This may be a live issue where the work necessary to conduct the litigation is beyond the client's ability to discharge it effectively and the barrister is not authorised to conduct litigation (see gC50 and **chapter 7**).

The barrister must not accept any instructions where there is a conflict between the barrister's interests and those of his prospective client (rC21.2). Where there is a conflict between the interests of a prospective client and those of an existing or past client, the barrister must not accept the instructions unless all affected clients give informed consent to him acting for the new client (rC21.3). The same principle applies where a conflict arises between the interests of two or more current clients, or two or more prospective clients (gC37). The barrister must make full disclosure to everyone of the nature and extent of the conflict in order for them to (possibly) give their informed consent to his continuing to act. It may be that he can continue to act for all clients or only some of them but all must consent to him continuing. If one client does not consent, the barrister must refuse the instructions or return them, as appropriate (see further gC69, rC25, rC27). The duty to respect client confidentiality may mean that the barrister cannot make the necessary full disclosure (see rC15.5 and **4.5**). In this situation, there is no possibility of informed consent, and the barrister will have no alternative but to refuse or return at least one set of instructions. In the situation where instructions are returned, the barrister would be under a duty to explain to the client his reasons for withdrawal (see rC27) but would need to be oblique to maintain client confidentiality.

## 4.4    Providing a competent standard of work and service

Core Duty 7 obliges the barrister to provide a competent standard of work and service to each client. As we will see in **4.6**, notions of competence under this heading cross over into issues of when a barrister can properly refuse to accept instructions, as well as representing the need to act in the client's best interests (CD2). So, rC21.8–9 make it clear that a barrister must not accept any instructions where he is not competent to tackle the matter or lacks the experience necessary to do so. Also, he must refuse the instructions if he does not have enough time to do what needs to be done, unless it will nevertheless be in the client's best interests for him to accept the instructions and do his best to provide a competent level of service. This is only likely to apply where there is very little time left either to find an alternative barrister or for any such barrister to get to court or do whatever work is needed.

So, time management is important for barristers and it is a key aspect of providing a competent standard of work and service. If a barrister realises that he will be unable to complete the work that he has been instructed to do by an agreed deadline, or within a reasonable time if there is no specific deadline, he must tell the professional client (or the lay client if dealing directly with him). Obviously, concomitant with this is the obligation to read one's instructions promptly upon receipt in order to consider the question of how much time will be required to perform the work to a competent standard. Guidance gC38.4 highlights this duty and makes the additional point that timely reading of one's instructions is vital because there will often be a time limit for action or even a limitation period that might expire soon. Clearly, it will not be in the client's interests to let those deadlines pass unfulfilled as the consequences may be extremely problematic for the client. The main aim here is to enable the client to make alternative arrangements so far as is possible, or take any other steps which could protect the interests of the client. The barrister has the same duty to inform others in situations where he realises that he simply will be unable to fulfil his commitment to the client at all; typically this will arise where he has a diary clash and needs to be in two places at once. One of the clients will need to be informed—it may be possible to apply for an adjournment of the hearing or there may be a need to instruct another barrister to attend it. See generally rC18 (gC52 links to the BSB guidance on the action that should be taken when it becomes apparent that the barrister has a listings clash).

No less important in terms of standard of service to the client is the need to advise and explain matters to each client in terms that they will understand, regardless of whether this is done orally in a meeting or through providing written advice. This will have special significance when dealing with a vulnerable client. When advising any type of client, sometimes bad news has to be given. This may need to be done face-to-face, either at court or at a meeting in chambers or in the offices of the professional client. Clearly, it will help the client if the possibility of the negative advice has been flagged up in advance as one would want to minimise any distress or upset that the client may feel on being told the bad news. It would also help if the barrister gives some thought to how the advice might affect the client and perhaps arranges for the meeting to be somewhere private, certainly if it takes place at court. In any event, the barrister should be mindful of the likely impact on the client and his possible reactions; try to see things from the client's perspective. The barrister should always act with courtesy and that is no less important in this type of situation. See generally gC38.

The barrister is providing a specialist and expert service to each client and therefore needs to keep up to date and be well-informed about legal developments. It is also necessary to maintain and seek to improve one's skill sets. This is another facet of the obligation to provide a competent service and standard of work. It really should go without saying that this process must go on continually throughout a professional career but of course the BSB has set down minimum requirements for continuing professional development ('CPD'; see further **chapter 11**). Guidance gC39 makes the point that CPD establishes a base level for maintenance and improvement—in terms of providing a competent standard of service, the barrister may well need to do more. Specific examples are given, of the need to undertake specialist training before the barrister can undertake advisory work at police stations or can handle public access work. Really these are forms of what might be called 'gateway' training, where the barrister cannot undertake that type of work at all until he or she is properly and effectively trained to do so. Perhaps what is the spirit of the guidance here is that the barrister should always be seeking to improve his knowledge, his know-how and his abilities, to make the best of himself and if he can continue to do this it will be to the benefit of all his clients.

## 4.5  Client confidentiality

This is a matter of fundamental importance, as reflected in Core Duty 6—the barrister 'must keep the affairs of each client confidential'. To an extent, we have considered this matter already, as it can easily arise in the context of a conflict of interest between clients where it may mean that new instructions cannot be accepted due to the possible jeopardy to a current or former client's confidential information which requires protection. The duty is clearly a continuing one that carries on after the relationship of barrister and client has formally ended. The duty is fleshed out more in Part 2, section C3 of the Handbook; see, for example, rC15.5—the barrister 'must protect the confidentiality of each client's affairs, except for such disclosures as are required or permitted by law or to which [the] client gives informed consent'.

This obligation can cause tensions with CD1 (duty to the court) and CD2 (duty to protect best interests of the client) in particular. We have considered some aspects of this already, in **chapter 2** (for example, gC8–13, in the context of the duty not to mislead the court). Guidance now makes it clear that 'confidentiality is central to the administration of justice' (gC42). There is an echo here of CD1, where the duty owed to the court is 'in the administration of justice'. But the dilemma for the barrister is that there may be occasions where respecting client confidentiality leads to either the risk or the actuality that the court will be misled. The key principle is that generally, the barrister must always respect the client's confidentiality; the same applies to the pupil of (or someone 'devilling' for) a self-employed barrister (gC46). In a position of dilemma, the Code solution is usually for the barrister to walk away—to return one's instructions and withdraw from the case. See for example, rC25.2–3 (further at **4.6.3**). The solution is *not* to take it upon oneself to make the disclosure.

There are exceptions, though. As gC42 states, confidentiality will be respected in 'normal circumstances'. Rule rC15.5 itself allows disclosures which are 'required or permitted by law' and disclosures where the client gives informed consent. The latter of course does not impact on the client's expectation of confidentiality as the client has waived it in those circumstances. In terms of situations where *unsanctioned* disclosure is required or permitted by law, the Handbook gives two examples. First, where the anti-money laundering provisions in the Prevention of Crime Act 2002 require a barrister to report concerns about possible money laundering activities by or on behalf of the client; see further **chapter 12**. Secondly, where the Handbook itself requires disclosure in breach of confidentiality—this may arise in the context of reporting *oneself* to the BSB for possible misconduct. The situation is different when considering reporting someone else for serious misconduct. See further rC64, gC93, and rC66; **chapter 8**.

Another situation of practical concern for barristers is where the lay client is in receipt of public funding and the barrister discovers that the financial statement made by the client has understated his finances, to the extent that he may not actually be entitled to receive public funding. In this situation, the barrister should advise the client to inform the Legal Aid Agency of the true position. Given the likely loss of public funding if he follows this advice, and the likely consequent loss of his legal representative, the lay client may decide not to follow the advice. In that situation, the barrister must withdraw from the case—the lay client is refusing to make a disclosure that the barrister has advised he must make (rC25.1). But the barrister's duty goes further than this—regulations made under the legal aid legislation make it clear that the lawyer is now under a duty to make the necessary disclosure to the Legal Aid Agency, regardless of the client's wishes. See, for example, SI 2013/457:

> The relationship between a provider [lawyer] and a legally aided person, and any privilege arising out of that relationship, does not preclude the provider from disclosing relevant information to the Lord Chancellor or the Director for the purposes of enabling or assisting them to carry out their functions under Part 1 of the [Legal Aid, Sentencing, and Punishment of Offenders] Act [2012].

Before leaving this topic, we must take note of rC21.4 and rC30: the barrister must not accept instructions where there is a real risk that a current (or former) client's confidential information will be relevant to a prospective client's case and the need to respect the confidentiality means that the barrister cannot act in the best interests of the prospective client. Further, in these circumstances, the 'cab rank' rule will not apply and the barrister is free (in fact is required) to decline the instructions from the prospective client.

## 4.6 Accepting and returning instructions

As we have seen already in this chapter, there may be situations where the barrister cannot take on a case, for example due to a lack of competence in the subject matter or because of a conflict of interest. There will also be situations that arise only after the barrister has accepted the instructions and has perhaps begun to work on the case or has even done a substantial amount of work on it. A fatal problem may even occur in mid-trial. To an extent, the obligation to *accept* instructions finds its most obvious form in the existence and scope of the 'cab rank' rule (see **4.6.5**). What we will look at here are those circumstances where for one reason or another, the barrister must in fact *refuse* to accept new instructions.

### 4.6.1 When the barrister must refuse instructions

This is governed primarily by rC21. The barrister is under an obligation not to accept instructions where:

- as the result of the instructions that one has from a current or former client, the barrister would not be able to act in the best interests of the prospective client
- there is a conflict of interest between the barrister and the prospective client

- there is a conflict of interest between current or former clients and the prospective client (and informed consent is not forthcoming from all clients involved)
- the barrister could not act in the best interests of the prospective client because of a real risk that confidential information of another client is relevant and that other client does not sanction its use or disclosure
- the instructions from the client seek to restrict the barrister's freedom to use his own authority and discretion over matters in court, or for other reasons there is a real prospect that he may be unable to maintain his independence
- the instructions would require the barrister to break the law or act in breach of his obligations under the Handbook, contrary to his obligation to the administration of justice
- the work required by the instructions is work that the barrister is not authorised or accredited to carry out (for example, the conduct of litigation, or criminal advocacy where the barrister is not appropriately accredited by QASA; see **4.7**)
- the barrister is not competent to handle the work required by the instructions or lacks the experience to do so (a reflection of the requirement to provide a competent level of work)—this will be an important consideration when the prospective client is vulnerable
- the barrister does not have enough time to deal with the matter, unless it would still be in the prospective client's best interests for him to undertake the work.

We can see that the fifth point in this list addresses the barrister's independence. The Handbook gives the example of a barrister who receives instructions to act as the advocate for a client but there is a risk that the barrister may be called as a significant witness in the case. The barrister should not accept the instructions here unless his withdrawal might jeopardise the client's interests; if so, then he should not withdraw. This is likely to be a potential problem where the issue arises very shortly before the relevant hearing (non-acceptance of instructions) or in the course of a trial (withdrawal, having previously accepted the instructions). See gC73.

The final point in the list has an important exception, concerned with protecting the client's best interests as far as possible. Guidance gC72 makes the point that sometimes a barrister will receive instructions so late in the day or so close to the deadline or court hearing that 'no suitable, competent advocate would have adequate time to prepare'. In this situation, there would be no purpose in refusing to take the case, other than to cause even more delay and leave the client either with no representation at all or with a barrister even less prepared than this one could be.

### 4.6.2    Setting the terms on which instructions are accepted

#### 4.6.2.1    Notifying the terms

When a barrister first accepts instructions in a matter, it is important to give written confirmation of the acceptance to either the professional client (if there is one) or the lay client; an email will suffice. This confirmation must include the terms on which the barrister is acting and the basis on which he will charge the client, and the procedure for making a complaint should that become relevant. Alternatively, the confirmation can direct the relevant client to the barrister's terms of service on chambers' website or to the standard terms of service which are set out on the Bar Council website; see <http://www.barcouncil.org.uk/media/185511/contractualterms.pdf>. The confirmation ought to be provided before work commences unless it is for some reason not reasonably practical to do so. The barrister's clerk can give the confirmation on his behalf.

#### 4.6.2.2    Varying the terms

If the client subsequently varies the instructions, there is no need to serve a fresh confirmation of acceptance as you will be deemed to have accepted on the same terms as before, unless it is specified to the contrary. See generally rC22–24 and gC75–82.

However, where a fundamental change is made to the basis of the barrister's remuneration, this should be treated as though the original instructions have been withdrawn and an offer of new instructions on different terms has been made (see gC87). In these circumstances, the barrister must first decide whether he is bound to accept the new instructions under the 'cab rank' rule. If he is so obliged, then he must accept them and that is an end to it. If he decides that he is not so obliged, then he may refuse the new instructions if he so chooses. If he does refuse the new instructions, this is not a return or withdrawal pursuant to rule rC25 or rC26 (see **4.6.3**) as the original instructions have been withdrawn by the client. On the 'cab rank' rule, see further **4.6.5**.

### 4.6.3    Returning your instructions

This topic can be divided into two sets of situations—those where the instructions *must* be returned, and those where they *may* be returned. The Handbook sometimes uses '*may*' where it plainly means '*must*' but here it is important to distinguish the two clearly.

#### 4.6.3.1    The instructions *must* be returned

Rule rC25 deals with situations where the barrister must return his instructions. It begins by cross-referencing all of the situations identified already where the barrister must not accept instructions (see rule rC21 and **4.6.1**). If one of these situations arises post-acceptance, then the same principle applies—the barrister must cease to act for the client and promptly return the instructions, including physically returning any paperwork supplied by the client. Rule rC25 adds three more situations to the original list:

- If the case is publicly funded but it becomes apparent to the barrister that this funding has been obtained wrongly, by either false or inaccurate information being supplied to the Legal Aid Agency, the barrister must draw this to the client's attention. If the client fails to take immediate action to rectify the position, the barrister must withdraw.

- If the barrister becomes aware of information which his duty to the court requires him to disclose (remember that the barrister must not mislead the court), again, the barrister must draw this fact to the client's attention. If the client refuses to sanction the disclosure, the barrister must withdraw.

- If, during the course of the case, the barrister learns of a document which should have been disclosed as part of the usual disclosure requirements in the case but it has in fact not been disclosed, the need to disclose it should be drawn to the client's attention. If the client then fails either to disclose it himself, or to permit the barrister to disclose it, then the barrister must withdraw.

Note that, in each of these three situations, the problem can be rectified by the client either making the appropriate disclosure or permitting the barrister to do so. Where neither of these events happens, the solution is usually *not* for the barrister to make an unsanctioned disclosure but instead he should withdraw from the case. Although the Handbook does not say so, the problem with public funding is actually an exception to the normal obligation to maintain client confidentiality. As we saw earlier, client confidentiality can be breached where required by law and this is a situation where the law does require that.

See further **4.6.4** on how to manage a withdrawal from a case.

#### 4.6.3.2    The instructions *may* be returned

This situation is governed by rule rC26. The use of the term '*may*' in this rule might denote some element of discretion or choice on the part of the barrister. This interpretation is reinforced by the guidance gC83 which states that when the barrister makes a decision under rule rC26 he should ensure that the client is not adversely affected by withdrawal because there is insufficient time for him to find other adequate legal assistance. If the client is likely to be so affected, then the barrister probably ought not to withdraw. That is subject to the overriding duty to the court which may mean that, regardless of the potential adverse effect to the client, the barrister actually has no alternative but to withdraw.

Rule rC26 sets out the grounds for possible withdrawal as follows:

- the professional conduct of the barrister is being called into question
- the client consents to withdrawal
- the barrister is a self-employed barrister and either
  - despite all reasonable efforts being made to avoid it, a hearing has become fixed for a date which he has already marked in his professional diary as one on which he is unavailable or
  - the barrister becomes unable reasonably to carry out the instructions because of illness, injury, pregnancy, childbirth, a bereavement or something similar to any of these situations or
  - the barrister is unavoidably required to perform jury service
- the barrister's fees are not paid when due, the client has been notified of this fact, given the chance to rectify it, told of the likely consequences should he fail to rectify it, and he has failed to do so
- the barrister becomes aware of material which is relevant to the matter on which he is instructed but the material is confidential or contained in privileged documents belonging to another person
- the barrister is conducting litigation, the client does not consent to the barrister ceasing to act in the matter but the court has approved the barrister's application to 'come off the record'
- there is 'some other substantial reason' for withdrawal (this category can only be exercised subject to rules rC27–29).

The barrister should not use the 'non-availability' ground above (essentially the 'diary clash') to break an agreement to provide legal services in order to attend or fulfil a non-professional engagement of any kind other than those identified above. See guidance gC85.

There is a rather obscure reference in the list to the barrister becoming aware of another person's confidential or privileged information. This in fact covers the situation where the barrister has come into possession of such material inadvertently, typically where it has been sent to him (or his instructing solicitor) by the other side in error. This might, and on occasion has, included confidential or privileged information such as unused witness statements, counsel's notes from a client conference, instructions to counsel, and counsel's written advice to the client. The guidance gC86 rather vaguely instructs the reader to have regard to relevant case law, including *English & American Insurance Co Ltd and ors v Herbert Smith* (1987) NLJ 148 and *Ablitt v Mills & Reeve (A Firm) and anor* (Times 24 October 1995). What the cases might be said to indicate is that if the lawyer realises the nature of what he has before reading it, he should not read it but should send it back to the other person unread. If he decides to read it, or begins to read it before realising its nature, there is a grave risk that when he does notify the opponent of the situation (remember he must not mislead any person: rule rC9.1), the opponent may apply for an injunction to prevent the lawyer from continuing to act in the matter. So, in a sense, this reason for withdrawal is a little like the barrister sending himself off the field of play before the referee does!

### 4.6.3.3 Withdrawal of the professional client

There is a further situation to be aware of, although it is not in the lists in **4.6.3.1** or **4.6.3.2**. Guidance gC84 states that where a barrister is working on a referral basis and thus has been instructed by a professional client on behalf of a lay client, if the professional client withdraws for any reason then the barrister is no longer instructed in the matter and cannot continue to act unless either he is appointed by the court dealing with the matter or he receives and accepts new instructions.

In a similar position under the old Code of Conduct, it was said that the barrister had 'a complete discretion' whether or not to carry on representing the lay client in this situation. Clearly, that position has been modified in the present scheme. If an offer of new instructions is forthcoming, no doubt this will need to be considered afresh but that should be done by applying the usual principles set out in rule rC21 (**4.6.1**) and subject to the 'cab rank' rule (**4.6.5**). Only if the court seeks to appoint the barrister might it still be said that he has a free choice of whether or not to accept the appointment.

### 4.6.4  How to handle withdrawal or the return of instructions

#### 4.6.4.1  The explanation

Rule rC27 states that, notwithstanding rules rC25 and 26, the barrister must not cease to act or return his instructions unless either he has his lay client's consent to this action or he has clearly explained, either to the professional client or lay client, his reasons for doing so. Given that often the lay client will be reluctant to see 'his' barrister departing the scene, either metaphorically or actually, the latter is likely to be the usual method of handling the matter.

Plainly, rule rC25 says that the barrister must withdraw and offers plenty of cogent examples of situations where that makes perfect sense. It would be illogical to then give the lay client the power of veto. That is not what rC27 does. It is suggested that it does not have that effect on the application of rule rC26 either. So, the upshot is that, when a barrister is withdrawing under either rC25 or rC26, he must first explain to the client(s) what he is doing and why. If after that has been done, the lay client consents, so be it. If he does not, that has no effect on the matter at all.

#### 4.6.4.2  Passing on the baton

When the barrister does withdraw, the lay client will be unrepresented (or at least under-represented) at least temporarily. No doubt, if so advised, he will seek to instruct another barrister. What must not happen is that the departing barrister simply returns his instructions to another barrister; it is not within his competence to make such a decision for the client(s). He can, of course, *propose* to the client another barrister who he feels could properly represent the client instead of himself. Whether the client acts on that suggestion probably depends on the state of the relationship between himself and the departing barrister at that point. If and only if the lay or professional client consents to it can the departing barrister return his instructions to another. Otherwise, he must do nothing else in the matter but simply return all case materials to the professional or lay client, as applicable.

### 4.6.5  The 'cab rank' rule and non-discrimination

The Handbook commences this subject with the non-discrimination principle (see rC28) and so shall we. In the course of one's professional practice, the barrister will probably encounter clients, lay and professional, for whom he does not care, or who he considers are unpleasant individuals. It may be that a prospective client has attracted considerable notoriety and public disapproval, and the barrister is afraid of the consequences for himself if he were to accept instructions to represent this individual and somehow be seen by a section of the public as being 'representative of' or in sympathy with this unattractive individual. The Bar has long held to the entirely commendable ideal that everyone is entitled to competent legal representation, regardless of their own nature, the nature of their case, the allegations against them, and a lawyer's personal feelings about them.

Nowadays, we have the Equality Act 2010 to provide a degree of protection against discrimination on the basis of a protected characteristic. That of course applies to the acceptance or refusal of instructions to provide legal services, just as it applies elsewhere. Rule rC28 sets out a broader principle though; it declares that the barrister must not withhold legal services for any of the following reasons:

- the nature of the case is objectionable to him or to any section of the public
- the conduct, opinions, or beliefs of the prospective client are unacceptable to him or to any section of the public
- the basis of funding for the instructions is not acceptable to him.

Generally, this should be quite clear and straightforward. The only matter which should require further explanation is the third prohibited reason—the financial basis for the case funding. In essence, what this says is that the barrister cannot refuse to take a publicly funded case, simply for that reason. See further guidance gC88. So much for non-discrimination.

The 'cab rank' rule is, it is suggested, something of which the Bar can rightly be proud (see rC29). The Legal Services Board commissioned research into the rule; the fascinating report that was published in January 2013 suggested that it was widely ignored or evaded, served no real purpose, and should be scrapped. The report noted, however, that the Bar 'strongly subscribes to it'. In response, the BSB published its own study, produced by barristers from Fountain Court chambers. In turn, this suggested that removal of the rule would constitute a major threat to justice. The then-Chair of the BSB, Baroness Deech, said that the rule gave everyone the chance to be represented by a barrister of *their* choice, which ought to help to ensure a fair trial. She added that the report's evidence showed that the rule protected the consumer (that is, the clients) and not the barrister, although the report did show that the rule helped to protect barristers from the wrath of the community as well. The Bar Council also published a report, written by Sir Sydney Kentridge QC, which was somewhat critical of the LSB's report, suggesting that it's authors did not 'see the Bar as an honourable profession whose members generally obey the ethical rules of their profession, and who do not seek to evade them. Indeed, throughout the [LSB] Report one finds not merely hostility to the ['cab rank'] rule but hostility to the Bar and sneers at its ethical pretensions.' After these responses, the Legal Services Board agreed to look at the rule once more. As the Handbook was given LSB approval in 2013, some months after that exchange took place, one would assume that the LSB is content for the rule to remain in place in the form that it takes in Part 2, section C3. All three reports are available on the respective websites of the LSB, BSB, and the Bar Council.

As its name implies, if a barrister is available for hire, much like a London hackney cab with its 'fare' sign illuminated, then he must accept any client who hails him. Of course, it is a little more complicated than getting a taxi, although both barrister and cabbie will have areas into which they will not venture, like south of the river, for example. So, let us examine how the 'cab rank' rule operates for barristers.

The relevant rule is rC29. It is important to note at the outset that we are looking only at *referral* work—the rule only applies to self-employed barristers who receive instructions from a professional client on behalf of a client. Therefore, it does not apply to public access work. 'Professional client' is to be given a broad interpretation; it should not be read as synonymous with 'solicitor'. This means that the 'cab rank' rule applies whenever a barrister is instructed by an authorised person who is regulated by another approved regulator. See the BSB guidance on the 'cab rank' rule: professional clients who are authorised persons not authorised by the Solicitors Regulation Authority.

If the instructions are appropriate to the barrister's experience, seniority, and field of practice then, unless there is a specific reason to disapply the 'cab rank' rule under rC30 (see **4.6.6**), the barrister must accept the instructions. This is the position regardless of the client's identity, the nature of the case, whether the client is paying privately or publicly, and irrespective of any belief or opinion that the barrister may have formed about the prospective client's character, reputation, conduct, cause, guilt, or innocence. This may well require the barrister to separate the personal from the professional; even a client that the barrister finds to be utterly unsympathetic and whose case is quite distasteful must be represented properly; indeed, this client must be represented 'fearlessly' and using 'all proper and lawful means' to protect his best interests (rC15.1). One might say that the 'cab rank' rule is a central plank of the commitment of both barrister and Bar to the administration of justice.

Having said that, as noted earlier, there are situations where the rule must be disapplied and it is to these that we now turn.

### 4.6.6   Disapplying the 'cab rank' rule

There are several grounds on which the 'cab rank' rule must be disapplied; they are set out in rule rC30.

First, the 'cab rank' rule is subordinate to rule rC21—all of those situations where the barrister must not accept instructions, largely on public interest grounds such as conflict of interest or maintenance of client confidentiality. The 'must not accept' in rC21 overrides the 'must accept' in rC29.

Secondly, the 'cab rank' rule can be disapplied if the instructions require the barrister to perform an activity or provide a service 'other than in the course of their ordinary working time'. This is not explained in the guidance but it is tentatively suggested that it has its origins in the equality provisions as applied to the Bar. If one looks at the BSB Handbook Equality Rules (a separate publication which supports the Handbook), one can see that there are provisions in there about equality and diversity, obviously, but specifically also covering issues around fair access to work, parental leave, flexible and part-time working. It may be that this ground for disapplication is aimed at giving barristers with non-professional commitments the ability to juggle more of the demands on their time. Certainly, it has traditionally been the position that a self-employed barrister would work on a case for as long as it took; the notion of the EU working time directive applying to such individuals would be well wide of the mark. But this mindset may be disadvantageous to some, especially those who simply cannot devote every waking moment to their professional practice. This ground for refusal may be an attempt to allow some degree of work/life balance to be achieved.

Thirdly, the rule can be disapplied if acceptance would result in a diary clash. There needs to be another commitment already in the diary for this ground to apply.

Fourthly, the barrister cannot be obliged to accept the instructions if they create a significant potential for professional negligence liability, such that it could exceed the cover which is reasonably available and which is likely to be available for that barrister. This is quite a pragmatic reason to set aside the rule but it protects the client as well as the barrister.

Fifthly, there is no obligation if accepting the instructions would require the barrister to undertake any foreign work, or to act for a foreign lawyer. Both of these terms are defined in Part 6 of the Handbook. A lawyer qualified in another EU member state or in an EFTA country, or from Northern Ireland or Scotland, is not a foreign lawyer for the purposes of this rule. There is no guidance on this ground; presumably it is justified by the likely lack of competence on the part of the barrister. If he is in fact competent to undertake the work, then he can choose to do so.

Sixthly, the identity of the professional client may be a reason for not having to accept the instructions. If the professional client is instructing you as a lay client and thus not in their professional capacity, then the rule does not apply to these facts. Next, if the professional client is not accepting liability for the barrister's fees, there is no obligation to accept the work. Why would you? Next, but related to the preceding reason, the barrister may refuse instructions if the professional client represents 'an unacceptable credit risk', in the barrister's reasonable opinion. Typically, this will arise if he is on the list of Defaulting Solicitors, that is solicitors who are problem payers.

Seventhly, the barrister can refuse to take a case if he has not been offered a proper fee for his services. What constitutes a proper fee is initially for the barrister to decide, usually in consultation with his clerk. Factors to consider include: how complex and difficult the case looks; how long it is likely to take; the barrister's ability, experience, and seniority; and the expenses that he will incur if he accepts the instructions. If a fee has been proposed by the professional client but the barrister does not respond within a reasonable time, then he cannot refuse the instructions on this ground. So, the onus will be on the barrister to act promptly or face being stuck with a poorly paid case. However, if the instructions are offered on the basis of either a conditional fee agreement or a damages-based agreement, then the barrister is entitled to refuse the instructions on the ground of not being offered a proper fee (gC90–91).

Eighthly, the barrister can refuse instructions where his fees have not been agreed (subject to the same caveat as above with the 'proper' fee). He can refuse where he required his fee to be paid prior to acceptance of the instructions and the fee has not been paid. Lastly, he can refuse where acceptance would mean that he is required to act other than on the Standard Contractual Terms for the Supply of Legal Services by Barristers to Authorised Persons 2012, as published on the Bar Council's website, or on his own published standard terms of work (if applicable). None of these last three bases for refusal can be used where the barrister is to be paid by either the Legal Aid Agency (public funding) or the Crown Prosecution Service.

In conclusion, this is rather a miscellany of grounds and it is impossible to see a common thread to them all. Most of them do seem to be justifiable in their own circumstances, aside perhaps from the foreign work embargo. It really is just a matter of knowing the list and when the 'cab rank' rule could be disapplied. It is suggested that, given the Bar's strong attachment to the rule, it should be disapplied very infrequently, despite the long list of situations permitting a barrister to do just that.

## 4.7   QASA—the quality assurance scheme for advocates

### 4.7.1   Introduction to QASA

For some time, concerns have been expressed within the legal profession about the standard of advocacy seen in court. Often, looking at media reports, it seems that this has manifested itself in judicial criticism of solicitor advocates. Whether any of that is merited or not, we should note that clients should 'have confidence in those who are instructed to act on their behalf' (outcome oC15). A joint advocacy group ('JAG') was formed by the BSB, the Solicitors Regulation Authority, and ILEX Professional Standards (Institute of Legal Executives). JAG developed, via several consultation stages, a new framework for advocates' ability to be objectively assessed—this is QASA. The scheme has been approved by the Legal Services Board and has been somewhat controversial. It was opposed by the Criminal Bar Association but survived an attempt at judicial review in June 2015 (see *R (on the application of Lumsdon and ors) v Legal Services Board* [2015] UKSC 41).

In its first incarnation, it applies only to those advocates undertaking 'criminal advocacy'. The Handbook indicates that 'criminal advocacy' has a particular meaning, defined in Part 6. It covers 'advocacy in all hearings arising out of a police-led or Serious Fraud Office-led investigation and prosecuted in the criminal courts by the Crown Prosecution Service or the SFO but does not include hearings arising out of Parts 2, 5, or 8 of the Proceeds of Crime Act 2002'.

### 4.7.2   Provisional and full QASA accreditation

QASA accreditation operates a bit like driving licences—one starts with a provisional and then hopes to progress on to a full one. As noted earlier, the scheme applies currently only to 'criminal advocacy' and that is intended to have a special meaning. If any hearing involves advocacy which falls substantially outside this definition, then a barrister may undertake 'criminal advocacy' even if he does not have provisional or full accreditation (rC32). With this exception, no barrister may undertake 'criminal advocacy' unless he holds either a provisional or full accreditation. The criminal work is divided into four levels and the accreditation held must be appropriate to the level of work being performed. The barrister can cover work at his level or below but generally cannot 'trade up' informally (rC33).

When a barrister successfully applies for registration at level 1 (the lowest level), he will be given full accreditation. Full accreditation is valid for five years from the date granted (rC35). For all other levels, successful registration is rewarded with provisional accreditation. The barrister must apply to convert this into full accreditation within 12 or 24 months of the date granted (rC34).

### 4.7.3 QASA applications

An application has to comply with the QASA Rules. An application form must be completed and the applicant must supply all information required and pay the prescribed fee. Before it makes a decision on the application, the BSB may appoint an independent assessor to assess the applicant's competence to undertake advocacy at the relevant QASA level (rC36–40).

### 4.7.4 QASA registration

A barrister who successfully applies for accreditation at level 1 is granted full accreditation. A successful application for accreditation to levels 2–4 results in provisional accreditation which will be valid for 24 months. Before that period expires, the barrister should apply to convert to full accreditation. This will be accomplished by the barrister being assessed in his first effective criminal trials at his QASA level and submitting the required number of completed evaluation forms which confirm that he is competent at that QASA level. However, the barrister must also enclose all completed evaluation forms from 'effective trials'. An 'effective trial' is not what we might expect but is one that allows for a QASA assessment to be completed, using the QASA standards (rC41.1–5).

If an application for full accreditation fails, the barrister will be granted *provisional* accreditation at the QASA level *below* and then has to apply to convert that into full accreditation within 24 months. It's a bit like snakes and ladders! The only exception is where the barrister drops from level 2 to level 1; here the fall is cushioned by getting *full* accreditation for level 1 immediately (rC41.7–8).

One particularly controversial aspect of QASA has been the inclusion of accreditation for non-trial advocacy, in other words an advocate who will undertake criminal advocacy but not criminal trials. This was something about which the Criminal Bar Association has expressed strong views. Nevertheless, it is in the scheme (rC41.9–11). A non-trial advocate will apply for registration on level 2. A successful application will get provisional accreditation which must then be converted to a full one. On obtaining full accreditation, the non-trial advocate will be allowed to undertake non-trial work up to QASA level 3 *and* trials at QASA level 1.

### 4.7.5 QASA progression

This refers to moving up a QASA level, not moving from provisional to full accreditation.

Once a barrister has full accreditation on a level, he can apply to move to the next level. Moving from QASA level 1 to 2 requires notifying the BSB of one's intention to progress to level 2—this will result in provisional accreditation at level 2. The barrister then has 24 months to convert it into full accreditation. He must be assessed in his first effective criminal trials at level 2, submit the required number of completed evaluation forms which confirm his competence in level 2 trials, and all completed evaluation forms obtained from effective trials. This means that the BSB can be assured that the barrister has shown level 2 competence in the requisite minimum number of trials but it also shows the BSB the full picture. A successful application results in the grant of full accreditation at level 2, valid for five years from date of grant (rC42.1–5).

Moving from level 2 to 3 or 3 to 4 involves a two-stage process. One first applies for provisional accreditation at the new higher level. This requires the barrister to submit the prescribed number of completed evaluation forms showing that he is *very competent* at his current level. As usual, all completed evaluation forms for effective trials must also be submitted, to show the full picture to the BSB. If successful, the barrister is awarded provisional accreditation at the higher level. This will be valid for 12 months. Before it expires, the barrister must apply to convert it to full accreditation. The procedure is essentially the same as above, although the barrister need only show competence at this level to convert. A successful application will result in the grant of full accreditation. An unsuccessful application means that the barrister can continue to conduct criminal advocacy at his current level until his accreditation expires (rC42.6–13).

**4.7.6    Re-accreditation, lapse of accreditation, variations, underperformance, and appeals**

4.7.6.1    Re-accreditation

Once a barrister has full accreditation for a QASA level, he can keep that for five years but must then apply for re-accreditation at that level. He will need to submit evidence, as prescribed, to show his continuing competence to undertake advocacy at the current QASA level. A successful application will result in another five-year grant of full accreditation. An unsuccessful application will result in a drop down to the level below on a provisional accreditation (unless dropping from QASA level 2 to level 1); that must be converted to a full accreditation at that lower level within 24 months (rC43–47).

4.7.6.2    Lapse of accreditation

If the barrister fails to apply to convert a provisional accreditation into a full one before it expires, the provisional accreditation will lapse. A timely application to convert means that the provisional accreditation will not lapse. A full accreditation will lapse after five years, in the absence of a timely application for re-accreditation. Once accreditation has lapsed, the barrister may not undertake 'criminal advocacy' (rC48–51).

4.7.6.3    Variation

A barrister may experience difficulties in getting enough completed evaluation forms within the prescribed period. In that situation, he may apply to the BSB for an extension to meet the requirement. If he simply is having problems in getting completed evaluation forms, he can ask the BSB to have him assessed by an independent assessor. He can then use that assessment in substitution for one completed evaluation form (rC52–53).

4.7.6.4    Underperformance

The BSB may have concerns about a barrister's competence under QASA. These may arise during an application by the barrister for registration, conversion, progression, or re-accreditation. Concerns may arise independently of action by the barrister—an evaluation form expressing concerns about him may go into the BSB at any time. Where the BSB has received concerns, it may appoint an independent assessor to conduct an assessment of the barrister's advocacy, or recommend that he undertakes a specified course of training, or revoke his current level of QASA accreditation. It may also refer him under the Fitness to Practise Rules or the Complaints Rules, for his health or conduct to be considered (rC54–55).

If accreditation is revoked under rC55, the barrister will drop down a QASA level and be put on a provisional accreditation, to be converted up to a full one within 24 months.

If the barrister has applied unsuccessfully for registration or re-accreditation at QASA level 1, he is not entitled to accept any instructions to conduct criminal advocacy and the BSB may recommend further training before any fresh application for registration or re-accreditation. This may affect his obligations under the 'cab rank' rule (see **4.6.5**).

4.7.6.5    Appeals

Any decision made by the BSB under the QASA Rules may be challenged by the barrister, who can appeal to the BSB.

# 5

## You and your regulator

### 5.1 Introduction

The regulator here is the BSB. Part 2, section C4, is intended to enable the BSB to perform its regulatory functions effectively. Specific aspects include ensuring that those regulated by the BSB pass the 'fit and proper person' test and continue to do so; also, that serious misconduct is reported to the BSB and that the BSB can effectively investigate such reports.

It is important that there is public confidence in those persons who are regulated by the BSB. It has to be able to get the information that it needs in order to be able to regulate effectively. With this in mind, any regulated person must respond promptly to the BSB, whether this relates to a requirement to provide information to it or to compliance with any decision or sentence imposed by it (or other body operating within the disciplinary or fitness to practise frameworks). The information that is requested may relate to oneself or any other BSB regulated person. Most importantly, the BSB may request information that is covered by legal professional privilege ('LPP'). In the first edition of the Handbook, the BSB took the view that this information must be supplied—in other words, client privilege is no barrier to disclosure. In the current, second, edition, the BSB says that the barrister is *not* entitled to disclose such information unless the client gives their consent to the disclosure. The barrister may ask the client if he is willing to waive the privilege and permit disclosure but there is a risk that the barrister has a conflict of interest in seeking permission from the client. If so, then the client should be advised to obtain independent advice on the issue. See section C4, gC93.

### 5.2 Reporting oneself to the BSB

We highlighted in **5.1** the need to *react* swiftly to requests or decisions made by the BSB. Here, we start to look at the duty to be proactive. It can apply to one's own circumstances or to instances of serious misconduct by another barrister or registered European lawyer (see **5.3**).

As we shall see in **chapter 11**, where we look at qualifying as a barrister, there are certain requirements and standards that an aspiring barrister must meet. Of necessity, these standards cannot be lowered once one has qualified. So, many of the matters that must be disclosed by those who aspire to become barristers and which ultimately may prevent them from fulfilling their ambition are also to be found in Part 2, section C4.

#### 5.2.1 What must be reported

The onus is on the barrister (or BSB regulated person) to tell the BSB if any of the following situations arises, and to do so promptly:

- He is charged with an indictable offence in England and Wales, or with an offence of comparable gravity anywhere else.
- He is convicted of, or accepts a caution for, any criminal offence anywhere in the world, other than a 'minor criminal offence' (one which may be dealt with by a fixed penalty or where the major element of the crime is unlawful parking).

- He knows that he (or an entity of which he is a manager) is the subject of disciplinary or other regulatory action by a regulator.
- He is a manager of a non-BSB authorised body which is subject to an intervention by its regulator.
- He is a registered European lawyer and he knows that his home regulator is investigating his conduct, or has charged him with a disciplinary offence, or has made a finding of professional misconduct against him, or his authorisation to practise is suspended in his home state.
- He is made bankrupt or is disqualified from being a company director, or such proceedings are initiated against him, or he enters into an arrangement with his creditors.
- He has been authorised to practise by another approved regulator.
- He has committed serious professional misconduct.

Where he considers that he has committed serious misconduct, he ought to take reasonable steps to mitigate its effects.

According to guidance gC94.1, a 'spent' conviction or caution does not need to be reported to the BSB under rC65. However, unless the conviction or caution becomes 'spent' immediately upon being imposed, then the BSB has to be notified 'promptly'. This is therefore likely to be a rarely applied exception to the reporting obligation. The group that are most likely to benefit will be those who have not yet begun the Bar Professional Training Course. The period before they fell under the aegis of the BSB may have been long enough for the conviction or caution to become 'spent'.

### 5.2.2   What is serious misconduct

There is an inclusive list in Part 2, at gC96. Many of the entries are quite obvious and infringe Core Duties but some are rather more surprising. 'Serious misconduct' includes:

- dishonesty
- assault or harassment
- trying to access confidential information relating to the opponent's case, including his instructions, without consent
- trying to access confidential information relating to someone else in chambers, whether a member, an employee, or a pupil, without consent
- knowingly or recklessly misleading a court or an opponent, or attempting to do so
- encouraging a witness to give untruthful or misleading evidence
- being under the influence of drink or drugs whilst in court
- conduct that poses a serious risk to the public
- failing to permit the Bar Council or BSB to have access to any premises from which you provide (or are believed to provide) legal services, or to any documents which relate to those premises or to your practice (rC70)
- failing to report another barrister (or registered European lawyer) where you have reasonable grounds to suspect that he is guilty of serious misconduct (rC66).

## 5.3   Reporting others to the BSB

The obligation is only to report serious misconduct where there are reasonable grounds to believe that another barrister or registered European lawyer is guilty of such misconduct (see **5.2.2**) and the barrister has a genuine and reasonably held belief to that effect (rC66–67). So, the reporting barrister's actions must be justifiable both objectively and subjectively.

However, the obligation to report is subject to the barrister's duty to keep his client's affairs confidential. There are several other circumstances where a report need not be made, even if the barrister would be objectively and subjectively justified in making a report.

No report need be made if the barrister considers that the facts are likely to have come to the attention of the BSB independently, by virtue of the fact that the matters that have led him to believe there has been serious misconduct by another are in the public domain. This sounds a little bit like discouraging 'nosy neighbours'. The barrister also has no duty to report if he is aware that the subject of the possible serious misconduct report has already reported themselves to the BSB. Where the events that lead the barrister to learn of another's serious misconduct are covered by their (presumably their client's) legal professional privilege, there is no duty to report and presumably one should in fact not report as to do so would breach the privilege. Finally, it is in the public interest that barristers are encouraged to make use of Bar Council advice helplines (for example the ethics helpline and the pupillage helpline); it is also important that when they do so, they are frank and open and the person advising them is able to give them fully informed advice. Thus, any BSB authorised person working on such a helpline who receives information in confidence has no duty to report to the BSB any misconduct which is thus disclosed to them. However, they are expected to encourage the caller to self-report to the BSB.

## 5.4  The Legal Ombudsman

If a barrister's client is unhappy with the service given by the barrister, they can complain. In the first instance, they should complain to the barrister using the chambers' complaints procedure (see **chapter 8**). If either no timely action is taken (allow at least eight weeks, according to the Legal Ombudsman website), or the client is unhappy with the final outcome, they have six months in which they can go to the Legal Ombudsman. The Ombudsman will then investigate the complaint; an investigator will be appointed and will first try to resolve the complaint informally and amicably, involving both client and barrister. Only if this fails will a recommendation report be produced; again, if the barrister and the client agree with the recommendation, the matter will be closed informally. If there is no agreement by both, then the matter will go to the Ombudsman for a formal decision. In order to facilitate the Ombudsman's procedures, it is incumbent on barristers to give 'all reasonable assistance' to the Ombudsman, when requested to do so (rC71). The rule is not explicitly limited to the barrister who is the subject of the complaint. For further information on the Legal Ombudsman scheme, see <http://www.legalombudsman.org.uk/helping-legal-service-providers/>.

# You and your practice

## 6.1 Introduction

This is quite a broad section, covering issues such as handling client money, professional insurance, outsourcing, and entering an association with others. It also looks at how the self-employed barrister's practice should be administered, and the administration of chambers and of BSB authorised bodies. The last two topics are contained in sections C5.3 and C5.4 respectively and neither are on the assessable syllabus published by the BSB for the Professional Ethics assessment on the BPTC.

The key outcome here is that the barrister's practice has to be run in a competent manner, compliant with the Core Duties, and to ensure that everyone working around the barrister—his clerks, employees, and pupils—understand and adhere to what they need to do so that the barrister meets *his* obligations under the Handbook (oC24).

## 6.2 Client money

### 6.2.1 The key principle

It has long been the tradition of the Bar that barristers do not handle client money. Even looking at the traditional design of the barrister's gown shows this—with the almost invisible pocket supposedly meant for payment, stitched onto the back of the gown where the barrister cannot really see it. The idea is that the client can just slip the money in and the barrister takes it on trust that the agreed, or reasonable, sum has been paid. Of course, that system has not been used for centuries, if at all. The attitude of the Bar towards client money can perhaps be illustrated by the fact that until relatively recently, a barrister's professional fee was described as an 'honorarium', a sort of tip or reward for doing a good job and could not be sued for as a sum due under a contract; also for the self-employed barrister, it was the clerk who dealt with fees—first agreeing a fee with solicitors, then demanding it via a fee note and collecting it before transmitting it onto the barrister. The situation has changed over the last few years but the Bar still has a very strict policy when it comes to keeping barristers apart from money and specifically money in which the client has an interest.

So we can see in rC73 a very strong statement about barristers and their clients' money:

> Except where you are acting in your capacity as a manager of an authorised (non-BSB) body, you must not receive, control or handle client money apart from what the client pays you for your services.

Not only can the barrister himself not handle client money but he cannot hold it through anyone else (gC103). De facto control is also prohibited (gC104).

### 6.2.2 What is client money?

This is defined in Part 6 and it covers money and other assets:

- which the client owns beneficially or
- which has been provided by, or for the benefit of, the client or
- which is intended by someone else to be transmitted to the client.

It does *not* include a fixed fee which has been paid to the barrister in advance; nor does it cover money which belongs to the employer of an employed barrister. It does not cover money paid in settlement of an accrued debt. Of these, probably the most problematic is the fixed fee paid in advance. Guidance gC106 is very explicit that this is not client money but the fact that gC107 goes on to explain this in greater detail suggests that the position can be confusing.

### 6.2.3    The fixed fee

The *fixed fee* referred to in this section of the Handbook basically relates to privately funded work. We can begin with the idea that a barrister should only be paid for work done and that the rate for that work is likely to vary according to factors such as the nature and complexity of the case, its duration, the time spent on it by the barrister, and the expertise that he has. There are essentially three ways that a barrister's remuneration can be paid: (i) in arrears after the work has been completed (which is really the traditional method), (ii) from time to time (where the work is spread over a substantial period and it would be difficult to manage cash flow without some money coming in), and (iii) in advance.

The norm is payment at the end of the case. Essentially, the barrister is extending credit to the client in this situation. That should not pose problems for payment. Usually, when the self-employed barrister is instructed by a professional client (typically a solicitor), the professional client is responsible for the barrister's fee. The professional client will usually be 'put in funds' by the client—that is, money is paid upfront by the lay client to the solicitor. That is not an issue for the barrister as he is not handling the lay client's money and it is not an issue for the professional client as they are subject to different rules about handling client money. Handling client money is a daily occurrence for solicitors and a necessary part of their practice; they have to be trained in how to handle it and account for it—such training is not a normal part of training for the Bar.

Where this becomes more problematic is when there is no professional client, no intermediary between the barrister and the lay client. So really we are looking at public access work here, where a lay client is directly instructing the barrister. No one has been 'put in funds' here so there is no guarantee for the barrister that money will be available at the end of the case to pay his fees. Payment in arrears seems less advisable here. The temptation for the barrister is that he seeks in effect to be 'put in funds' himself by the lay client. He may ask for payment in advance and, in order to make that more acceptable to the lay client, he may ask for a fixed fee to be paid. This can be attractive to a lay client as they know precisely what their own legal fees are going to be.

The risk with the fixed fee is that someone is likely to feel short-changed at the end of the matter, either the barrister thinks he has undercharged when he looks at the work he has put in, or the client feels that he has overpaid. The likely solution is that the barrister will seek a fixed fee at the upper range of what he would expect to be paid for the anticipated work and will assure the client that, once the work has been completed, whatever balance is left from the fee after his *actual* fee has been calculated and deducted will be repaid to the client. In essence, the fee is capped but the actual fee might eventually turn out to be less than the cap. At this point, we see the dilemma for the barrister: he is now holding client money. He has not yet done the work so he hasn't earned his fee and, if he is agreeing with the client to repay any surplus, there is a real risk that a court may think that he is holding some of the money on trust for the lay client. This is exactly what the rule prohibits, of course.

The Handbook addresses this in gC107. As long as several criteria are satisfied, there will be no breach of the rule:

- There must be a clear written agreement between the barrister and the client, made in advance, as to the way that payment will work.
- The agreement must stipulate that:
  - the barrister's fee for any work will be calculated according to the time spent on it
  - a fixed fee will be paid by the lay client in advance
  - once the work has been done, any difference between the fixed fee and the fee that has been earned will be repaid by the barrister and

- ◦ the difference between the two will *not* be held on trust by the barrister for the client.
- The lay client must be one who can reasonably be expected to understand the implications of the agreement.

The barrister should also give consideration to whether such an agreement is in the client's best interests (CD2) and whether the client fully understands its implications. The guidance states that where the amount of work that will be needed is unclear, it may be better to agree a scheme of staged payments to be paid as the proceedings continue, rather than a fixed fee paid in advance. The guidance advises that a barrister 'should take extreme care if contracting with a client in this way'. If the barrister abuses the position by overestimating the sum likely to be due to himself, sets the fixed fee too high and thus holds more money than is reasonable at the start of the case, he is very likely to be found to be holding client money and thus in breach of rC73.

### 6.2.4  Third party services

As noted earlier, the barrister is forbidden to have even de facto control over a client's money (gC104). Thus, having the ability to determine the use or destination of funds, whether paid by or for the benefit of the client or intended by another party to be transmitted to your client, will breach the prohibition. This is so regardless of whether or not the funds are (a) beneficially owned by the client and (b) held in an account of the barrister.

In light of this, if the barrister uses a third party payment service in order to make payments either to, from, or on behalf of the client, he must take care to ensure that the arrangement will not result in him handling client money. He should only use the third party service to make payments to, from, or on behalf of the client for legal services; he should carry out reasonable checks to make sure that use of this service is consistent with both his duty to act competently and in his client's best interests (rC74; gC109–111).

## 6.3  Insurance

As one might expect, a barrister must have adequate insurance cover for the legal services he provides (rC76.1). The BSB may stipulate a minimum level of insurance cover and/or minimum terms for the insurance that must be taken out by 'BSB authorised persons'. This category covers practising barristers, pupils in their 'second six', and registered European lawyers.

When acting as a self-employed barrister (a practising barrister who is self-employed), the barrister must belong to the Bar Mutual Indemnity Fund (or 'BMIF'). As a member, it is your obligation promptly to pay the insurance premiums and supply such information as BMIF requires. However, if a pupil is covered by his pupil supervisor's professional insurance then the pupil does not need to be a member of BMIF; nor does a registered European lawyer who has been called to the Bar under Qualification Rule rQ94.

If the barrister is working in an authorised (non-BSB) body, the insurance cover that the body must have will be determined by its approved regulator. An employed barrister working for a non-authorised body need not be insured if he is only providing legal services to his employer. If he is providing legal services to other people as part of his job, then he needs to consider whether his employer's insurance cover is adequate to cover claims made in respect of those services, including any *pro bono* work (gC115–116).

## 6.4  Associations with others

The principle here is quite simple—you cannot avoid the obligations placed upon you as an individual simply by practising in an 'association'. 'Association' is defined in Part 6 to cover the situation where several 'BSB authorised individuals' are practising as a set of chambers. 'BSB authorised individual' is synonymous with 'BSB authorised person'. As noted earlier, this can be a practising barrister, a 'second six' pupil, or a registered European lawyer. There is also an 'association' where BSB authorised persons and people who are not such 'persons' share premises and/or costs and/or use a common means for obtaining or distributing work in such a way that the association is not required to be authorised as an entity under the Legal Services Act 2007.

Where a barrister is in an association, the BSB must be notified and supplied with whatever details are required. The barrister should not enter into an association with anyone where, simply by being associated with him, the barrister may reasonably be considered as bringing the profession into disrepute, or diminishing public trust in himself and the profession.

To protect clients (and barristers) from a possible conflict of interest, where the barrister proposes to refer a client to an organisation in which he has a 'material commercial interest', he must inform the client in writing about that interest before making the referral and keep a record of all such referrals in case the BSB wishes to review them. He should only make the referral where it is in the client's best interest. Similarly, if an organisation in which the barrister has a material commercial interest is proposing to refer a client to the barrister, then the barrister (not the organisation) must make a written declaration of his interest to the client before accepting the referral and keep a record of all such referrals, as well as having a clear agreement with the organisation addressing how any conflicts of interest are to be resolved. A 'material commercial interest' is defined as one where an objective and fully-informed observer would reasonably conclude that it might potentially influence the barrister's judgment (rC79–85). The guidance states that the purpose behind these rules is to ensure that clients and the public are not confused by such associations; it should always be clear who is responsible for doing the work and how and by whom that person is being regulated.

## 6.5  Outsourcing

In the same way that being in an association does not absolve the barrister from his individual obligations under the Handbook, neither does outsourcing any support services in connection with his supply of legal services. He remains responsible for compliance and must ensure that the contract between himself and the third party protects client confidentiality to a similar degree as provided in the Handbook, as well as complying with any other obligations which may be affected by the outsourcing (see rC86). This rule does not apply where the barrister instructs a pupil or 'devil' to undertake work on his behalf; see instead rC15 (C3: You and your client).

## 6.6  Administration and conduct of self-employed practice

A barrister must take reasonable steps to ensure that his practice is administered efficiently and properly and that proper records are kept. Records relevant to any fees charged or claimed must be kept at least until either the fees are paid or any determination or assessment of costs has been done and the time for an appeal has passed, whichever comes later. The client should be provided with enough detail of the work done as is reasonably necessary to justify the fees charged (C5.2).

## 6.7  Administration of chambers

This is covered in the Handbook at C5.3. It is not on the BPTC syllabus.

The thrust of the rules here is the onus is on the individual barrister to ensure that chambers' administration is competent and efficient, that chambers has appointed someone to liaise with the BSB about any regulatory requirements, that chambers does not employ someone who has been disqualified from such employment, that pupils and pupillages are dealt with properly, and that there are proper arrangements for managing any conflicts of interest that arise and ensuring that clients' affairs remain confidential (rC89–90).

# Dealing with the client without a solicitor—public access and licensed access work

## 7.1 Introduction

It almost goes without saying that there are particular pressures involved in dealing directly with the client. Most barristers are unused to the proximity of the client, there may be issues around the conduct of litigation—what is involved, who is responsible—and of course there may be concerns about client money. It follows that in order to be operating in the public interest, it is important that barristers undertaking this type of work possess the necessary skills and experience (oC30). Proper records need to be kept of all such work and appropriate systems need to be in place for this. See generally Part 2, D2, of the Handbook.

It is important to make sure that clients only use public access to instruct a barrister when this is in their best interests and they have a full understanding of what they will need to do as the matter progresses. So, there will inevitably need to be an introductory contact where these issues are explored and resolved, either with the client continuing to instruct via public access, or moving to a more traditional relationship and instructing a professional client, as well as or instead of the barrister.

The BSB has produced detailed guidance on public access work—see 'Public access guidance for barristers' on the BSB website.

The BSB has also provided guidance for barristers' clerks on the rules on public access and licensed access work. One of the important matters raised by this guidance is the need to be alert for signs of money laundering, although it does make the point that responsibility for ensuring compliance with the Proceeds of Crime Act 2002 and the Money Laundering Regulations remains at all times with the barrister and cannot be delegated to the clerk. See <https://www.barstandardsboard.org.uk/media/1580341/public_access_and_licensed_access_guidance_for_clerks_-_jan_2014.pdf>.

## 7.2 Public access work

### 7.2.1 Qualification to do public access work

In order to accept public access work, a barrister must hold a full practising certificate, so it follows that a pupil barrister cannot undertake public access work. In addition, the barrister must have satisfactorily completed the appropriate training to do such work, be registered with the BSB as a public access practitioner, and have adequate insurance cover.

Although a pupil barrister cannot undertake public access work, a very junior barrister who has successfully completed his pupillage can do so. If a barrister of less than three years' standing wishes to undertake public access work, then he must fulfil an additional requirement—he must have an experienced 'qualified person' available to guide and support him in his work. See further rC121 and rS22.

### 7.2.2    Accepting public access instructions

By definition, there is no professional client involved here. It follows that the 'cab rank' rule does not apply here and no barrister is obliged to accept any public access instructions. Nevertheless, he must still comply with his obligations under CD 8, rC12, and rC28.

Before accepting public access instructions, the barrister must take reasonable steps to check whether it would be in the client's interests (or in the interests of justice) to instruct a solicitor or other form of professional client. This is a continuing obligation; if the barrister subsequently forms the opinion that it would be in the client's interests (or in the interests of justice) to instruct a solicitor or other professional client, he must tell the client this and he must withdraw from the case unless the client acts on his advice by instructing a solicitor or other professional client to act on his behalf. The barrister must also check that the client is able to make an informed decision about whether to apply for public funding or to go ahead with the public access instructions.

Once the barrister has accepted the public access instructions, he must inform the client forthwith, clearly and in writing, of:

- the work that he has agreed to perform and the fact that, in performing it, he will be subject to the conduct rules and scope of practice rules, in Parts 2 and 3 of the Handbook
- the fees which the barrister proposes to charge for the work or the basis on which the fee will be calculated
- the contact arrangements for the barrister
- the barrister's complaints procedure
- the fact that the barrister may be prevented from completing the work if a conflict of interest arises or there is a real risk that by maintaining confidential information of another client, he may not be able to act in the public access client's best interests and what can be expected of him in that situation. Typically, this means that the barrister will withdraw from the case (rC21).

Further, the client must be told that the barrister is not allowed to perform the functions of a solicitor in relation to the conduct of litigation, unless the barrister has been authorised by the BSB to do so (via a litigation extension; see **chapter 10**). There is a model letter on the BSB website that will cover all of the foregoing matters.

Having accepted public access instructions, the barrister must keep a record of the case. This must include the dates that the instructions were received and accepted, the client's name, the case name, and the dates of all subsequent correspondence, for example when an advice was sent or when there was a telephone conversation.

Unless otherwise agreed, the barrister is entitled to take and keep copies of all documents sent by the client but must return all documents received if and when the client demands their return, whether or not he has been paid for any work done (so the barrister has no lien over the paperwork). On the other hand, the barrister need not deliver any documents he has drafted until he has been paid for all work done for the client. Where instructed in a civil matter, the barrister may take a proof of evidence from the client.

See generally Part 2, section D2.1, rC119–131.

## 7.3    Licensed access work

This was originally launched in 1990, when it was known as direct professional access. The basic idea was that certain professions, such as accountants and surveyors, might be capable of and interested in instructing barristers without using a solicitor as an intermediary. The scheme has been extended since then and is now known as licensed access. This work is governed by the Licensed Access Recognition Regulations. A licensed access client is any person or organisation that has applied to the BSB and been approved as such a client in accordance with the Regulations. Once approved, the BSB will issue the licence.

A self-employed barrister can accept instructions from a licensed access client if, and only if, the client is identified at the time of giving the instructions and at the same time sends the barrister a copy of the licence that has been issued by the BSB. The licence can vary considerably, as to its terms, its duration, and the type of matter on which the licensed client can instruct a barrister, so when a licensed access client seeks to instruct a barrister they need to supply a copy of the licence. If the barrister and his chambers are not able to provide the services that the licensed access client requires, he should not accept the instructions. If the barrister considers that it is in the client's best interests (or in the interests of justice) that an intermediary (such as a solicitor) be instructed, either in addition to the barrister or in substitution for him, he should decline the licensed access instructions. If the barrister, at any subsequent time, forms such an opinion, he should inform the client forthwith.

When a barrister accepts instructions from a licensed access client, he must promptly send the client either a statement that the instructions have been accepted on the standard terms previously agreed in writing with the client or on the standard Licensed Access Terms of Work. If neither of these applies, then the barrister must send the client a written copy of the agreement, setting out the terms on which he has agreed to do the work and specifying the basis on which he is to be paid. In any event, the client must be told that the barrister is not allowed to perform the functions of a solicitor in relation to the conduct of litigation, unless of course he has been authorised by the BSB to do so (via a litigation extension).

Having accepted the instructions, if the barrister at any point considers that there are substantial grounds to believe that the client has failed to comply with the terms of their licence, that failure shall be reported to the BSB forthwith.

Either the barrister or the licensed access client must retain for six years following the date of the last item of work done, copies of the instructions, copies of all advices and documents drafted, a list of all documents enclosed with instructions, and notes of all conferences and telephone advice.

See Part 2, section D2.2; rC132–141.

## 7.4  Barristers and immigration advisors

In June 2015, the BSB issued some guidance for barristers who supervise immigration advisors. Under the Immigration and Asylum Act 1999, as amended, a barrister can now act as a supervisor for the purposes of immigration advice and services. From the client's perspective, such advice is likely to come from an advisor, with the barrister remaining in the background, advising the advisor, and having no direct role in the advisor–client relationship. However, the BSB considers that the supervisory role of the barrister is something relied upon by the client with the result that the barrister is personally responsible for the work undertaken by the advisor. This will be seen as a form of public access work and it should therefore not be undertaken unless the barrister is registered as a public access practitioner.

When acting as a supervisor, the barrister must comply with all relevant provisions of the Code of Conduct, including the Core Duties. This will include informing the client in writing when instructed (or at the next reasonable opportunity) of the right to make a complaint (see rC99).

# 8

## Complaints

### 8.1 Introduction

Complaints to the BSB are addressed in Part 5 of the Handbook, entitled 'Enforcement Regulations'. Part 5, Section A contains the Complaints Regulations; in particular, it sets out the powers and functions of the Professional Conduct Committee ('PCC'). So, regard should be had for these provisions when considering the question of a complaint about misconduct and the procedure that will be adopted to resolve the complaint. However, Part 5 is not on the syllabus for the BPTC. What *is* on the syllabus is Part 2, section D1.1—the *complaints rules*. The difference between the two is basically that the PCC handles complaints about non-compliance with the Handbook whilst the complaints rules are there for a client to complain about the legal services he received from his barrister. If a client does complain to the PCC about their barrister, then the PCC must refer it on to the Legal Ombudsman without further consideration. The rest of this chapter will confine itself to the complaints rules under Part 2, section D1.1.

### 8.2 The complaints rules

Basically, clients must be told clearly that they can complain if they are unhappy with the service they have received and they must be informed how to complain. Any complaint must be addressed promptly and the client must be kept up-dated about its progress (oC26–27).

The BSB says that there are three types of complaint—about poor service, about misconduct, and about professionally negligent work. Misconduct matters should go to the BSB as per the Conduct Regulations. Professional negligence should probably be addressed through legal proceedings. The complaints rules address complaints about poor level of service.

When a barrister is instructed, he must inform the client in writing of the right to complain, how to complain and to whom, and any time limits for doing so. If the client has the right to complain to the Legal Ombudsman, that must be stated clearly. If it is impractical to provide this information when instructed, it must be given at the next appropriate opportunity.

In the case of referral work, the client should be told that he does not need to go through solicitors but can complain to chambers directly. It is not necessary to give a professional client the written information in a separate letter but it should be provided in the ordinary terms of reference supplied when the barrister accepts instructions in the matter.

Chambers' complaints procedure should be displayed on chambers' literature and its website.

The procedure for making a complaint should be convenient and easy to use. When a complaint is received, it must be acknowledged promptly, telling the complainant who will be dealing with it and their role in chambers. The complainant must be given a copy of chambers' complaints procedure and a deadline by which they will next hear from chambers about the complaint.

Once a complaint has been dealt with by chambers, the complainant must be given written notice of any right that they have to complain to the Legal Ombudsman, how to do so, and any time limit. Presumably, this is only likely to be of any relevance where the complaint has been rejected or the complainant is dissatisfied for some other reason.

All records relating to complaints must be kept confidential and material should be disclosed only for the purpose of dealing with the complaint, or where chambers conducts an internal review to improve its complaints handling, or where the BSB requires the information for an audit. A record should be kept for six years from the date on which the complaint was resolved.

See further the BSB Guidance on first tier complaints handling.

# 9

# The unregistered barrister

## 9.1 Introduction

An unregistered barrister is a barrister who has been called to the Bar by an Inn of Court, has not subsequently ceased to be a member of the Bar but who does *not* hold a practising certificate. A practising certificate could be a full practising certificate, a provisional one, a limited one, a European lawyer's practising certificate, or a temporary one issued by the Bar Council. Rule rI7 states that the Handbook applies to unregistered barristers. The Handbook Part 2, section D, sets out the rules which apply to particular groups of regulated people. D4 covers unregistered barristers.

The Core Duties apply to unregistered barristers; in particular Core Duties 5 and 9 apply to them at all times. However, the Conduct Rules in Part 2 do not apply to them, except where the rules state clearly that they do so apply. Other rules that *do apply* to unregistered barristers include:

- rC3.5: must ensure the ability to act independently is not compromised
- rC4: duty to act in client's best interests is subordinate to the duty owed to the court
- rC8: must not do anything which could reasonably be seen by the public to undermine one's honesty, integrity, and independence
- rC16: duty to act in client's best interests is subordinate to duty to the court, obligation to act with honesty and integrity, and to maintain one's independence
- rC19: must not mislead clients about nature and scope of legal services being provided, the terms on which they are being provided, who is legally responsible, whether one is entitled to supply the services, whether one is regulated and if so by whom, and the extent to which one is covered by insurance. This is probably the key provision for the unregistered barrister
- rC64–70: in summary, rules relating to the relationship between the barrister and the Bar Standards Board.

## 9.2 The unregistered barrister and the inexperienced client

An unregistered barrister must fulfil certain obligations towards an inexperienced client (rC144). An 'inexperienced client' is an individual, a micro-enterprise business, a charity with an annual net income of less than £1 million, a trustee of a trust with assets valued at less than £1 million, a club or association managed by its members with an annual net income of under £1 million, or the personal representative or beneficiary of the estate of a deceased who had not themselves complained to the Legal Ombudsman (gC153).

An inexperienced client who receives legal services from an unregistered barrister must understand that the barrister is not subject to the same regulatory framework as a practising barrister, so that the safeguards are not the same. So, the client must be told that the barrister is not acting as a barrister (this probably means a practising barrister), that he is not subject to certain parts of the Code and the Handbook, and that in the event of a complaint to the BSB, it will only be considered if it relates to the Core Duties or those specific parts of the Handbook that apply to the unregistered barrister. The inexperienced client must also be told that the unregistered barrister is not covered by professional indemnity insurance (unless he is so covered), and that he has the right to complain, how to do so, and to whom and any deadline for doing so but that he has no right to complain to the Legal Ombudsman about the legal services being supplied (rC144).

The obligations to inform the inexperienced client, as set out above, do not apply where the unregistered barrister supplies legal services as the employee or manager of an authorised body, or of a body which is regulated by a professional body or regulator. An 'authorised body' is a partnership, a limited liability partnership, or a company, which has been authorised or licensed by an approved regulator (other than the BSB) to undertake reserved legal activities (rC145).

## 9.3 The unregistered barrister and the provision of legal services

An unregistered barrister is able to supply legal services but must not engage in any reserved legal activities. These terms are defined in the Legal Services Act 2007. The most obvious forms of reserved legal activity are exercising rights of audience and conducting litigation. A practising barrister with a practising certificate could engage in these reserved legal activities and, if he had a 'litigation extension' to his practising certificate he could 'conduct litigation'. If an unregistered barrister engaged in reserved legal activities, he would be committing a crime under the Legal Services Act 2007. On the subject of reserved legal activities, see further **chapter 10**.

The unregistered barrister is allowed to represent clients at a tribunal hearing, since this does not involve any exercise of a right of audience. Furthermore, the unregistered barrister is allowed to act as a mediator, to lecture on law, and to write law books, since these activities are not even regarded as legal services.

## 9.4 Holding yourself out as a barrister

It is not permitted to practise as a barrister unless you hold a practising certificate (see rS8). If you hold yourself out as a barrister whilst providing legal services, this would amount to practising as a barrister. You would be considered to have held yourself out as a barrister if you described yourself as a barrister to a client, perhaps on a business card, or if you attended court robed as a barrister and sat in the seats reserved for barristers.

See further the BSB guidance for unregistered barristers (barristers without practising certificates)—supplying legal services and holding out.

# 10

# The scope of practice

## 10.1 Introduction

Part 3 of the Handbook covers the scope of practice and the authorisation and licensing rules. Of the five substantive sections, the Ethics syllabus issued by the BSB whittles this list down. We need only be concerned about 3B—the scope of practice rules and 3C—the fundamentals of the rules about practising certificates. This will, of course, be reflected in the coverage in this chapter.

## 10.2 Scope of practice

Section B is fairly short but quite important. It addresses what work you are allowed to do and the circumstances under which it must be done. It covers the provision of legal services and reserved legal activities; these are crucial elements within the regulatory framework set up by the Legal Services Act 2007 ('LSA').

### 10.2.1 Reserved legal activities and legal services

'Reserved legal activities' are ones which are regulated by the LSA 2007 and a person (including an unincorporated body and a body corporate) can only carry on a reserved legal activity if entitled to do so (LSA 2007, s 12; rS6 in Section 3B of the Handbook). One is entitled to do so if *authorised* or exempt (LSA 2007, s 13). The following are the reserved legal activities under LSA 2007, s 12:

- exercising a right of audience in a court
- the conduct of litigation
- reserved instrument activities
- probate activities
- notarial services
- oath administration.

The first of these is straightforward. The second is the sort of litigation work that is traditionally carried out by solicitors (see further **10.3.6**). Probate activities and the administration of oaths are also reasonably familiar work, albeit not often carried out by most self-employed barristers. 'Reserved instrument activities' is probably the most vague term here; it is defined in LSA 2007, Sch 2, as 'preparing any instrument of transfer or charge for the purposes of the Land Registration Act 2002', or making an application or lodging a document for registration under that Act, or preparing any other instrument relating to real or personal property for the purposes of the law of England and Wales. It also includes preparing a contract for the sale or other disposition of land, other than in a will or other form of testamentary disposal.

'Legal services' are defined in Part 6 as including giving legal advice; representing a client; and drafting or settling a statement of case, witness statement, or other legal document. They do not include sitting as a judge, acting as a mediator, giving free legal advice to friends, being a 'libel reader' for the press, teaching law, or writing law books or articles.

## 10.2.2    Authorisation to carry out reserved legal activities

An 'authorised person' is defined in LSA 2007, s 18, as a person who is authorised to carry on a reserved legal activity by an approved regulator. Part 6 of the Handbook has several overlapping definitions of persons who are 'authorised'. An 'authorised body' means an 'authorised (non-BSB) body'. 'Authorised (non-BSB) person' also means an 'authorised (non-BSB) body'. An 'authorised (non-BSB) body' is a partnership, limited liability partnership, or company which has been authorised or licensed by an approved regulator *other than the BSB* to undertake reserved legal activities. On the other hand, an 'authorised individual' and a 'BSB authorised person' are both 'BSB authorised individuals'. Finally (!), a 'BSB authorised individual' is any individual who is authorised by the BSB to carry on reserved legal activities; this includes practising barristers and 'second six' pupils, and registered European lawyers.

So, there is a lot of authorisation of a variety of different bodies here. To a great extent, authorisation by the BSB really turns on whether or not an individual has a practising certificate.

If you supply 'legal services' and either:

* you are an individual and have a practising certificate
* you hold yourself out as a barrister or a registered European lawyer or
* you manage, or own, an authorised (non-BSB) body and are required by the regulator of that body to hold a practising certificate issued by the Bar Council

then you are practising as a barrister or a registered European lawyer. If you are an individual and *do not* have a practising certificate, then you must not practise as a barrister or a registered European lawyer, and you are *not* authorised by the BSB to carry out any reserved legal activity.

A 'first six' pupil is not eligible for a practising certificate. The 'scope of practice' rules do not prevent a 'first six' pupil from accepting a noting brief for court, if permission to do so is granted by either his pupil supervisor or head of chambers (rS11).

## 10.2.3    Providing reserved legal activities and other legal services

Currently, there are only four capacities in which one may carry on a reserved legal activity or provide other legal services: first, as a self-employed barrister; secondly, as the manager of an authorised (non-BSB) body or as an 'employed barrister (authorised non-BSB body)'; thirdly, as an 'employed barrister (non-authorised body)'; and fourthly, as a registered European lawyer.

We will examine each in turn but before doing so, we should note two points.

First, a 'second six' pupil will have a provisional practising certificate and may supply legal services or exercise any right which he has by virtue of being a barrister (for example, a right of audience) but only if granted permission to do so by either his pupil supervisor or head of chambers (rS19).

Secondly, if you are a barrister of less than three years' standing and you either supply legal services, exercise any right of audience, or conduct litigation, then generally you will need a more experienced lawyer who is readily available to guide you (a 'qualified person'). See rS20–22 for details.

### 10.2.3.1    Scope of practice as a self-employed barrister

The first matter to consider here is—who can instruct you? Essentially, you may only supply legal services if you are instructed (i) by a court, (ii) by a professional client, (iii) by a licensed access client, or (iv) in any other situation you may supply legal services only if the matter is public access work or relates to the conduct of litigation. If you have a licensed access client, you must abide by the licensed access rules. To accept public access instructions, you must be entitled to do so, have notified the BSB that you are willing to accept such work, and abide by the public access rules. Where you are instructed to conduct litigation but not by a professional client or a licensed access client, you must have a litigation extension to your practising certificate (see **10.3.6**) and have informed the BSB that you are willing to accept instructions from lay clients.

Secondly, in summary, you must not undertake the management, administration, or general conduct of a client's affairs (rS25). Traditionally, this is solicitor's work, not done by barristers. Usually, we are neither trained nor qualified to offer these services. There is an exception—where this is 'foreign work', performed by you at a base outside England and Wales. See generally Part 3, B3.

### 10.2.3.2    Scope of practice as an employed barrister (non-authorised body)

This applies where a practising barrister is employed by a non-authorised body under a contract of employment, or on a fixed-term contract for services, or by virtue of an office under the Crown (a civil servant), or by an EU institution (EU civil servant) and who supplies legal services as a barrister in the course of employment.

You may only supply legal services as follows:

- to your employer, or to staff of your employer on matters concerning that person's employment
- if you are employed by a foreign lawyer, to any client of your employer if the legal services consist of 'foreign work' (any legal services relating either to legal proceedings taking place outside England and Wales, or to any matter not subject to the law of England and Wales)
- if you are employed in a government department, to any government Minister
- if you are employed by a trade association, to a member of the association
- if you are performing the functions of a Justices' clerk, to the Justices
- if you are employed at a Legal Advice Centre, you can supply legal services to its clients
- if you work pro bono or are employed by the Legal Aid Agency, you may supply legal services to members of the public.

### 10.2.3.3    Scope of practice for registered European lawyers

If a registered European lawyer is working in either of the two preceding categories, then the equivalent limitations that would have applied if he was practising as a barrister in that category shall equally apply to him in his practice (rS16.6).

### 10.2.3.4    Legal advice centres

For the time being, Legal Advice Centres are allowed to provide reserved legal activities without being authorised to do so. We have already seen that an employed barrister may supply legal services to Legal Advice Centres (**10.2.3.2**). You may also supply legal services at a Centre on a voluntary or part-time basis. In these situations, you will be treated as though you were employed by the Centre and the Handbook will apply as appropriate.

Where you are so treated as an employee, with the exception of a salary paid to you by the Centre, you must not receive any fee or reward for providing legal services to any client of the Centre. You must have no financial interest in the Centre and any fees that come in for legal services provided by you must accrue and be paid to the Centre or to charity, as prescribed by the Lord Chancellor.

A self-employed barrister who does work for a Centre does not need to tell the BSB that he is doing so. See generally Part 3, section B9.

## 10.3    Practising certificates

### 10.3.1    Who is covered and what can they have

Two categories of lawyer can apply for a practising certificate—barristers and registered European lawyers. In both cases, they must not be currently suspended from practice or have been disbarred. Since 1 April 2015, they must also meet one of the following conditions:

- within the previous five years, they have
  - held a practising certificate or
  - satisfactorily completed either the first six months of pupillage or the full 12 months (or been exempted from the requirement to complete either period) or
- have complied with whatever training requirements have been laid down by the BSB.

Assuming that the above factors are satisfied, the lawyer can then aim for one of four different practising certificates—the full certificate, the provisional, the limited certificate, or the registered European lawyer's certificate. Each has separate qualifying criteria. We shall examine each in turn.

### 10.3.2   The full practising certificate

This authorises the barrister to exercise a right of audience before every court, covering all proceedings. A 'right of audience' means the right to appear before and address a court, and the right to call and examine witnesses; see LSA 2007, Sch 2, para 3.

There are four alternative ways to be eligible for the full certificate. First, the barrister has completed the full 12 months of pupillage satisfactorily. Secondly, the barrister has been exempted from the need to complete 12 months' pupillage. Thirdly, on 30 July 2000, the barrister was entitled to exercise full rights of audience by virtue of being a barrister. Finally, the barrister was called to the Bar before 1 January 2002 and, before 31 March 2012, the barrister had (i) notified the Bar Council that he wished to exercise rights of audience before every court and covering all proceedings, and (ii) complied with training requirements as laid down by the Bar Council or BSB (or had been informed that he need not comply with such requirements).

### 10.3.3   The provisional practising certificate

This authorises a 'second six' pupil to exercise a right of audience before every court, covering all proceedings. In order to get the certificate, the pupil must have completed their first six, or been exempted from it and be registered with the BSB as a pupil at the time of applying for the certificate. See further the BSB guidance for pupils and newly qualified barristers, on the BSB website.

### 10.3.4   The limited practising certificate

The limited certificate only allows a barrister to exercise any rights of audience which he had by reason of being a barrister and was entitled to exercise on 30 July 2000. A barrister is entitled to this certificate if he was called to the Bar before 1 January 2002 and is otherwise unable to meet the eligibility requirement for a full certificate (see **10.3.2**).

### 10.3.5   The registered European lawyer's practising certificate

A 'registered European lawyer' is a European lawyer who has been registered as such, seemingly by the Bar Council and by one of the Inns of Court (Part 6 *but see* **10.4**). Once registration is complete, the lawyer is entitled to this certificate.

The certificate allows the lawyer to engage in the same reserved legal activities as a full practising certificate allows a barrister, except that the European lawyer can only exercise a right of audience or conduct litigation (see **10.3.6**) if he acts in conjunction with a solicitor or barrister who is entitled to practise in the relevant forum and who can legitimately exercise that right. There is also a limited class of European lawyers who can be paid to produce an instrument creating or transferring an interest in land.

### 10.3.6 Litigation extensions

A litigation extension can be added to a practising certificate (other than a provisional one) where the certificate holder wants to be able to conduct litigation. This will allow the holder to conduct litigation in every court and for all proceedings. A registered European lawyer will need to be 'paired up' as mentioned in **10.3.5**. The ability to 'conduct litigation' has the same meaning as in the LSA 2007, Sch 2, para 4—it means that one can issue, commence, prosecute, and defend proceedings before any court in England and Wales, and perform any necessary ancillary functions.

A barrister is eligible for a litigation extension if he satisfies the criteria in rS47. He must be more than three years' standing, know the relevant procedural requirements well enough to be able to conduct litigation competently, and have the necessary admin systems set up so that he can provide legal services direct to clients and cover the administrative demands involved in conducting litigation. Where the barrister is less than three years' standing, he can still have a litigation extension if his principal place of business is in chambers, which is also the principal place of business of a 'qualified person' who is on hand to provide guidance as necessary. Alternatively, his principal place of practice can be in the office of an organisation where an employee, manager, partner, or director is a 'qualified person' who will be on hand to provide swift guidance.

A 'qualified person' is defined in Part 3, section B2, rS22.3; put simply it is a fairly senior barrister who has the right to conduct litigation and has practised as a barrister for at least six of the last eight years. He must have made his practice his primary occupation for the last two years and he must not act as a qualified person to more than three people.

See further the BSB guidance for barristers—conducting litigation.

### 10.3.7 Applying for a practising certificate

Essentially what is required here is to:

- complete the application form
- provide all information required
- pay the appropriate fee.

See rules rS48–49.

There are slightly different requirements for the information to be provided, depending on whether one is applying for a practising certificate or a litigation extension.

The applicant is personally responsible for the content of the application and, of course, no application should be submitted unless the applicant believes it contains full and accurate information.

The applicant can request a reduced fee when applying for a practising certificate, if on a relatively low income: presently a gross annual income in the preceding 12 months of less than £40,000 for a self-employed barrister and £30,000 for an employed barrister.

## 10.4 Registration of European lawyers

This is covered in the Handbook at Part 3, section D. As noted at **10.1**, this discrete topic is *not* on the BSB syllabus for Professional Ethics. However, there have been several references to registered European lawyers in the preceding sections of this chapter (for example, **10.3.5**), so some consideration must be given to this topic in order to give some context.

One slightly odd wrinkle comes in the question of who has the competence to register a European lawyer. Part 6 defines a 'registered European lawyer' as a European lawyer who has been registered by the Bar Council and by an Inn of Court, as per Part 3, section D. This is the definition that was used earlier at **10.3.5**. However, if one examines Part 3, section D itself, the position is different. This says that the lawyer should apply to the BSB for registration and, provided that it is satisfied that the requirements have been met, it is the BSB who will register him as a registered European lawyer, not the Bar Council, with no mention of registration by an Inn.

Why would one register as a European lawyer? As we have seen in **10.3.5**, it opens up entitlement to a practising certificate. It is appropriate, as rS78 says, if one is a European lawyer who wishes to practise in England and Wales on a permanent basis under a home professional title. 'Home professional title' means the professional title that he holds in his home EU state and under which he is authorised in his home state to pursue professional activities.

The European lawyer must apply on the appropriate form (available at <https://www. barstandardsboard.org.uk/qualifying-as-a-barrister/forms-and-guidelines/bar-training-waivers-and-exemption-forms/#Panel1>), supply a certificate that he is registered with the competent authority in an EU member state as a lawyer qualified to practise in that state under a professional title, and of course pay the prescribed fee. He must also make a declaration that, in effect, he is a fit and proper person to be registered (rS79).

As an alternative to registration, the European lawyer may decide to apply to be called to the Bar, in which case he will not be practising under his home professional title but will instead be practising as a barrister. See <https://www.barstandardsboard.org.uk/qualifying-as-a-barrister/transferring-lawyers/european-lawyers/> for further information.

# The Qualification Rules

## 11.1 Introduction

These are to be found in Part 4 of the Handbook. They divide into two discrete parts—the rules which govern training for the Bar, and the rules that provide the framework for Continuing Professional Development ('CPD'). Although both sections are very important to the profession and to those aspiring to enter it, the syllabus for the BPTC considerably reduces the assessable content of this part. The syllabus requires students to know the CPD rules and the rules that relate specifically to the conduct of students. These will therefore form the major part of this short chapter.

Before turning to examine those sections, it is important to give a sense of the overall framework for training for the Bar.

The Bar Training Rules ('BTR') apply to everyone who wishes to qualify to practise and be called to the Bar, to pupil supervisors, and to approved training organisations. An 'approved training organisation' is one which is approved by the BSB to provide professional training (pupillage) and fairly obviously this can include, but is not limited to, sets of chambers. The fundamental purpose of the BTR is to ensure that anyone who qualifies to practise as a barrister is both competent to do so and is a fit and proper person.

One *practises* as a barrister if one is supplying legal services and is either an individual with a practising certificate or holds oneself out as a barrister (or one is a manager or owner of an authorised (non-BSB) body and is required by that body's regulator to hold a practising certificate issued by the Bar Council). In order to be qualified to *practise* as a barrister, one must have been called to the Bar by one of the four Inns of Court—Inner Temple, Middle Temple, Lincoln's Inn, or Gray's Inn. One must also have completed pupillage and meet any further requirements in Part 3 of the Handbook. In order to be called to the Bar, one must belong to an Inn, have a qualifying law degree (or a qualifying degree and the conversion course), pass the Bar Professional Training Course (or be exempted from the academic and vocational stages), and fulfil all requirements about attending qualifying sessions (usually attendance at educational and collegiate events organised by one's Inn).

The BTR set out the criteria to be eligible for admission to an Inn of Court; probably the most important point is that the applicant is certified as a person of good character by two professional people or people who are of good standing in their community. The applicant must be a *fit and proper person*—this will need to be considered if he has been convicted of a criminal offence (other than one that can be dealt with by a fixed penalty or one that consists of unlawful parking), has been made bankrupt, disqualified from being a company director, or if there is anything else that calls into question his fitness to be a practising barrister.

## 11.2 Student conduct

This is governed by Part 2, section B8. The student must immediately notify his Inn if any of the following situations arise:

- He is convicted of, or is charged with, a criminal offence (as defined in **11.1**), or is on bail, in custody, or on the run in connection with a criminal offence.

- He becomes the subject of pending disciplinary proceedings or is convicted of a disciplinary offence by a professional or regulatory body.
- He is made bankrupt, enters an IVA, or is disqualified from being a company director.
- He is found guilty by his BPTC provider of cheating or other misconduct on the BPTC.

It may come to the attention of the student's Inn that he has, or may have, made a false statement in his admission declaration (or call declaration) or that whilst a student he has or may have committed a breach of Inn regulations on conduct and discipline, been convicted of a criminal offence or of a disciplinary offence, been made bankrupt, been found guilty of misconduct on the BPTC, or is otherwise guilty of any conduct discreditable to a member of the Inn. In this situation, the Inn shall make enquiries and can require the student to provide any information that it thinks fit. The Inn will then consider if the matter is a serious one or not. It is a serious matter if it involves any of the foregoing situations except a breach of Inn regulations, or if in the opinion of the Inn the matter raises the issue of whether the student is a fit and proper person.

If it is not a serious matter, the Inn may use its internal disciplinary procedure. In this case, the Inn may dismiss any complaint against the student, or decide that no action is necessary. Alternatively, the Inn may advise the student as to his future conduct, or reprimand him, or ban him from using Inn facilities for a specified time. The student may go to the Inns' Conduct Committee ('ICC') to appeal a decision made against him.

If it is a serious matter, it must be referred to the ICC which will then make a determination. If the ICC finds that a serious matter has been proved, it may advise the student as to his future conduct, reprimand him, order that his call to the Bar be postponed, or direct that he be expelled from his Inn. The student may seek a review of the decision from the BSB under Part 4, B10.

## 11.3  The CPD rules

The BSB takes continuing professional development ('CPD') very seriously. Every practising barrister must report the details of his CPD to the BSB using the prescribed form and by the deadline specified by the BSB. Looking at the reports of professional misconduct findings on the BSB website, it would seem that this is one of the more frequent reasons for a barrister to find himself the subject of disciplinary proceedings. So, clearly the BSB does check up that barristers are meeting their CPD obligations and takes action when it finds a shortcoming. Measures reported against non-compliant barristers include fines, suspension, and even disbarment.

Since 1 October 2001, after any pupillage year (a calendar year in which the barrister was a pupil for any time) has ended, in the first three calendar years in which the barrister holds a practising certificate he must complete at least 45 hours of CPD. It does not matter when the hours are done, just that at the end of this three-year period, a total of 45 hours has been achieved.

Thereafter, if the barrister holds one or more practising certificates through a whole calendar year, he must complete at least 12 hours of CPD during that period. If he only holds a practising certificate for part of a calendar year, he must complete one hour of CPD in that year for each month that he held the certificate.

## 12

# The Proceeds of Crime Act 2002

## 12.1  The problem posed by the Proceeds of Crime Act 2002

Since it came into force, the Proceeds of Crime Act 2002 ('POCA 2002') has caused considerable anxiety for lawyers. Following the decision of the Court of Appeal in *Bowman v Fels* [2005] EWCA Civ 226, the main remaining area of concern for lawyers is the reporting obligation under s 330 when working in 'the regulated sector'. However, there is also the need to advise the client when he or she is at risk of liability under s 327 and/or s 329. Further new legislation appeared subsequently, in the form of the Money Laundering Regulations 2007, which came into force on 15 December 2007. The Bar Standards Board has money laundering on the BPTC syllabus as an outline topic only. However, the syllabus makes reference to POCA 2002, the Regulations, and Guidance issued as well. This is a lot of content for an outline topic and it is difficult to gauge accurately what needs to be known and understood for the purpose of the assessment. In the past, there has been guidance on the Bar Council website but that has now been replaced by a statement directing the reader to the website of the Chancery Bar Association. If you should wish to visit that website, the address to access the relevant guidance is <http://www.chba.org.uk/for-members/library/professional-guidance/aml-guidance-part-1-final.pdf>. Rather oddly, when you get there, you will still be able to access the Bar Council guidance! That was last updated in 2008. The CBA information is stated to be most recently revised in May 2013. However, when you read it, you will see that it still refers to the Bar Council guidance that was last updated in 2008 and is no longer accessible. Anyway, you can find detailed guidance on POCA and on the Regulations. Together, these two documents from the Chancery Bar Association come to almost 100 pages. This seems a lot to absorb for a topic that is assessed in outline form only. It is therefore tentatively suggested that the rest of this chapter may suffice for the purposes of the BPTC assessment. When embarking on the post-BPTC stage of your professional career, whether self-employed or perhaps as an employee of an LLP, you would be well advised to visit the CBA website once more and embark on a more concentrated reading of the material that you find there. One does not currently need to be a member of the CBA to have access to their guidance, which is remarkably generous of them.

To discuss the legislation, this chapter uses the specific example of ancillary relief. Ancillary relief is the process by which divorcing spouses obtain financial resolution of their affairs from the court. However, that should make it no less applicable to other situations. In ancillary relief, the client is in practice obliged to tell his or her adviser about all of his or her assets and income because of the obligation to the court of full and frank disclosure. The problem is that this process may disclose that some of those assets are the proceeds of crime.

In order for there to be proceeds of crime, somebody (usually the client or another party in the context of legal proceedings) must have engaged in 'criminal conduct' (s 340(2)). It is not necessary that he or she has actually been convicted of an offence, and your client does not necessarily need to have personally engaged in the criminal conduct, only (for example) to be in possession of criminal property (see **12.2.2**).

It may be that the client has, for example, been involved in mainstream drug dealing. More commonly, there may be issues of tax evasion; for example, the client receives money 'cash in hand'. This is not in itself 'criminal conduct'—anyone can pay their bills in cash or by cheque—but it becomes an offence if he or she fails to disclose these earnings to HM Revenue & Customs. Tax evasion is a crime, as is benefit fraud.

A number of problems face the lawyer as a result of the POCA 2002. First, there are the 'principal offences' under Part VII of the POCA 2002 (ss 327, 328, and 329) and the secondary offences under ss 333A–D (tipping off) and s 342 (prejudicing an investigation). The lawyer will need to advise the client of potential liability under these sections. There is a *small* residual risk of lawyers being liable under s 328 despite the judgment in *Bowman*. Secondly, since 15 December 2007, lawyers have been subject to the Money Laundering Regulations 2007, and thus may be a 'relevant person' in terms of the Regulations, while also being in the 'regulated sector' in terms of the Act (as defined by Sch 9—definitions of these terms are the same in the Act and the Regulations). Being in the regulated sector exposes lawyers to the risk of criminal liability for breach of s 330 of the POCA 2002 (ie failure to disclose). The risks are more acute for solicitors owing to the nature of their work (after all, they usually have first, and continuous, contact with the client and handle the client's money) but, for certain types of work, the Bar is also under specific obligations and at risk of criminal liability.

The Bar Council issued guidance to barristers in respect of the POCA 2002 and the Money Laundering Regulations 2007, most recently in 2008. This has now been subsumed into the Explanatory Notes provided by the Chancery Bar Association; see **12.6** for finding the latest version.

## 12.2    Principal offences

### 12.2.1    Key differences between the principal and secondary offences

Sections 327, 328, and 329 set out the principal offences in Part VII of the POCA 2002. They differ from the secondary offences (considered later) in a number of key respects:

- Disclosure in respect of the principal offences is 'authorised disclosure' under s 338 (not 'protected disclosure' under s 337 which relates to the secondary offences).

- The disclosure defence under s 338 requires not only 'authorised disclosure' but also the 'appropriate consent' under s 335. Section 337 does not require a consent because of the fundamental difference in the duties between ss 327–9 and 330: in ss 327–9, disclosure is made in order to exonerate the discloser from criminal responsibility for what he or she would otherwise do; s 330 on the other hand is a general duty (arising from the fact of one's practice in the regulated sector) to disclose the fact that someone is involved in money laundering and in that sense is separate from any activity with which the discloser himself is involved.

### 12.2.2    Definitions

'Criminal conduct' is defined in s 340(2) (s 340 is in fact the definition section for Part VII of the POCA 2002). It covers conduct which would constitute an offence in any part of the UK—so, for example, tax evasion is a criminal offence in UK law. It also covers conduct which occurs abroad but would be an offence in the UK if it had occurred there, but in those circumstances defendants charged under ss 327, 328, 329, and 330 may be able to take advantage of the defences in those sections. These provide that if the defendant knew or believed on reasonable grounds that the relevant conduct had occurred in a particular country or territory outside of the UK, *and* that conduct was not criminal according to *local* laws at the time it occurred, *and* it was not conduct of a type prescribed by order of the Secretary of State, the defendant has not committed the offence.

'Criminal property' (s 340(3)) is that which constitutes 'a person's benefit from criminal conduct or . . . represents such a benefit (in whole or part and whether directly or indirectly)', and the alleged offender (ie the person accused of facilitating money laundering, etc) knows or suspects that it constitutes or represents such a benefit.

If, for example, in an ancillary relief claim, the matrimonial home had been partially paid for by 'criminal property' in the form of unpaid tax monies—say, by paying the mortgage instalments partly with these monies—the house could 'represent' the benefit from criminal conduct. The same might be the case for other assets.

### 12.2.3  Sections 327, 328, and 329

Sections 327, 328, and 329 of the POCA 2002 may affect your client, and the client will need to be advised of this. Section 327 provides that:

> *(1) A person commits an offence if he—*
>
> > *(a) conceals criminal property;*
> >
> > *(b) disguises criminal property;*
> >
> > *(c) converts criminal property;*
> >
> > *(d) transfers criminal property;*
> >
> > *(e) removes criminal property from England and Wales or from Scotland or from Northern Ireland.*
>
> *[. . .]*
>
> *(3) Concealing or disguising criminal property includes concealing or disguising its nature, source, location, disposition, movement or ownership, or any rights with respect to it.*

Section 328 provides that:

> *(1) A person commits an offence if he enters into or becomes concerned in an arrangement which he knows or suspects facilitates (by whatever means) the acquisition, retention, use or control of criminal property by or on behalf of another person.*

As discussed later, 'being concerned in an arrangement' was once thought to include involvement in litigation which resulted in a settlement or an order of the court in relation to proceeds of crime. The Court of Appeal in *Bowman* made it quite clear that s 328 is not intended to affect 'the ordinary conduct of litigation by legal professionals. That includes any step taken by them in litigation from the issue of proceedings and the securing of injunctive relief or a freezing order up to its final disposal by judgment', and that such activities are not to be regarded as 'being concerned in an arrangement'. Subject to the points made at **12.7.2** et seq, s 328 now clearly does not apply to the involvement of a lawyer in litigation or the resolution of litigation by agreement.

However, the client may still have committed the offence in relation to an arrangement over property, *independent of the litigation process*, for example a sham property transaction designed to conceal the proceeds of crime.

Section 329 provides:

> *(1) A person commits an offence if he—*
>
> > *(a) acquires criminal property;*
> >
> > *(b) uses criminal property;*
> >
> > *(c) has possession of criminal property.*

For example, a wife in an ancillary relief claim who had not personally committed the criminal offence of tax evasion could potentially be accused of the s 329 offence—acquiring, using, or possessing criminal property—if the house that she jointly owns with her tax-evading husband was bought with money he had not declared to tax—unless she makes an authorised disclosure under s 338. The husband could conceivably be accused of both s 327 and s 329 offences, as well as tax evasion itself. In order to protect herself, the wife should make an 'authorised disclosure' under s 338.

### 12.2.4  Defences to the principal offences

The client (and the barrister, in the rare situation that disclosure is required of him) can obtain a complete defence by making an 'authorised disclosure' under s 338 (in the manner prescribed by s 339), *and* by getting the 'appropriate consent' (s 335).

Generally speaking, disclosure is to the National Crime Agency (NCA). The way that consent works is as follows:

- The NCA may consent within seven days of disclosure being made, in which case the client can continue with the act or transaction in question.
- If not, the client is required to wait for seven working days from the working day after disclosure. Once that period has passed without a notice of refusal from the NCA, the consent is deemed and the client can continue with the act or transaction.
- If the NCA gives notice of refusal within the seven-day period, there is then a moratorium period of 31 calendar days from the day on which refusal is received. Thereafter, the client is free to continue with the act or transaction.

Specific guidance is given by the Chancery Bar Association in its Explanatory Notes on the Substantive Law of Money Laundering; see paragraphs 44–50 and note paragraphs 51–5 on *Shah v HSBC Private Bank* [2010] EWCA Civ 31, [2012] EWHC 2183.

### 12.2.5    Does s 328 apply to the activities of lawyers?

The judgment in *Bowman* was handed down by the Court of Appeal on 8 March 2005. It is authority of considerable public importance since this was the first full examination by the Court of Appeal of the impact of the POCA 2002 on legal professional privilege between lawyer and client. It effectively overrules *P v P (Ancillary Relief; Proceeds of Crime)* [2003] EWHC Fam 2260.

#### 12.2.5.1    Background

Prior to this decision, the word 'arrangement' was believed to cover litigation, including settlement of such litigation by agreement. Where a lawyer knew or suspected that money or assets being the subject of litigation were the proceeds of crime, then he or she could only escape criminal liability under s 328 by making an 'authorised disclosure'—in other words, by notifying the NCA of the suspected criminal activity and obtaining the appropriate consent to proceed with the arrangement. For lawyers, it seemed that the fundamental principle of legal professional privilege had been fatally undermined—not only would a lawyer be obliged to report suspected money laundering by the other party, but he or she would also be compelled to make disclosure to a third party of suspected money laundering by his or her own client.

#### 12.2.5.2    The central question in *Bowman*

The Court of Appeal identified the following issues (para 24):

- whether s 328 applied to the ordinary conduct of legal proceedings at all
- whether Parliament could have been taken, without using clear words to that effect, to have intended to override the very important principles of legal professional privilege.

#### 12.2.5.3    The decision in *Bowman*

The Court of Appeal concluded as follows:

- (para 83) Section 328 is not intended to affect 'the ordinary conduct of litigation by legal professionals. That includes any step taken by them in litigation from the issue of proceedings and the securing of injunctive relief or a freezing order up to its final disposal by judgment.' In other words, conducting litigation does not involve 'becoming concerned in an arrangement' within the meaning of s 328, and s 328 is therefore inapplicable to such activities.
- (para 87) The Court of Appeal further stated that even if the above conclusion was wrong, it was quite clear that on a proper construction s 328 does not override legal professional privilege.

- (paras 99 and 100) The Court of Appeal also came to the view that resolution of the whole, or any aspect of, legal proceedings by agreement would equally be outside the scope of s 328.

Clearly, this guidance has brought considerable clarity to an area which caused enormous concern to lawyers involved in litigation when the POCA 2002 was first enacted. A lawyer can advise and represent a client in the vast majority of situations without fear of being obliged to breach legal professional privilege by reporting suspected money laundering to the authorities. However, there remain some situations where s 328 could apply to lawyers. These are discussed at **12.7**.

## 12.3  Secondary offences

### 12.3.1  The Money Laundering Regulations 2007

A barrister acting in the course of business who is a 'relevant person' as defined in the Regulations will be subject to additional requirements and liability. Barristers most likely to fall within the ambit of the Regulations are members of the Chancery Bar involved in non-contentious advisory work, especially in relation to business or taxation or property transactions and the setting up of companies and trusts.

#### 12.3.1.1  When is counsel deemed to be a 'relevant person'?

Regulation 3(1) sets out a list of relevant persons, including at (c) 'tax advisers' and at (d) 'independent legal professionals'. 'Independent legal professional' is further defined in reg 3(9) as being a firm or practitioner providing legal services in financial or real property transactions concerning: at (a) the buying and selling of real property or business entities; and at (e) the creation, operation, or management of trusts, companies, or similar structures.

Most barristers will not find themselves falling within the definition of 'relevant person' under these regulations. In particular the Bar Council considered that definition will not cover employed barristers, barristers providing advice *after* a relevant transaction, barristers conducting litigation arising from a relevant transaction, or barristers advising in connection with an agreement intended to compromise a genuine dispute. See Appendix 1 to the Chancery Bar Association's Explanatory Notes for further detail.

The Regulations are transaction based; therefore counsel has to consider for every piece of work undertaken whether he or she is a relevant person.

Barristers must be astute to determine whether any particular piece of work undertaken by them falls within the Regulations, as an error in this regard and consequential failure to implement the requisite systems will result in the commission of a criminal offence, punishable by a fine or up to two years' imprisonment.

#### 12.3.1.2  Additional requirements under the Regulations

The additional requirements for a relevant person when conducting business include the carrying out of:

- due diligence procedures
- record-keeping procedures
- internal reporting procedures and training of employees.

The final set of requirements above are of less significance to the Bar than to other businesses in the regulated sector, because barristers in private practice are individuals, neither employing nor acting in association with any other person and are solely responsible for their own professional practice. Most of these latter requirements either do not apply or such individuals are exempted.

In terms of due diligence, record-keeping, and identification procedures, this will usually have been carried out by the UK solicitor or other regulated professional, and counsel's duty will often be discharged by ensuring that in the instructions a letter or certificate is included which confirms that the relevant process has been carried out. Where this is not the case, a barrister must carry out his own checks. Guidance and pro forma letters in respect of these matters can be found in the appendices to the Chancery Bar Association guidance (see **12.6**).

### 12.3.2    Liability under s 330 for barristers operating within the regulated sector

Since barristers are considered to be in the 'regulated sector', they are open to criminal liability under s 330, which is the offence of 'failure to disclose' by a person in the 'regulated sector'. However, the section includes a defence relating to legal privilege, which means that it will not catch most barristers engaged in the ordinary conduct of litigation. Section 330(1)–(5) (as amended) reads as follows:

> *(1) A person commits an offence if the conditions in subsections (2) to (4) are satisfied.*
>
> *(2) The first condition is that he—*
>
> > *(a) knows or suspects, or*
> >
> > *(b) has reasonable grounds for knowing or suspecting,*
> >
> > *that another person is engaged in money laundering.*
>
> *(3) The second condition is that the information or other matter—*
>
> > *(a) on which his knowledge or suspicion is based, or*
> >
> > *(b) which gives reasonable grounds for such knowledge or suspicion*
> >
> > *came to him in the course of a business in the regulated sector.*
>
> *(3A) The third condition is—*
>
> > *(a) that he can identify the other person mentioned in subsection (2) or the whereabouts of any of the laundered property, or*
> >
> > *(b) that he believes, or it is reasonable to expect him to believe, that the information or other matter mentioned in subsection (3) will or may assist in identifying that other person or the whereabouts of any of the laundered property.*
>
> *(4) The fourth condition is that he does not make the required disclosure to—*
>
> > *(a) a nominated officer, or*
> >
> > *(b) a person authorised for the purposes of this Part by the Director General of the National Crime Agency,*
> >
> > *as soon as practicable after the information or other matter mentioned in subsection (3) comes to him.*
>
> *(5) The required disclosure is a disclosure of—*
>
> > *(a) the identity of the other person mentioned in subsection (2), if he knows it,*
> >
> > *(b) the whereabouts of the laundered property, so far as he knows it, and*
> >
> > *(c) the information or other matter mentioned in subsection (3).*

Note first that, unlike in other parts of Part VII, the standard is objective, not subjective. If you have failed to 'know' or 'suspect' personally, you can be liable if there were 'reasonable grounds' on which you should have known or suspected. In other words, the 'moron' defence (that the grounds were there but you simply failed to notice them) is not available to you.

So, for any piece of work you do, you have to consider your obligations under s 330. If the conditions in ss 2–4 apply then, subject to the defences described below, you may have an obligation to make a 'protected' disclosure under s 337.

### 12.3.3    Defences

There are in fact two defences available for a failure to disclose under s 330(6):

- you have a reasonable excuse for not making disclosure
- you are a professional legal adviser and the information (the identity of the other

person in subsection (2), or the whereabouts of the laundered property, or the information or matter in subsection (3)) has come to you in privileged circumstances.

In other words, there is a legal professional privilege defence to s 330. Section 330(10) clarifies the circumstances in which it applies. However, it is to some degree limited by s 330(11), which provides that legal professional privilege will not apply where 'information . . . is communicated or given with the intention of furthering a criminal purpose'. It is not clear whose intention is relevant for the purposes of this section. Given the wide manner in which criminal behaviour prohibited by ss 327, 328, and 329 is drafted, the lawyer will have to look very closely at what the client is intending to achieve in communicating information to the lawyer. Certainly, in telling you that her husband is taking cash in hand and not declaring it for tax purposes, an ancillary relief client probably is not intending to further a criminal purpose; rather she is telling you this in order to maximise her recovery in the ancillary relief—the sole or dominant purpose of her giving you this information being the conduct of the family proceedings. For further guidance, see the Chancery Bar Association Explanatory Notes (see **12.6**).

If you do make disclosure under s 337 ('protected disclosure'), provided that you comply with the conditions of s 337, you will be protected against litigation by the client for breaching confidentiality by s 337(1). Check that you have (or should have) suspicion based on real grounds, as opposed to mere speculation, or you may be at risk that your disclosure is not in accordance with s 337 and thus leave yourself vulnerable to successful litigation by the client.

## 12.4  Other secondary offences

There are two other secondary offences which merit consideration. These arise particularly in the context of discussing the issue of disclosure with the client.

### 12.4.1  Sections 333A–D—'tipping off'

The offence of 'tipping off' has been amended and now only applies within the regulated sector. Essentially, it relates to a situation where you know or suspect that a disclosure has been made (for example, your solicitor has made a disclosure already). The offence cannot be committed in relation to a disclosure that is yet to be made (as to which, see s 342 below). Where you 'make a disclosure which is likely to prejudice any investigation which might be conducted' as a result of the primary disclosure, you may be guilty of an offence. The 'disclosure' you make could be to your client, or to the other side, the point being that by revealing what you know or intend to do, you could enable a criminal or money launderer to cover his or her tracks, conceal the evidence, etc. Defences are available—those most likely to be relevant to a barrister are set out in s 333D. Disclosure to the Bar Council or to further a proper investigation is permissible as is disclosure made without knowing or suspecting that it might prejudice an investigation under the Act. Also permitted is a disclosure made to your client and 'for the purpose of dissuading the client from engaging in conduct amounting to an offence' (s 333D(2)(b)). It is not clear how this will work in practice; it is submitted that its purpose is to enable the avoidance of an absurd, 'quasi-entrapment' scenario, where a legal adviser would be forced to stand dumbly by and watch a client commit a criminal offence that is bound to be detected, which would not be committed at all if the adviser could advise the client as to the reality of the situation.

### 12.4.2  Section 342—prejudicing an investigation

Unlike ss 333A–D, this offence *can* be committed in advance of a disclosure being made, and relates to conduct, including making disclosures, which could prejudice an investigation which is being made or is contemplated. (Other conduct could include, for example, concealing or falsifying or destroying relevant documents.)

A variety of defences are available, including legal professional privilege. Again, legal professional privilege is limited where there is an intention to further a criminal purpose, and again the relevant intention is that of the lawyer.

In the circumstances, it may be hard to see how a lawyer could be considered to be furthering a criminal intention of his own (in relation to 'tipping off' and the prejudicing of investigation offences) in simply advising a client of the state of the law with regard to his or her position, for example the risk of the client committing an offence under s 329.

## 12.5  Penalties

### 12.5.1  Section 334

| | |
|---|---|
| Sections 327, 328, and 329 | on summary conviction, imprisonment of up to six months or a fine or both; on indictment, a fine or imprisonment of up to 14 years. |
| Sections 330 and 333A–D | on summary conviction, imprisonment of up to six months or a fine or both; on indictment, a fine or imprisonment of up to five years. |

### 12.5.2  Section 342

| | |
|---|---|
| Section 342 | on summary conviction, imprisonment of up to six months or a fine or both; on indictment, a fine or imprisonment of up to five years. |

Clearly, it pays to get it right. And note that the mere fact that you advise the solicitor that he has a reporting obligation under the POCA 2002 does not discharge your own obligations. However, it is perfectly possible to make joint disclosure to the NCA on the part of the solicitor, counsel, and possibly the client. In addition, the NCA's predecessor entity, the Serious Organised Crimes Agency, indicated in its guidance that if a solicitor has made a report in advance of instructing counsel and counsel's report would be based on the exact same facts, there is no obligation on counsel to report further.

## 12.6  Sources of useful information

(a) The Chancery Bar Assocation (<http://www.chba.org.uk/for-members/library/professional-guidance>)—under the section 'Guidance' you can obtain four documents which are the CBA's current guidance on these areas. These are the Explanatory Notes on the Substantive Law, and on the Money Laundering Regulations; also the Bar Council's guidance from 2008 and a draft letter for use.

(b) *Bowman v Fels* [2005] EWCA Civ 226 can be accessed through the Court Service website (<http://www.hmcourts-service.gov.uk>)—search under the 'Legal/Professional' section—or go directly to <http://www.bailii.org>.

(c) The Law Society (<http://www.lawsociety.org.uk/support-services/advice/practice-notes/aml/>)—there is much helpful guidance on this site, under the 'Practice Notes' link on the home page, and it has been updated to take account of the replacement of SOCA by the NCA in October 2013.

(d) National Crime Agency (<http://www.nationalcrimeagency.gov.uk/crime-threats/money-laundering>)—for information such as how to go about making a report, and for NCA guidance.

## 12.7    Areas in which counsel remains at risk of liability under the POCA 2002

The decision in *Bowman v Fels* [2005] EWCA Civ 226 has provided considerable clarity on an issue of acute concern to litigators. However, lawyers still need to tread carefully in certain areas—and in others, confusion remains. References to paragraph numbers in the following are to paragraphs in *Bowman*.

### 12.7.1    Section 330 and the regulated sector

Lawyers will have to continue to keep possible liability under s 330 in mind when operating in the regulated sector (principally in relation to financial and real estate transactions). This will be of particular concern to certain sectors of the Bar, such as tax specialists and Chancery practitioners who are routinely involved in such work—although every lawyer needs to be aware of the potential application of s 330, since it is transaction based; in other words, its applicability depends on the subject matter of every individual transaction rather than the lawyer's general area of work. It may well be that specialist Bar associations issue future guidance specific to their areas in relation to s 330 obligations. Of course, availability of the legal professional privilege defence is likely to mean that you are very rarely obliged to report money laundering by the client. As pointed out in the Bar Council guidance, it is apparent from the reasoning in *Bowman* that the ordinary conduct of litigation or its consensual resolution does not fall within the 'regulated sector' for the purposes of s 330 in any event, and so s 330 really only applies to non-contentious advisory work within the 'regulated sector'.

### 12.7.2    Negotiation and agreement in the absence of issued proceedings

At paras 99–102, the Court of Appeal considered resolution of the whole, or part, of legal proceedings by agreement. The obvious point was made that if the ordinary conduct of litigation was to be treated as outside the scope of s 328, as the court had already concluded, then it would be inconsistent and illogical to nevertheless treat any step in such proceedings taken by *agreement*, or a settlement of the litigation obtained by agreement, as subject to s 328. Given the considerable emphasis on resolution of litigation by agreement not only in domestic law (the 'Woolf reforms') but also in international law, the court concluded that consensual steps—including final resolution by agreement—were not subject to s 328.

However, the court indicated (para 101) that the situation might be different where the agreed settlement was *independent* of litigation. The court was careful to use the phrase 'in a litigious context' when discussing consensual agreement. This appears to extend to situations of *existing or contemplated legal proceedings* only. As the court pointed out (para 101), this is in line with the language of the relevant European directives, as well as relevant sections of the POCA 2002. It does, however, leave something of a grey area. Surely a lawyer with his or her client's interests foremost in his mind will attempt to negotiate a settlement without recourse to legal proceedings. At what point would a court regard him or her as negotiating in the context of 'contemplated' legal proceedings (and thus beyond the reach of s 328)? Will lawyers have to threaten legal proceedings as a first step to attempting negotiation in all cases in order to escape the confines of s 328?

There is considerable emphasis on the use and observance of pre-action protocols since the Woolf reforms. It is suggested that observance of such protocols (the purpose of which is to avoid litigation where possible by agreed settlement) could, and would, be considered by a court as negotiation in the context of contemplated legal proceedings. Clearly, legal proceedings are the likely result if negotiation under the protocol fails, and protocols additionally have as their aim the efficient preparation of the case for litigation in the event of failed negotiation. It may be that this aspect of the applicability, or not, of s 328 will serve to emphasise and increase use of the protocols.

### 12.7.3    Sham litigation

While not expressing a concluded view on the point, the Court of Appeal referred to the possibility that s 328 could potentially apply to lawyers in the situation where they were:

> concerned with a settlement which did not reflect the legal and practical merits of the parties' respective positions in the proceedings, and was known or suspected to be no more than a pretext for agreeing on the acquisition, retention, use or control of criminal property. [para 102]

This would be an entirely logical position on the basis of the court's interpretation of the legislation. First, s 330, used by the court to illuminate the intentions of the legislator in respect of s 328, clearly provides for a situation where legal professional privilege does not apply (s 330(11)), whereby if the client intends to further a criminal purpose (such as concealing proceeds of crime) in communicating the relevant information to his lawyer, privilege does not attach and the lawyer working in the regulated sector must report. Secondly, recital 17 of the 2001 Directive (Directive 2001/97/EC amending Council Directive 91/308/EEC on prevention of the use of the financial system for the purpose of money laundering), on which the court placed so much reliance in interpreting the applicability of s 328 to litigation, states:

> *legal advice remains subject to the obligation of professional secrecy unless the legal counsellor is taking part in money laundering activities, the legal advice is provided for money laundering purposes, or the lawyer knows that the client is seeking legal advice for money laundering purposes.*

The consequences are that a lawyer conducting litigation must be astute to the possibility that the litigation is a sham in order to pursue money laundering. A good indication might be that the settlement did not substantially reflect the merits of each side's case. The Court of Appeal further made the point that this still leaves the question of at what point the s 328 offence could be said to have been committed by the lawyer. In paras 67 and 68 of the judgment, the court took the view that an offence under s 328 could not have been committed until the 'arrangement' was actually made.

### 12.7.4    Transactions resulting from the judgment

The Court of Appeal stated at para 59 that:

> while legal advice may be given in any area, one would not often expect legal professionals assisting in the planning or execution of or acting for a client in respect of a financial or real estate transaction of a kind specified in Article 2a(5) to have received from, or obtained on, their client relevant information 'in the course of performing their task of defending or representing that client in, or concerning judicial proceedings'.

This viewpoint is doubtless entirely accurate in relation to many situations. However, the question arises, what is the position in relation to the 'fruits' of litigation? More often than not, the implementation of an order, or an agreed resolution to litigation, will involve lawyers in transactions—financial, commercial, real property. An example could be an ancillary relief case, involving the transfer of a house, or a shareholding, to one of the parties. This is clearly within the meaning of 'transaction' in Art 2a(5) of the 2001 Directive, and therefore subject to s 330. Quite often (if not always), the law firms involved in the litigation will be those dealing with the transactions required to finally resolve the dispute. To what degree could the knowledge of a client's wrongdoing gained by the litigation team be imputed to the team dealing with the transactions flowing from resolution of the litigation? Or perhaps even more acutely, what about the situation of a sole practitioner dealing with the litigation and the transactions flowing from it?

One answer to this dilemma seems to depend on how one interprets the reference to 'ordinary course of litigation' in the judgment. If it includes those transactions required to give effect to the order or agreement, then the difficulty is removed. Support for such an interpretation comes from para 62 of the judgment. Reference is made to the function of litigation—'resolving the rights and duties of two parties according to law'. Such 'resolution' would be threatened if parties were deterred from litigating due to a fear of a report of their activities at the stage of actually effecting the remedy obtained. More importantly, the court's reference to assets, being proceeds of money laundering, being 'retained *or used to satisfy any liability according to the outcome of proceedings*' seems to suggest that execution of the order or agreement would not be 'carrying out' a 'transaction' relating to money laundering.

Of course, such transactions, subject as they are to s 330, will benefit from the defence in s 330(6) and (10)—that the information has come to the lawyer in privileged circumstances and so disclosure will not be required. However, under s 330(11), privilege will afford no defence to the obligation to disclose if the client's purpose in communicating the information is a criminal purpose, and it may well be here that the problem arises.

### 12.7.5  Conclusion

Clearly, *Bowman* and its subsequent consideration has provided considerable clarity to lawyers in terms of their obligations under ss 328 and 330 of the POCA 2002 and the Money Laundering Regulations 2007 and to their clients in terms of legal professional privilege. However, some caution may still be required with regard to the situations suggested herein. As ever, it is crucial that you are familiar with, and remain up to date with, suitable professional guidance.

# The letter and spirit of the Code: Professional ethics and personal values

## 13.1 The lawyer joke

> *A layperson, an accountant and a lawyer were all asked: 'What do two and two make?'*
> *The layperson replied: 'Four, of course.'*
> *The accountant replied: 'Four—or five.'*
> *The lawyer replied: 'What do you want it to make?'*

Lawyers are the butt of many jokes, many of which flow from a perception that lawyers are capable of acting quite unethically in pursuit of their client's interests. While this perception has, fortunately, never developed in the UK to the extent that it has in the USA, the characteristics of practice in common law jurisdictions expose lawyers to many ethical dilemmas, and responses to these vary. This chapter (and indeed this manual) will provide you with some answers, but in other areas it will simply provide you with a framework within which you will still have to make your own decisions. In these cases it should provide you with tools and ideas that may help you to arrive at conclusions that satisfy the ethical demands of practice.

The issues have been neatly presented by Ross Cranston:

> An important policy issue is the extent to which the Code of Conduct ought to be infused by wider ethical notions. There are two aspects to this. One is encapsulated in the question: 'Can a good lawyer be a bad person?'. In other words, are the standards in the Code of Conduct untenable when laid alongside ethical thought or common morality? The second aspect is that if there is a discrepancy between the Code of Conduct and secular ethical thought, what is special about barristers that exempts them from the precepts of the latter? To put it another way, how is it that barristers can decide ethically on a course of action for a client which is different from that which they would adopt for themselves?
>
> (Cranston, R (ed.), *Legal Ethics and Professional Responsibility* (Oxford: Clarendon, 1996)

The Bar Standards Board recognises this dilemma. Amongst the things it requires you to achieve on the BPTC are 'knowledge and understanding of the philosophical issues and purposes underpinning ethical behaviour'. These and other quotations are from the BPTC Handbook, section 2.2.4, accessible at <https://www.barstandardsboard.org.uk/media/1689434/bar_professional_training_course_and_covers_sept_15__revised_.pdf>. More specifically, you are expected to 'understand and appreciate the core professional values which underpin practice at the Bar of England and Wales, particularly the additional moral responsibilities held by the profession (over and above the population in general) due to decision-making roles, functions and authority which are key to practice at the Bar'.

## 13.2 The Code of Conduct

The Bar Code of Conduct can be found in Part 2 of the BSB Handbook. It provides you with the duties, rules, and guidance that should inform all aspects of your practice at the Bar. It differs from a statute (the form of rule with which you will probably be most familiar) in that it contains Core Duties as well as Conduct Rules, that these are supported by Guidance and finally, that each section of the Conduct Rules is supported by the Outcomes that the rules are designed to achieve. These are valuable sources of assistance in interpretation.

These distinctive characteristics should remind you that you should not approach the Code as you would any other piece of legislation. Why should you not do so? It stems from the underlying principle within UK substantive law that all actions are permitted unless they are forbidden. Thus Acts that regulate behaviour are to be construed in a restrictive manner and loopholes may properly be exploited.

For example, the Theft Act 1968, s 9 provides:

(1) A person is guilty of burglary if:

    (a)   he enters any building or part of a building as a trespasser and with intent to steal anything in the building or part of a building in question, to inflict on any person in it any grievous bodily harm or to rape any woman in it, or to do unlawful damage to the building or anything in it; or

    (b)   having entered any building or part of a building as a trespasser, he steals or attempts to steal anything in the building or that part of it or inflicts or attempts to inflict on any person in it any grievous bodily harm.

Your client has entered a building as a trespasser but with no particular intention, and, once inside decides to do unlawful damage to property within the building. Your advice to him should be to plead not guilty to a charge of burglary. This is because his actions fall within neither paragraph of the subsection even though his actions have produced the same result as behaviour that would lead to guilt (had he formed the intention to cause the damage before, rather than after entering the building). This conclusion may be hard for a layperson to understand but would be natural to any lawyer versed in statutory interpretation.

To adopt the same approach to following the Code may enable you to avoid successful disciplinary proceedings by the BSB. In other words, in so far as it acts in an analogous manner to a criminal statute, the Code may be treated in the same way. However, to approach the Code in this way could carry dangers for the reputation of the profession. Your interpretation of the Code should be informed by the desire to achieve its indicated outcomes and by ethical values, and where the Code permits a variety of responses your choice between them should be similarly informed. This is why the BSB requires that you understand these underpinning values.

An example of how the Code regulates your professional response arises from rC9:

(2) you must not draft any statement of case, witness statement, affidavit or other document containing:

    …

    (c)   any allegation of fraud, unless you have clear instructions to allege fraud and you have reasonably credible material which establishes an arguable case of fraud;

The concept of 'reasonably credible material' inherently carries a degree of subjectivity. Suppose that you have been instructed by your lay client that the opponent has been perpetrating a fraud. It is not uncommon for hostility between the parties to lead to all sorts of allegations that are discovered later to be impossible of formal proof. That being the case, it would be unwise to incorporate such an allegation into any draft on the client's assertion alone. What, however, if the client (who has behaved in a temperate manner throughout) tells you that the opposing party has admitted to committing fraud, but no other independent evidence is available? What if, in addition, the client is prepared to make a statement of truth in respect of this allegation? Would such a statement be 'reasonably credible material' given that it is in essence no more than the original assertion presented formally in a way that is admissible in court? Should you still insist on some independent evidence?

In practical terms you would doubtless advise your professional client to seek independent evidence to corroborate your lay client's oral evidence before settling a statement of case that contained an allegation of fraud. If it is not forthcoming, should you pursue the allegation? The guidance section of this part of the Code offers no further assistance. The outcomes (oC6–9) are too general to help further. The assertion of an intemperate client would clearly be inadequate (it is the mischief the rule is designed to avoid). To rely on a statement of truth may be sufficient to avoid a finding of misconduct (although if there were no other evidence the client should be advised of the dangers of pressing the matter in court: a wasted costs order may loom). However, to refuse to incorporate such an allegation in those circumstances will upset your client, and is likely to upset them more if the allegations are in fact well founded. You must not let your independence be compromised (rC8), yet you should act in the best interests of your client (CD2 and rC15).

No doubt you should err on the side of caution and advise that further evidence should be obtained if possible, but it may not be available. Moreover, if, after settling the statement of case, it becomes clear that there is no credible evidence of fraud (for example, the opposing party may have made the admission to provoke a reaction or as an act of bravado) or if other facts come to light showing that the allegation of fraud has no prospect of success, you will no doubt recognise that the fraud allegation should no longer be pursued. It is submitted that the proper approach is not to seek a 'way around' the provisions of the Code, but to consider underlying values, so that your response is likely to assist to maintain the Bar's reputation as a thoroughly ethical profession (oC6). Fortunately, problems as awkward as this should not be a daily occurrence, and you should remember that advice will be available from your Head of Chambers or from the Bar Council.

An understanding of the underpinning values will give you a basis for deciding ethical questions beyond what the Code provides. Remember that behaviour prohibited by the Code is not made acceptable by a contrary underpinning value, but an underpinning value might validate conduct upon which the Code is silent or in circumstances that generate conflict between its provisions. Ultimately, where, having thought through matters in this degree of depth, you remain uncertain as to the proper way of proceeding, you should contact the Bar Council Ethical Enquiries Service available for advice in emergencies. Note that this service is only available for barristers and not for students.

## 13.3  Underpinning values

Here are a number of values that may be said to underpin the Code of Conduct. It is not intended to be exhaustive:

- justice
- respect for the law
- client autonomy
- confidentiality
- honesty.

How these values apply to the demands of practice at the Bar may best be understood by reading them in the context of the core principles identified by the Bar Standards Board in the previous edition of the Code of Conduct (NB: eighth edition of the Bar Code of Conduct (obsolete since 2014)). These were:

- the principle of professional independence
- the principle of integrity
- the principle of duty to the court
- the principle of loyalty to the lay client
- an understanding of the problems and perception of conflict of interest
- the principle of non-discrimination on grounds of race, colour, ethnic or national origin, nationality, citizenship, sex, sexual orientation, marital status, disability, age, religion or belief and
- commitment to maintaining the highest professional standards of work, to the proper and efficient administration of justice, and to the Rule of Law.

### 13.3.1  Conflict in underpinning values

Conflict between values is inherent in legal practice. Lord Reid makes this clear in his opinion in *Rondel v Worsley* [1969] 1 AC 191, 227:

> Every counsel has a duty to his client fearlessly to raise every issue, advance every argument and ask every question, however distasteful, which he thinks will help his client's case. But, as an officer of the court concerned with the administration of justice, he has an overriding duty to the court, to the standards of his profession, and to the public, which may and often does lead to a conflict with his client's wishes or what the client thinks are his personal wishes.

Consider a concrete situation. If your client in a criminal matter has provided you with information that is relevant (but adverse) to your case you will be faced with a conflict between maintaining confidentiality and not misleading the court. A perusal of the Code will throw up relevant provisions.

The Core Duties, in particular:

> CD1 -
>
> You must observe your duty to the *court* in the administration of justice
>
> CD2 -
>
> You must act in the best interests of each *client*
>
> CD3 -
>
> You must act with honesty and integrity
>
> CD4 -
>
> You must maintain your independence
>
> CD5 -
>
> You must not behave in a way which is likely to diminish the trust and confidence which the public places in you or in the profession
>
> CD6 -
>
> You must keep the affairs of each *client* confidential

Also:

> rC3 -
>
> You owe a duty to the court to act with independence in the interests of justice. This duty overrides any inconsistent obligations which you may have (other than obligations under the criminal law). It includes the following specific obligations which apply whether you are acting as an advocate or are otherwise involved in the *conduct of* litigation in whatever role (with the exception of Rule C3.1 below, which applies when acting as an advocate):
>
> > 1 - you must not knowingly or recklessly mislead or attempt to mislead the *court*;
> >
> > 2 - you must take reasonable steps to avoid wasting the *court's* time;
> >
> > 3 - you must ensure that your ability to act independently is not compromised;
> >
> > 4 - you must take reasonable steps to ensure that the court has before it all relevant decisions and legislative provisions;
> >
> > 5 - you must ensure that your ability to act independently is not compromised.
>
> rC4 -
>
> Your duty to act in the best interests of each *client* is subject to your duty to the *court*.
>
> rC5 -
>
> Your duty to the *court* does not require you to act in breach of your duty to keep the affairs of each *client* confidential.

These rules are helpful in identifying what is expected in relation to each of the underlying values. However, they provide little guidance as to how conflicts should be resolved. While on the one hand your duty to the court is described as overriding (rC3), it does not require breach of client confidentiality (rC5). rC6 provides further detail:

rC6 -

Your duty not to mislead the court or to permit the court to be misled will include the following obligations:

you must not:

a - make submissions, representations or any other statement; or

b - ask questions which suggest facts to witnesses, which you know, or are instructed, are untrue or misleading.

2 - you must not call witnesses to give evidence or put affidavits or witness statements to the *court* which you know, or are *instructed*, are untrue or misleading, unless you make clear to the *court* the true position as known by or instructed to you.

The Code then provides further guidance:

gC6 -

You are obliged by CD2 to promote and to protect your client's interests so far as that is consistent with the law and with your overriding duty to the court under CD1. Your duty to the court does not prevent you from putting forward your client's case simply because you do not believe that the facts are as your client states them to be (or as you, on your client's behalf, state them to be), as long as any positive case you put forward accords with your instructions and you do not mislead the court. Your role when acting as an advocate or conducting litigation is to present your client's case, and it is not for you to decide whether your client's case is to be believed.

gC7 -

For example, you are entitled and it may often be appropriate to draw to the witness's attention other evidence which appears to conflict with what the witness is saying and you are entitled to indicate that a court may find a particular piece of evidence difficult to accept. But if the witness maintains that the evidence is true, it should be recorded in the witness statement and you will not be misleading the court if you call the witness to confirm their witness statement. . . .

gC8 -

As set out in Rule C4, your duty to the court does not permit or require you to disclose confidential information which you have obtained in the course of your instructions and which your client has not authorised you to disclose to the court. However, Rule rC6 requires you not knowingly to mislead the court or to permit the court to be misled. There may be situations where you have obligations under both these rules.

In fact, the conflict identified occurs so regularly in practice that a proper way of responding is well established. You will not necessarily be required to withdraw unless your client wishes you to present information you now know (as opposed to believe) to be incorrect. Your precise duties will depend on the nature of the information being withheld. This may range from a full confession to dishonesty in obtaining public funding (where you may have a statutory duty to disclose) or an indication of past offences of which the prosecution appears to be unaware. You will find detailed guidance as to how to respond ethically to these different situations in the Code of Conduct.

By contrast, in civil litigation the demands of the Civil Procedure Rules and the overriding obligation expect full and frank disclosure during the pre-trial procedures. Thus, obligations of disclosure differ as between civil and criminal cases. This itself throws up an important value, associated with client autonomy and justice. Our adversarial system of justice requires as close as possible an approach to equality of arms. The assumption is that representation by competent and qualified lawyers achieves that equality. In a civil matter the parties are to some extent equal (although one may be able to spend more money than the other in preparing the case). In a criminal matter, however, it is normal to find individuals (often impecunious and possibly facing loss of liberty) with all the forces and resources of a powerful state arranged against them. This goes some way to explaining:

- the 'cab-rank' rule (rC29), which requires barristers to accept any case which is within their competence and ability to undertake (there are exceptions—see rC30) and

- the lesser expectations to disclose adverse factual information in criminal, as opposed to civil matters (given that the task is for the prosecution to prove the case, not for the defendant to prove his innocence).

So your response to a clash of underlying values may need to differ depending on the context. You may find yourself in a situation where you face such a clash of values or where you are challenged by a client holding different values to your own. Consider the following situations.

---

**EXAMPLE**

**What if my client is impecunious and facing a wealthy opponent?**

For example, you are acting pro bono for an unemployed client who claims to have been unfairly dismissed for fighting at work. Your professional client instructs you to contact the respondent's lawyers in order to seek a settlement. The evidence from a number of witnesses and from personnel records suggests that your client had, indeed, been fighting, had done so on many occasions, and was only dismissed after proper warnings had been given. In conference, however, your client continues to deny the allegation while offering no explanation for the evidence against him. You are confident that should the matter proceed to trial your client will lose. You are, however, aware that many cases can result in a technical finding of unfair dismissal for procedural failings, even if the compensation in such cases is likely to be minimal. Your lay client has indicated that he is willing to accept £4,000 in settlement. You recognise, moreover, that for the employer to defend the claim, should you make many demands on them for disclosure or further questions, will cost them well over £4,000.

Should you contact the employer, pointing out that the hearing will be a long one and that you will be requiring considerable disclosure of documents and answers to detailed questions about personnel practices in the firm, suggesting that your client will withdraw the case if they pay £4,000 in settlement? To do so would promote the value of client autonomy and (by subverting the normal consequences of inequalities in wealth) promote a particular view of social justice.

Should you, instead, avoid putting that pressure on the employer when negotiating, recognising that this might make it less likely that the employer will settle for £4,000? To do so would promote the values of respect for the law and a particular (but different) perception of justice.

The Code does not prevent either course, provided you are acting on your client's instructions after giving proper advice. This is thus one example where your own values may have an impact on your choice of whether to use the 'we'll make this expensive for you' tactic.

**What if my client is seeking to achieve, by instructing me, a goal which I regard as immoral?**

For example, your clients, who are a couple seeking to have an exceptionally bright child, wish to carry out genetic checks to screen out any foetuses that appear not to be intelligent. You feel strongly that this is an abuse of the genetic research that has been done. Although the motive appears to be one that is forbidden under the relevant legislation you understand that similar checks (which are permitted) can indirectly provide information that would enable them to screen for intelligence.

Should you simply advise them that their proposed course of action would contravene the law and that they should not therefore attempt to pursue it? To do so may promote the value of (your particular view of) morality. This itself will be based on a value such as the integrity of the individual (in this case the unconceived child).

Should you, instead, indicate how they might achieve their goal without technically breaking the law? To do so would promote the value of client autonomy.

When considering the propriety of your response you must remember that your duty is to act for your client and you should not make moral judgments about your client's actions. You should also consider what your client needs to know in order to make a properly informed decision. These principles are addressed in the Code and clearly prioritise the value of client autonomy.

**What if my client is seeking to achieve, by instructing me, a goal which involves a breach of the law?**

For example, you are instructed by solicitors to advise a corporate client which wishes to reduce some of its production costs. The proposed savings will significantly increase the risk of a release of toxic chemicals into a river. Such a release will constitute a breach of regulations designed to protect the environment and expose the client company to the risk of fines. However, you are aware that the local authority with responsibility for enforcing those regulations is extremely short of finance and is unable to make regular checks. A minor release is therefore unlikely to be noticed, although it will probably be environmentally damaging.

> Should your advice be to explain the legal situation and simply point out that the proposed cost reductions place the company at risk of committing an illegal action for which they might suffer a penalty? To do so may promote the value of respect for the law.
>
> Should your advice extend to your assessment of the very small risk of discovery? To do so may promote the value of client autonomy.
>
> Does the principle indicated in the previous example (that you should not make moral judgments about your client's actions) apply equally here, when the proposed action involves your client committing a criminal offence? The Code indicates that you must do nothing dishonest or bring the profession into disrepute. Incitement to break the law clearly falls within that concept. You can therefore protect yourself from breach of the Code by giving clear advice not to break the law. However, you may be doing that in the realistic knowledge that your client may well ignore you and break the law. Note that if this has occurred to you it is probably your own sensitivity to ethical issues that alerts you to the risk that this may have the effect of indirectly inciting a breach of the law.

You will see that none of these three examples produces a single, clearly correct answer. Regrettably, this may well arise in practice. I have my personal preferences as to the most appropriate response in each case, but you may well take a different view. Any such difference will flow in part from the personal values that you or I espouse. For this reason we need to be aware of those values and how they impact on our responses when faced with ethical dilemmas (as we undoubtedly will be). At the same time it is important that we remember that we must not apply our personal values unrestrained. As barristers, we are bound by the Code and that recognition may assist when you are faced with a conflict of potentially applicable values. You cannot justify a departure from the clear requirements of the Code by pleading an inconsistent personal value, no matter how strongly you espouse it.

## 13.4  Role morality

One concept which may assist in resolving conflicts of this sort is that of role morality. A lawyer may be required to do something for a client which she could not morally justify doing for herself. That proposition may initially appear to be wrong, or at least counterintuitive. However, it is explained to a degree by the recognition that the basis of litigation in the UK is adversarialism. The lawyer is the skilled partisan advocate of the client and is (in theory) opposed by a similarly skilled partisan advocate for the opponent. The neutral decision-maker is neither lawyer but the tribunal.

This concept only works if the lawyer is genuinely partisan and the parties are equitably resourced. A client whose lawyer adopts a neutral role will be severely disadvantaged if opposed by a client whose lawyer adopts a partisan approach. In order to shoulder this burden properly, lawyers may well have to seek to achieve conclusions of which they disapprove, or carry out actions that they would not carry out on their own behalf. To justify this, many have introduced the idea of 'role morality'. This concept prioritises the value of client autonomy and is the source of the 'cab-rank' rule (see rC29). Many lawyers regard it as enabling them to do for their clients what they would not do for themselves.

It may have surprising consequences. As Boon and Levin point out:

> Paradoxically, whilst lawyers are expected to act cooperatively, altruistically and ethically when dealing *with* their clients, they are expected to be uncooperative, selfish and possibly unethical in pursuing the objectives *of* their clients. This creates considerable moral strain, . . .

> (Boon, A and Levin, J, *The Ethics and Conduct of Lawyers in England and Wales)* (Oxford: Hart, 2nd ed, (2008) at 192)

That moral strain will alert you to the fact that while the concept of role morality may justify your doing for your client what you would not do for yourself, it does not give you guidance as to how far you can go. Take an example.

---

**EXAMPLE**

It may well be that if you clearly owed a debt you would not take advantage of the limitation provisions to evade it. However, would you apply the same moral judgment if it were your client who owed the debt? Suppose, for example, your client is very short of money and had forgotten the debt, which is owed to a large corporation? Suppose, instead, your client is the large corporation and the person owed the debt is impecunious?

---

Your view may be identical in those two situations or you may regard their relative wealth as a key issue. That is a matter for you. However, identifying the issue should make it clear that role morality, while potentially justifying actions which you would feel uncomfortable about on your own behalf, does not resolve questions about whether a particular course of action is ethically acceptable. For that, once again, you need to follow the Code and, where necessary, consider your underlying values.

The underpinning principle here is client autonomy. The Code permits you to do whatever your client wants provided that it is not illegal, you are not dishonest, and you give the court the full benefit of your knowledge of the law, whether helpful to your case or not. Equally, you must provide your client with advice that helps him or her to take an informed decision as to whether to pursue a case or not. It would be improper (as with the second example at 13.**3.1**) to prioritise your views over those of your client. There is nothing to stop you identifying ethical considerations to your client, but the decision must remain with the client.

The adversarial nature of the UK legal system may be some justification for a barrister behaving differently in professional and personal contexts, but it also carries its own limits to professional behaviour. Because (unlike in an inquisitorial system) the court does not have the resources to explore the truth for itself, it relies on the honesty of advocates and their ability to research the law fully. This is the source of the requirements not to mislead the court and to cite authorities that go against your client's interests. This should identify two insights:

(a) A claim to role morality does not justify all behaviour. A balance between conflicting values must still be maintained. This is clear from the Marre Report (para 6.1):

> The client is frequently acting under physical, emotional or financial difficulties and may well wish to take every step he can, whether legal or extra-legal, to gain advantage over the other party. In this situation the lawyer has a special duty and responsibility to advise his client as to the legal and ethical standards which should be observed and not to participate in any deception or sharp practice.

> (Lady Marre, CBE, *A Time for Change: Report of the Committee on the Future of the Legal Profession* (General Council of the Bar and Council of the Law Society, London: 1998))

This is helpful guidance, but leaves much to the individual lawyer.

(b) No advocate will be able to meet the standards expected unless the requisite knowledge, understanding, and skills have been mastered. The knowledge, understanding, and skills that you have acquired in your undergraduate study and which you are now developing on your Bar Professional Training Course are central to your effectively meeting the demands of an adversarial system. Competence itself is an ethical issue.

For further discussions of role morality, see Nicolson, D and Webb, J, *Professional Ethics: Critical Interrogations* (Oxford: OUP, 2000) at 169–171.

---

## 13.5 Ethical behaviour and self-interest

It is often said that ethical behaviour is in the individual lawyer's best interest because 'the Bar is a small profession and your reputation will quickly get around'. Barely hidden behind this assertion is the suggestion that if you acquire a reputation for poor ethical standards opponents will not trust you and you will find it increasingly difficult to meet your clients' needs. This may be true. However, it is important to recognise that ethics and self-interest should not be equated.

Some help may be available from the recognition that taking a long-term view of self-interest is highly likely to be an ethically safer approach than taking a short-term view. Thus, an approach which ensures that you have a reputation for honesty is likely to enable you to represent many future clients in negotiation. It is also therefore likely to enhance your long-term income. Willingness to deceive an opponent may achieve something your current client values but will inhibit your ability to come to desirable solutions for future clients. Not only would this inhibit long-term income, it would involve a breach of the Code (rC8, rC9).

One other aspect of self-interest is worth addressing here. You have an interest in your profession continuing to be perceived as in good ethical standing. If you comply with the provisions of the Code, this will preserve you from the risk of disciplinary proceedings. However, where the Code provides a framework within which different courses of action are permitted you should be alert to maintain the highest possible ethical standards.

This insight helps us to identify those aspects of self-interest that will assist us to maintain high ethical standards, but relying on self-interest is altogether insufficient. It ignores most of the underpinning values that we have identified earlier and leaves the individual lawyer without ethical guidance. Thus it remains necessary to comply with the requirements of the Code and to consider its underpinning values in those situations where conflicts nevertheless arise.

## 13.6    The lawyer joke again

So which of the three was acting most ethically? I have no problem with the layperson's response and am sufficiently ignorant to accept that there may be justification for the accountant's response. However, to judge the lawyer I need to go back to my core values again. If I prioritise client autonomy, this lawyer may be responding perfectly correctly. There are few situations in reality where one simple answer is the only one available. The lawyer here is seeking the client's instructions as to what the desired outcome is. It may be that that outcome is not legally available, in which case the lawyer should advise the client to that effect. It may be readily available, in which case the lawyer is in the fortunate position of giving the client good news. It is just as likely, however, that the answer is somewhere between the two. How far should you go to achieve the client's desired result? That is a matter of your professional responsibility. The Code of Conduct provides guidance:

> Other rules deal with specific aspects of your obligation to act in your client's best interests (CD2) while maintaining honesty, integrity (CD3) and independence (CD4), such as rule C21.10 (not acting where your independence is compromised), rule C10 (not paying or accepting referral fees) and C21 (not acting in circumstances of a conflict of interest or where you risk breaching one *client's* confidentiality in favour of another's) (gC15), . . .

which makes it clear that you should not allow your personal values to override the requirements of the Code. However, within the boundaries provided by the Code, the Guidance available on the Bar Council and Bar Standards Board websites, and always remembering the availability of the Ethical Queries Helpline, the final decision is your responsibility.

## SUGGESTED FURTHER READING

Andrew Boon: *The Ethics and Conduct of Lawyers in England and Wales* (3rd ed. Oxford, Hart, 2014). This is the most authoritative of the books suggested and explores the principles underlying the ethics of solicitors and barristers. It looks critically at the conflicts that may arise and the ways in which the ethical principles apply in different areas of lawyers' work.

Andrew Boon: *Lawyers' Ethics and Professional Responsibility* (Oxford, Hart, 2015). This is a student text that has the advantage of many examples and problems to help you to understand the ethical dilemmas that lawyers may encounter.

Adrian Evans: *The Good Lawyer: A Student Guide to Law and Ethics* (Cambridge, CUP, 2014). Although written from an Australian perspective, this book addresses the same issues as the UK-published books and takes your personal values as its starting point. It also contains many examples and problems.

Donald Nicolson and Julian Webb: *Professional Legal Ethics: Critical Interrogations* (Oxford, OUP, 2000). This is a more theoretical book that provides a wide-ranging and critical analysis of the ethical principles of the English legal professions.

# 14

# Professional conduct problems

## Question 1

A solicitor seeks to instruct you to act for notoriously bad landlords in an action for possession of premises occupied by a highly regarded charitable organisation. The case is likely to draw adverse publicity. You hold yourself out to act in landlord and tenant cases, you have no connection with either party or with the premises, you have no conflicting professional commitment, and the fee offered is a proper fee for you and for the case. Your clerk tells you that he wishes you to refuse the instructions because:

(a) it is chambers' policy not to act for landlords and
(b) he fears that your normal professional clients will be reluctant to instruct you in future cases as their clients (tenants, consumers, etc) would refuse to have as counsel one who had acted for these particular claimants.

What do you do?

## Question 2

You are instructed in a family law matter. You act for a white father whose former wife, who is also white, is now cohabiting with a black African boyfriend. Your client instructs you to resist her application for contact with the parties' son on grounds which you consider to be racist. Can you refuse to put forward instructions even if wrapped up as seeking to avoid 'exposing his son to a cultural environment totally alien to him . . . '?

## Question 3

You have successfully appeared for the claimants in an action where the unsuccessful defendants now wish to seek a Part 20 indemnity or contribution from a third party who was not a party to the original action. The defendants' solicitors were impressed with your performance and want you to be able to use your knowledge of the case against the third party. Do you accept the instructions?

## Question 4

A solicitor, who regularly instructs you and your chambers, telephones you and instructs you to attend at a particular police station where a lay client is about to be interviewed and to advise the client as necessary. The solicitor undertakes to pay you a proper fee. If the matter leads to a charge or charges being preferred, the brief is likely to come into chambers for someone of your experience.

(a) Can you act?

(b) Would it make any difference if the brief would certainly be beyond your competence?

## Question 5

You have received and accepted instructions to appear in case 'A' (a civil case fixed to be heard on 20 April). You have done a lot of preparatory work upon it and have seen the professional and lay clients in conference on a number of occasions. You have also accepted instructions to defend in a serious criminal case (case 'B'), expected to be tried in the week beginning 1 April and to last for five days, but which may well go on longer. Before you have conferred with the client in case 'B', you learn that it will not be heard until the week beginning 15 April. Both solicitors assert priority and both clients are anxious to have your services. Which case do you do? Why?

## Question 6

You have represented your client successfully in court. After the hearing, the client stuffs a £20 note in your pocket and tells you to enjoy a drink on him.

(a) Do you keep the money?

(b) Would it make any difference if your client instead sent you a bottle of whisky?

## Question 7

(a) The defendant in a rape case instructs you that sexual intercourse took place between him and the victim with her consent. At trial, he tells you that he did not have sexual intercourse with her and gives you names of alibi witnesses.

(b) Your client has mental health problems. His instructions differ each time you speak to him.

What should you do in these circumstances?

## Question 8

You act for the claimant in civil proceedings. In the course of his evidence-in-chief, he produces several documents from his pocket which he alleges support his claim. You have never seen them before nor have they been disclosed to the defence. What do you do?

## Question 9

You receive a set of instructions to advise and settle civil proceedings for a claimant from X and Co, a firm of solicitors who have instructed you on a number of occasions and are among your best clients. It is apparent that they have been negligent in handling the claimant's affairs. It appears to you that the claimant's chances have not been badly affected and he is likely to succeed in the litigation, but he has at least been prejudiced in the sense that, if the relevant matter 'surfaces' in the litigation, the defendants will be able to make use of it to reduce the damages or to obtain a better settlement than would otherwise have been open to them. (For example, there has been a failure to secure evidence relevant to proving the amount of the claimant's loss and damage.) What, if anything, should you do?

## Question 10

You are defending in a trial at the Crown Court. In the course of giving his evidence, the defendant makes an allegation which, although it is in your instructions, you had not put to the victim. It is apparent that it should have been, and the victim has gone on holiday and cannot be recalled. The judge is furious. What do you do?

## Question 11

You are asked to advise, in conference, upon the acceptability of an offer of £3,000 in settlement of your clients claim for damages in a personal injury case. The medical report, which has been disclosed to the defence, is now ten months old. In the course of the conference, your client informs you that the doctor's prognosis was unduly pessimistic as his condition has improved since the report was prepared. In the circumstances, the offer is generous and more than your client is likely to receive from the court.

(a) What advice do you give?
(b) Would it make any difference if the client's information was contained in a more recent, but undisclosed medical report?

## Question 12

You are instructed to represent the defendant in proceedings for damages for breach of contract. Upon your arrival at court, your instructing solicitor informs you that one of your witnesses has just telephoned his office to say that she is ill and cannot attend court to give evidence. Her testimony is vital to the defendant's case. You have no option but to seek an adjournment. At that moment, your opponent approaches you and asks if he can have a word with you. He indicates that he has witness difficulties and invites you to agree to an adjournment of the hearing for two weeks. In so doing:

(a) Do you inform your opponent and the court of your own witness difficulties?
(b) If not, do you make an application for the claimant to pay the defendant's costs thrown away by the adjournment?

# APPENDIX 1
# EXCERPTS FROM THE BAR STANDARDS BOARD HANDBOOK

THE BAR STANDARDS BOARD HANDBOOK

2nd Edition

April 2015

Bar Standards Board

## Part 2
# The Code of Conduct

# CONTENTS

# A. APPLICATION

## R  Rules

**rC1**   Who?

.1   Section 2.B (Core Duties): applies to all *BSB regulated persons* except where stated otherwise, and references to "you" and "your" in Section 2.B shall be construed accordingly.

.2   Section 2.C (Conduct Rules):

.a   Applies to all *BSB regulated persons* apart from *unregistered barristers* except where stated otherwise.

.b   Rules C3.5, C4, C8, C16, C19 and C64 to C70 (and associated guidance to those rules) and the guidance on Core Duties also apply to *unregistered barristers*.

References to "you" and "your" in Section 2.C shall be construed accordingly

.3   Section 2.D (Specific Rules): applies to specific groups as defined in each sub-section and references to "you" and "your" shall be construed accordingly.

**rC2**   When?

.1   Section 2.B applies when practising or otherwise providing *legal services*. In addition, CD5 and CD9 apply at all times.

.2   Section 2.C applies when practising or otherwise providing *legal services*. In addition, rules C8, C16 and C64 to C70 and the associated guidance apply at all times.

.3   Section 2.D applies when practising or otherwise providing *legal services*.

.4   Sections 2.B, 2.C and 2.D only apply to *registered European lawyers* in connection with professional work undertaken by them in that capacity in England and Wales.

# B. THE CORE DUTIES

**CD1**    You must observe your duty to the court in the administration of justice [CD1].

**CD2**    You must act in the best interests of each client [CD2].

**CD3**    You must act with honesty and integrity [CD3].

**CD4**    You must maintain your independence [CD4].

**CD5**    You must not behave in a way which is likely to diminish the trust and confidence which the public places in you or in the profession [CD5].

**CD6**    You must keep the affairs of each client confidential [CD6].

**CD7**    You must provide a competent standard of work and service to each client [CD7]

**CD8**    You must not discriminate unlawfully against any person [CD8].

**CD9**    You must be open and co-operative with your regulators [CD9].

**CD10**   You must take reasonable steps to manage your practice, or carry out your role within your practice, competently and in such a way as to achieve compliance with your legal and regulatory obligations [CD10].

| **G** | **Guidance** |
|---|---|

**Guidance to the core duties**

**gC1**    The Core Duties are not presented in order of precedence, subject to the following:

     .1    CD1 overrides any other core duty, if and to the extent the two are inconsistent. Rules C3.5 and C4 deal specifically with the relationship between CD1, CD2 and CD6 and you should refer to those rules and to the related Guidance;

     .2    in certain other circumstances set out in this Code of Conduct one Core Duty overrides another. Specifically, Rule C16 provides that CD2 (as well as being subject to CD1) is subject to your obligations under CD3, CD4 and CD8.

**gC2**    Your obligation to take reasonable steps to manage your *practice*, or carry out your role within your *practice*, competently and in such a way as to achieve compliance with your legal and regulatory obligations (CD10) includes an obligation to take all reasonable steps to mitigate the effects of any breach of those legal and regulatory obligations once you become aware of the same.

*Act accordance with CD, R, G → then you will achieve the outcome.*

# C. THE CONDUCT RULES

## C1.  You and the *court*

### O  Outcomes

**oC1**  The *court* is able to rely on information provided to it by those conducting litigation and by advocates who appear before it.

**oC2**  The proper administration of justice is served.

**oC3**  The interests of *clients* are protected to the extent compatible with outcomes oC1 and oC2 and the Core Duties.

**oC4**  Both those who appear before the *court* and *clients* understand clearly the extent of the duties owed to the *court* by advocates and those conducting litigation and the circumstances in which duties owed to *clients* will be overridden by the duty owed to the *court*.

**oC5**  *The public* has confidence in the administration of justice and in those who serve it.

### R  Rules

**rC3**  You owe a duty to the *court* to act with independence in the interests of justice. This duty overrides any inconsistent obligations which you may have (other than obligations under the criminal law). It includes the following specific obligations which apply whether you are acting as an advocate or are otherwise involved in the conduct of litigation in whatever role (with the exception of Rule C3.1 below, which applies when acting as an advocate):

  .1    you must not knowingly or recklessly mislead or attempt to mislead the *court*;

  .2    you must not abuse your role as an advocate;

  .3    you must take reasonable steps to avoid wasting the *court's* time;

  .4    you must take reasonable steps to ensure that the *court* has before it all relevant decisions and legislative provisions;

  .5    you must ensure that your ability to act independently is not compromised.

**rC4**  Your duty to act in the best interests of each *client* is subject to your duty to the *court*.

**rC5**  Your duty to the *court* does not require you to act in breach of your duty to keep the affairs of each *client* confidential.

### Not misleading the court

**rC6**  Your duty not to mislead the *court* or to permit the *court* to be misled will include the following obligations:

.1     you must not:

    .a     make submissions, representations or any other statement; or

    .b     ask questions which suggest facts to witnesses

    which you know, or are instructed, are untrue or misleading.

.2     you must not call witnesses to give evidence or put affidavits or witness statements to the *court* which you know, or are *instructed*, are untrue or misleading, unless you make clear to the *court* the true position as known by or instructed to you.

## G     Guidance

### Guidance on Rules C3 – C6 and relationship to CD1 and CD2

**gC3**     Rules C3 – C6 set out some specific aspects of your duty to the *court* (CD1). See CD1 and associated Guidance at gC1

**gC4**     Knowingly misleading the *court* includes inadvertently misleading the *court* if you later realise that you have misled the *court*, and you fail to correct the position. Recklessness means being indifferent to the truth, or not caring whether something is true or false. The duty continues to apply for the duration of the case.

**gC5**     Your duty under Rule C3.3 includes drawing to the attention of the *court* any decision or provision which may be adverse to the interests of your *client*. It is particularly important where you are appearing against a litigant who is not legally represented.

**gC6**     You are obliged by CD2 to promote and to protect your *client's* interests so far as that is consistent with the law and with your overriding duty to the *court* under CD1. Your duty to the *court* does not prevent you from putting forward your *client's* case simply because you do not believe that the facts are as your *client* states them to be (or as you, on your *client's* behalf, state them to be), as long as any positive case you put forward accords with your *instructions* and you do not mislead the *court*. Your role when acting as an advocate or conducting litigation is to present your *client's* case, and it is not for you to decide whether your *client's* case is to be believed.

**gC7**     For example, you are entitled and it may often be appropriate to draw to the witness's attention other evidence which appears to conflict with what the witness is saying and you are entitled to indicate that a *court* may find a particular piece of evidence difficult to accept. But if the witness maintains that the evidence is true, it should be recorded in the witness statement and you will not be misleading the *court* if you call the witness to confirm their witness statement. Equally, there may be circumstances where you call a hostile witness whose evidence you are instructed is untrue. You will not be in breach of Rule C6 if you make the position clear to the *court*. See further the guidance at gC14.

**gC8**     As set out in Rule C4, your duty to the *court* does not permit or require you to disclose confidential information which you have obtained in the course of your *instructions* and which your *client* has not authorised you to disclose to the *court*. However, Rule C6 requires you not knowingly to mislead the *court* or to permit the *court* to be misled. There may be situations where you have obligations under both these rules.

**gC9**     Rule C3.5 makes it clear that your duty to act in the best interests of your *client* is subject to your duty to the *court*. For example, if your *client* were to tell you that he had committed the crime with which he was charged, in order to be able to ensure compliance with Rule C4 on the one hand and Rule C3 and Rule C6 on the other:

.1      you would not be entitled to disclose that information to the *court* without your *client's* consent; and

.2      you would not be misleading the *court* if, after your *client* had entered a plea of 'not guilty', you were to test in cross-examination the reliability of the evidence of the prosecution witnesses and then address the jury to the effect that the prosecution had not succeeded in making them sure of your *client's* guilt.

**gC10**     However, you would be misleading the *court* and would therefore be in breach of Rules C3 and C6 if you were to set up a positive case inconsistent with the confession, as for example by:

.1      suggesting to prosecution witnesses, calling your *client* or your witnesses to show; or submitting to th*e jury*, that your *client* di*d* not commit the crime; or

.2      suggesting that someone else had done so; or

.3      putting forward an alibi.

**gC11**     If there is a risk that the *court* will be misled unless you disclose confidential information which you have learned in the course of your *instructions*, you should ask the *client* for permission to disclose it to the *court*. If your *client* refuses to allow you to make the disclosure you must cease to act, and return your *instructions*: see Rules C25 to C27 below. In these circumstances you must not reveal the information to the *court*.

**gC12**     For example, if your *client* tells you that he has previous *convictions* of which the prosecution is not aware, you may not disclose this without his consent. However, in a case where mandatory sentences apply, the non-disclosure of the previous *convictions* will result in the *court* failing to pass the sentence that is required by law. In that situation, you must advise your *client* that if consent is refused to your revealing the information you will have to cease to act. In situations where mandatory sentences do not apply, and your *client* does not agree to disclose the previous *convictions*, you can continue to represent your *client* but in doing so must not say anything that misleads the *court*. This will constrain what you can say in mitigation. For example, you could not advance a positive case of previous good character knowing that there are undisclosed prior *convictions*. Moreover, if the *court* asks you a direct question you must not give an untruthful answer and therefore you would have to withdraw if, on your being asked such a question, your *client* still refuses to allow you to answer the question truthfully. You should explain this to your *client*.

**gC13**     Similarly, if you become aware that your *client* has a document which should be disclosed but has not been disclosed, you cannot continue to act unless your *client* agrees to the disclosure of the document. In these circumstances you must not reveal the existence or contents of the document to the *court*.

### R   Rules

### Not abusing your role as an advocate

**rC7**     Where you are acting as an advocate, your duty not to abuse your role includes the following obligations:

.1      you must not make statements or ask questions merely to insult, humiliate or annoy a witness or any other person;

.2      you must not make a serious allegation against a witness whom you have had an opportunity to cross-examine unless you have given that witness a chance to answer the allegation in cross-examination;

.3    you must not make a serious allegation against any person, or suggest that a person is guilty of a crime with which your *client* is charged unless:

.a    you have reasonable grounds for the allegation; and

.b    the allegation is relevant to your *client's* case or the credibility of a witness; and

.c    where the allegation relates to a third party, you avoid naming them in open *court* unless this is reasonably necessary.

.4    you must not put forward to the *court* a personal opinion of the facts or the law unless you are invited or required to do so by the *court* or by law.

## C2.   Behaving ethically

### O   Outcomes

oC6   Those and entities regulated by the *Bar Standards Board* maintain standards of honesty, integrity and independence, and are seen as so doing.

oC7   The proper administration of justice, access to justice and the best interests of *clients* are served.

oC8   Those and entities regulated by the *Bar Standards Board* do not discriminate unlawfully and take appropriate steps to prevent *discrimination* occurring in their practices.

oC9   Those and entities regulated by the *Bar Standards Board* and *clients* understand the obligations of honesty, integrity and independence.

### R   Rules

#### Honesty, integrity and independence

 rC8   You must not do anything which could reasonably be seen by the public to undermine your honesty, integrity (CD3) and independence (CD4).

 rC9   Your duty to act with honesty and integrity under CD3 includes the following requirements:

.1   you must not knowingly or recklessly mislead or attempt to mislead anyone;

.2   you must not draft any statement of case, witness statement, affidavit or other document containing:

   .a   any statement of fact or contention which is not supported by your *client* or by your *instructions*;

   .b   any contention which you do not consider to be properly arguable;

   .c   any allegation of fraud, unless you have clear instructions to allege fraud and you have reasonably credible material which establishes an arguable case of fraud;

   .d   (in the case of a witness statement or affidavit) any statement of fact other than the evidence which you reasonably believe the witness would give if the witness were giving evidence orally;

.3   you must not encourage a witness to give evidence which is misleading or untruthful;

.4   you must not rehearse, practise with or coach a witness in respect of their evidence;

.5   unless you have the permission of the representative for the opposing side or of the *court*, you must not communicate with any witness (including your *client*) about the case while the witness is giving evidence;

.6   you must not make, or offer to make, payments to any witness which are contingent on his evidence or on the outcome of the case;

.7   you must only propose, or accept, fee arrangements which are legal.

**G**    Guidance

### Guidance on Rules C8 and C9 and their relationship to CD1, CD2, CD3, CD4 and CD5

**gC14**    Your honesty, integrity and independence are fundamental. The interests of justice (CD1) and the *client's* best interests (CD2) can only be properly served, and any conflicts between the two properly resolved, if you conduct yourself honestly and maintain your independence from external pressures, as required by CD3 and CD4. You should also refer to Rule C16 which subjects your duty to act in the best interests of your *client* (CD2) to your observance of CD3 and CD4, as well as to your duty to the *court* (CD1).

**gC15**    Other rules deal with specific aspects of your obligation to act in your *client's* best interests (CD2) while maintaining honesty, integrity (CD3) and independence (CD4), such as rule C21.10 (not acting where your independence is compromised), rule C10 (not paying or accepting *referral fees*) and C21 (not acting in circumstances of a conflict of interest or where you risk breaching one *client's* confidentiality in favour of another's).

**gC16**    Rule C3 addresses how your conduct is perceived by the public. Conduct on your part which the public may reasonably perceive as undermining your honesty, integrity or independence is likely to diminish the trust and confidence which the public places in you or in the profession, in breach of CD5. Rule C8 is not exhaustive of the ways in which CD5 may be breached.

**gC17**    In addition to your obligation to only propose, or accept, fee arrangements which are legal in Rule C9.7, you must also have regard to your obligations in relation to *referral fees* in Rule C10 and the associated guidance.

Examples of how you may be seen as compromising your independence

**gC18**    The following may reasonably be seen as compromising your independence in breach of Rule 8 (whether or not the circumstances are such that Rule C10 is also breached):

    .1    offering, promising or giving:

        .a    any commission or referral fee (of whatever size) – note that these are in any case prohibited by Rule C10 and associated guidance; or

        .b    a gift (apart from items of modest value),

        to any *client*, *professional client* or other *intermediary*; or

    .2    lending money to any such *client*, *professional client* or other *intermediary*; or

    .3    accepting any money (whether as a loan or otherwise) from any *client*, *professional client* or other *intermediary*, unless it is a payment for your professional services or reimbursement of expenses or of disbursements made on behalf of the *client*;

**gC19**    If you are offered a gift by a current, prospective or former *client*, *professional client* or other *intermediary*, you should consider carefully whether the circumstances and size of the gift would reasonably lead others to think that your independence had been compromised. If this would be the case, you should refuse to accept the gift.

**gC20**    The giving or receiving of entertainment at a disproportionate level may also give rise to a similar issue and so should not be offered or accepted if it would lead others reasonably to think that your independence had been compromised.

**gC21**    Guidance C18 to C20 above is likely to be more relevant where you are a *self-employed barrister*, a *BSB authorised body*, an *authorised (non-BSB) individual*, an *employed barrister (BSB authorised body)* or a *BSB regulated manager*. If you are a *BSB authorised individual* who is a an *employee* or *manager* of an *authorised (non-BSB) body* or you are an *employed barrister (non-authorised body)* and your *a*pproved regulator* or *employer* (as appropriate) permits payments to which Rule C10 applies, you may make or receive such payments only in your capacity as such and as permitted by the rules of your *approved regulator* or *employer* (as appropriate). For further information on referral fees, see the guidance at C32).

**gC22**    The former prohibition on *practising barristers* expressing a personal opinion in the media in relation to any future or current proceedings in which they are briefed has been removed. *Practising barristers* must, nevertheless, ensure that any comment they may make does not undermine, and is not reasonably seen as undermining, their independence. Furthermore, any such comment must not bring the profession, nor any other *barrister* into disrepute. Further guidance is available on the *Bar Standards Board's* website (https://www.barstandardsboard.org.uk/regulatory-requirements/bsb-handbook/code-guidance/) or by clicking on the relevant link.

*Examples of what your duty to act with honesty and integrity may require*

**gC23**    Rule C9 sets out some specific aspects of your duty under CD3 to act with honesty and integrity.

**gC24**    In addition to the above, where the other side is legally represented and you are conducting correspondence in respect of the particular matter, you are expected to correspond at all times with that other party's legal representative – otherwise you may be regarded as breaching CD3 or Rule C9.

*Other possible breaches of CD3 and/or CD5*

**gC25**    A breach of Rule C9 may also constitute a breach of CD3 and/or CD5. Other conduct which is likely to be treated as a breach of CD3 and/or CD5 includes (but is not limited to):

.1    subject to Guidance C26 below, breaches of Rule C8;

.2    breaches of Rule C10;

.3    criminal conduct, other than *minor criminal offences* (see Guidance C27);

.4    seriously offensive or discreditable conduct towards third parties;

.5    dishonesty;

.6    unlawful *victimisation* or *harassment*; or

.7    abuse of your professional position.

**gC26**    For the purposes of Guidance C25.7 above, referring to your status as a *barrister*, for example on professional notepaper, in a context where it is irrelevant, such as in a private dispute, may well constitute abuse of your professional position and thus involve a breach of CD3 and/or CD5.

**gC27**    Conduct which is not likely to be treated as a breach of Rules C8 or C9, or CD3 or CD5, includes (but is not limited to):

.1    *minor criminal offences*;

.2    your conduct in your private or personal life, unless this involves:

.a    abuse of your professional position; or

.b    committing a *criminal offence*, other than a *minor criminal offence*.

**gC28** For the purpose of Guidance C27 above, *minor criminal offences* include:

.1 an offence committed in the United Kingdom which is a fixed-penalty offence under the Road Traffic Offenders Act 1988; or

.2 an offence committed in the United Kingdom or abroad which is dealt with by a procedure substantially similar to that for such a fixed-penalty offence; or

.3 an offence whose main ingredient is the unlawful parking of a motor vehicle.

## R  Rules

### Referral fees

**rC10** You must not pay or receive *referral fees*.

## G  Guidance

### Guidance on Rule C10 and their relationship to CD2, CD3, CD4 and CD5

**gC29** Making or receiving payments in order to procure or reward the referral to you by an intermediary of professional *instructions* is inconsistent with your obligations under CD2 and/or CD3 and/or CD4 and may also breach CD5.

**gC30** Moreover:

.1 where *public* funding is in place, the *Legal Aid Agency's* Unified Contract Standard Terms explicitly prohibit contract-holders from making or receiving any payment (or any other benefit) for the referral or introduction of a *client*, whether or not the lay *client* knows of, and consents to, the payment;

.2 whether in a private or publicly funded case, a *referral fee* to which the *client* has not consented may constitute a bribe and therefore a *criminal offence* under the Bribery Act 2010;

.3 *referral fees* and inducements (as defined in the Criminal Justice and Courts Act 2015) are prohibited where they relate to a claim or potential claim for damages for personal injury or death or arise out of circumstances involving personal injury or death personal injury claims: section 56 Legal Aid, Sentencing and Punishment of Offenders Act 2012 and section 58 Criminal Justice and Courts Act 2015

**gC31** Rule C10 does not prohibit proper expenses that are not a reward for referring work, such as genuine and reasonable payments for:

.1 clerking and administrative services (including where these are outsourced);

.2 membership subscriptions to ADR bodies that appoint or recommend a person to provide mediation, arbitration or adjudication services; or

.3 advertising and publicity, which are payable whether or not any work is referred. However, the fact that a fee varies with the amount of work received does not necessarily mean that that it is a referral fee, if it is genuinely for a marketing service from someone who is not directing work to one provider rather than another, depending on who pays more.

**gC32** Further guidance is available at https://www.barstandardsboard.org.uk/regulatory-requirements/bsb-handbook/code-guidance/

**R** | **Rules**

### Undertakings

**rC11**    You must within an agreed timescale or within a reasonable period of time comply with any undertaking you give in the course of conducting litigation.

**G** | **Guidance**

### Guidance on Rule C11

**gC33**    You should ensure your insurance covers you in respect of any liability incurred in giving an undertaking.

**R** | **Rules**

### Discrimination

**rC12**    You must not discriminate unlawfully against, victimise or harass any other person on the grounds of race, colour, ethnic or national origin, nationality, citizenship, sex, gender re-assignment, sexual orientation, marital or civil partnership status, disability, age, religion or belief, or pregnancy and maternity.

**G** | **Guidance**

### Guidance on Rule C12

**gC34**    Rules rC110 and associated guidance are also relevant to equality and diversity. The BSB's Supporting Information on the BSB Handbook Equality Rules are available on the BSB website: https://www.barstandardsboard.org.uk/media/1562168/bsb_equality_rules_handbook_corrected.pdf.

**R** | **Rules**

### Foreign work

**rC13**    In connection with any *foreign work* you must comply with any applicable rule of conduct prescribed by the law or by any national or local Bar of:

.1    the place where the work is or is to be performed; and

.2    the place where any proceedings or matters to which the work relates are taking place or contemplated;

unless such rule is inconsistent with any requirement of the Core Duties.

**rC14**    If you solicit work in any jurisdiction outside England and Wales, you must not do so in a manner which would be prohibited if you were a member of the local Bar.

## G    Guidance

### Guidance on Rules C13 and C14

**gC35**    When you are engaged in *cross border activities* within a *CCBE State* other than the UK, you must comply with the rules at 2.D5 which implement the part of the *Code of Conduct for European Lawyers* not otherwise covered by this Handbook as well as with any other applicable rules of conduct relevant to that particular *CCBE State*. It is your responsibility to inform yourself as to any applicable rules of conduct.

## C3. You and your client

### O   Outcomes

oC10   *Clients* receive a competent standard of work and service.

oC11   *Clients'* best interests are protected and promoted by those acting for them.

oC12   *BSB authorised persons* do not accept instructions from *clients* where there is a conflict between their own interests and the *clients'* or where there is a conflict between one or more *clients* except when permitted in this *Handbook*.

oC13   *Clients* know what to expect and understand the advice they are given.

oC14   Care is given to ensure that the interests of vulnerable *clients* are taken into account and their needs are met.

oC15   *Clients* have confidence in those who are instructed to act on their behalf.

oC16   *Instructions* are not accepted, refused, or returned in circumstances which adversely affect the administration of justice, access to justice or (so far as compatible with these) the best interests of the *client*.

oC17   *Clients* and *BSB authorised persons* and *authorised (non-BSB)* individuals and *BSB regulated managers* are clear about the circumstances in which *instructions* may not be accepted or may or must be returned.

oC18   *Clients* are adequately informed as to the terms on which work is to be done.

oC19   *Clients* understand how to bring a *complaint* and *complaints* are dealt with promptly, fairly, openly and effectively.

oC20   *Clients* understand who is responsible for work done for them

### R   Rules

#### Best interests of each client, provision of a competent standard of work and confidentiality

rC15   Your duty to act in the best interests of each *client* (CD2), to provide a competent standard of work and service to each *client* (CD7) and to keep the affairs of each *client* confidential (CD6) includes the following obligations:

.1   you must promote fearlessly and by all proper and lawful means the *client's* best interests;

.2   you must do so without regard to your own interests or to any consequences to you (which may include, for the avoidance of doubt, you being required to take reasonable steps to mitigate the effects of any breach of this *Handbook*);

.3   you must do so without regard to the consequences to any other person (whether to your *professional client*, *employer* or any other person);

.4   you must not permit your *professional client*, *employer* or any other person to limit your discretion as to how the interests of the *client* can best be served; and

.5    you must protect the confidentiality of each *client's* affairs, except for such disclosures as are required or permitted by law or to which you *client* gives informed consent.

**rC16**    Your duty to act in the best interests of each *client* (CD2) is subject to your duty to the *court* (CD1) and to your obligations to act with honesty, and integrity (CD3) and to maintain your independence (CD4).

## G    Guidance

### Guidance on Rules C15 and C16 and their relationship to CD2, CD6 and CD7

**gC36**    Your duty is to your *client*, not to your *professional client* or other *intermediary* (if any).

**gC37**    Rules C15 and C16 are expressed in terms of the interests of each *client*. This is because you may only accept *instructions* to act for more than one *client* if you are able to act in the best interests of each *client* as if that *client* were your only *client*, as CD2 requires of you. See further Rule C17 on the circumstances when you are obliged to advise your *client* to seek other legal representation and Rules C21.2 and C21.3 on conflicts of interest and the guidance to those rules at gC69.

**gC38**    CD7 requires not only that you provide a competent standard of work but also a competent standard of service to your *client*. Rule C15 is not exhaustive of what you must do to ensure your compliance with CD2 and CD7. By way of example, a competent standard of work and of service also includes:

CD7

.1    treating each *client* with courtesy and consideration; and

.2    seeking to advise your *client*, in terms they can understand; and

.3    taking all reasonable steps to avoid incurring unnecessary expense; and

.4    reading your instructions promptly. This may be important if there is a time limit or limitation period. If you fail to read your instructions promptly, it is possible that you will not be aware of the time limit until it is too late.

**gC39**    In order to be able to provide a competent standard of work, you should keep your professional knowledge and skills up to date, regularly take part in professional development and educational activities that maintain and further develop your competence and performance and, where you are a B*SB authorised body* or a *manager* of such body, you should take reasonable steps to ensure that *managers* and *employees* within your *organisation* undertake such *training*. Merely complying with the minimum Continuing Professional Development requirements may not be sufficient to comply with Rule C15. You should also ensure that you comply with any specific training requirements of the *Bar Standards Board* before undertaking certain activities – for example, you should not attend a police station to advise a suspect or interviewee as to the handling and conduct of police interviews unless you have complied with such training requirements as may be imposed by the *Bar Standards Board* in respect of such work. Similarly, you should not undertake public access work without successfully completing the required training specified by the *Bar Standards Board*.

**gC40**    In addition to Guidance gC38 above, a *BSB authorised body* or a *manager* of such body should ensure that work is allocated appropriately, to *managers* and/or *employees* with the appropriate knowledge and expertise to undertake such work.

**gC41**    You should remember that your *client* may not be familiar with legal proceedings and may find them difficult and stressful. You should do what you reasonably can to ensure that the *client* understands the process and what to expect from it and from you. You should also try to avoid any unnecessary distress for your *client*. This is particularly important where you are dealing with a vulnerable *client*.

**gC42**    The duty of confidentiality (CD6) is central to the administration of justice. *Clients* who put their confidence in their legal advisers must be able to do so in the knowledge that the information they

give, or which is given on their behalf, will stay confidential. In normal circumstances, this information will be privileged and not disclosed to a *court*. CD6, rC4 and Guidance C8 and C11 to C13 provide further information.

**gC43**    Rule C15.5 acknowledges that your duty of confidentiality is subject to an exception if disclosure is required or permitted by law. For example, you may be obliged to disclose certain matters by the Proceeds of Crime Act 2002. Disclosure in those circumstances would not amount to a breach of CD6 or Rule C15.5 In other circumstances, you may only make disclosure of confidential information where your *client* gives informed consent to the disclosure. See the Guidance to Rule C21 at gC68 for an example of circumstances where it may be appropriate for you to seek such consent.

**gC44**    There may be circumstances when your duty of confidentiality to your *client* conflicts with your duty to the *court*. Rule C4 and Guidance C8 and C11 to C13 provide further information.

**gC45**    Similarly, there may be circumstances when your duty of confidentiality to your *client* conflicts with your duty to your regulator. Rule C64 and Guidance C92 to C93 in respect of that rule provide further information. In addition, Rule C66 may also apply.

**gC46**    If you are a *pupil* of, or are *devilling* work for, a *self-employed barrister*, Rule C15.5 applies to you as if the *client* of the *self-employed barrister* was your own *client*.

**gC47**    The section You and Your Practice, at 2.C5, provides for duties regarding the systems and procedures you must put in place and enforce in order to ensure compliance with Rule C15.5.

**gC48**    If you are an *authorised individual* or a *manager* working in a *BSB authorised body* your personal duty to act in the best interests of your *client* requires you to assist in the redistribution of *client* files and otherwise assisting to ensure each *client's* interests are protected in the event that the *BSB authorised body* itself is unable to do so for whatever reason (for example, insolvency).

**R    Rules**

**rC17**    Your duty to act in the best interests of each *client* (CD2) includes a duty to consider whether the *client's* best interests are served by different legal representation, and if so, to advise the *client* to that effect.

**G    Guidance**

### Guidance on Rule C17

**gC49**    Your duty to comply with Rule C17 may require you to advise your *client* that in their best interests they should be represented by:

.1    a different advocate or legal representative, whether more senior or more junior than you, or with different experience from yours;

.2    more than one advocate or legal representative;

.3    fewer advocates or legal representatives than have been instructed; or

.4    in the case where you are acting through a *professional client*, different *solicitors*.

**gC50**    Specific rules apply where you are acting on a public access basis, which oblige you to consider whether *solicitors* should also be instructed. As to these see the public access rules at Section 2.D2 and further in respect of *BSB regulated bodies* Rule S28 and the associated guidance.

**gC51**    CD2 and Rules C15.5 and C17 require you, subject to Rule C16, to put your *client's* interests ahead of your own and those of any other person. If you consider that your *professional client*, another *solicitor* or *intermediary*, another *barrister*, or any other person acting on behalf of your *client* has been negligent, you should ensure that your *client* is advised of this.

**R**    **Rules**

*at CO2.*

**rC18**    Your duty to provide a competent standard of work and service to each *client* (CD7) includes a duty to inform your *professional client*, or *your client* if instructed by a *client*, as far as reasonably possible in sufficient time to enable appropriate steps to be taken to protect the *client's* interests, if:

*clash.*

.1    it becomes apparent to you that you will not be able to carry out the *instructions* within the time requested, or within a reasonable time after receipt of *instructions*; or

.2    there is an appreciable risk that you may not be able to undertake the *instructions*.

**G**    **Guidance**

**Guidance on Rule C18**

**gC52**    For further information about what you should do in the event that you have a clash of listings, please refer to our guidance which can be accessed on the *Bar Standards Board's* website at https://www.barstandardsboard.org.uk/regulatory-requirements/bsb-handbook/code-guidance/.

**R**    **Rules**

**Not misleading clients and potential clients**

**rC19**    If you supply, or offer to supply, *legal services*, you must not mislead, or cause or permit to be misled, any person to whom you supply, or offer to supply, *legal services* about:

.1    the nature and scope of the *legal services* which you are offering or agreeing to supply;

.2    the terms on which the *legal services* will be supplied, who will carry out the work and the basis of charging;

.3    who is legally responsible for the provision of the services;

.4    whether you are entitled to supply those services and the extent to which you are regulated when providing those services and by whom; or

.5    the extent to which you are covered by insurance against claims for professional negligence.

**G**    **Guidance**

**Guidance on Rule C19**

**gC53**    The best interests of *clients* (CD2) and public confidence in the profession (CD5) are undermined if there is a lack of clarity as to whether services are regulated, who is supplying them, on what terms, and what redress *clients* have and against whom if things go wrong. Rule C19 may potentially be infringed in a broad variety of situations. You must consider how matters will appear to the *client*.

**gC54**    *Clients* may, by way of example, be misled if *self-employed barristers* were to share premises with *solicitors* or other professionals without making sufficiently clear to *clients* that they remain separate and independent from one another and are not responsible for one another's work.

**gC55**    Likewise, it is likely to be necessary to make clear to *clients* that any entity established as a "ProcureCo" is not itself able to supply *reserved legal activities* and is not subject to regulation by the *Bar Standards Board*.

**gC56**    A set of *chambers* dealing directly with unsophisticated lay *clients* might breach Rule C19 if its branding created the appearance of an entity or *partnership* and it failed to explain that the members of *chambers* are, in fact, self-employed individuals who are not responsible for one another's work.

**gC57**    Knowingly or recklessly publishing advertising material which is inaccurate or likely to mislead could also result in you being in breach of Rule C19. You should be particularly careful about making comparisons with other persons as these may often be regarded as misleading.

**gC58**    If you carry out public access work but are not authorised to *conduct litigation*, you would breach Rule C19 if you caused or permitted your *client* to be misled into believing that you are entitled to, or will, provide services that include the *conduct of litigation* on behalf of your *client*.

**gC59**    If you are a *self-employed barrister*, you would, for example, likely be regarded as having breached Rule C19 if you charged at your own hourly rate for work done by a *devil* or *pupil*. Moreover, such conduct may well breach your duty to act with honesty and integrity (CD3).

**gC60**    If you are an *unregistered barrister*, you would breach Rule C19 if you misled your *client* into thinking that you were providing *legal services* to them as a *barrister* or that you were subject to the same regulation as a *practising barrister*. You would also breach the rule if you implied that you were covered by insurance if you were not, or if you suggested that your *clients* could seek a remedy from the *Bar Standards Board* or the *Legal Ombudsman* if they were dissatisfied with the services you provided. You should also be aware of the rules set out in Section D5 of this Code of Conduct and the additional guidance for *unregistered barristers* available on the *Bar Standards Board* website which can be accessed here https://www.barstandardsboard.org.uk/regulatory-requirements/bsb-handbook/code-guidance/.

**gC61**    Rule C19.3 is particularly relevant where you act in more than one capacity, for example as a *BSB authorised individual* as well as a manager or employee of an *authorised (non BSB) body*. This is because you should make it clear to each *client* in what capacity you are acting and, therefore, who has legal responsibility for the provision of the services.

**gC62**    If you are a *pupil*, you should not hold yourself out as a member of *chambers* or permit your name to appear as such. You should ensure the *client* understands your status.

**gC63**    A number of other rules impose positive obligations on you, in particular circumstances, to make clear your regulatory status and the basis and terms on which you are acting. See, for example, Rule C23 and guidance C74.

**R**    **Rules**

**Personal responsibility**

**rC20**    Where you are a *BSB authorised individual*, you are personally responsible for your own conduct and for your professional work. You must use your own professional judgment in relation to those matters on which you are instructed and be able to justify your decisions and actions. You must do this notwithstanding the views of your *client*, *professional client*, *employer* or any other person.

## G Guidance

### Guidance on Rule C20

**gC64** It is fundamental that *BSB authorised individuals* and *authorised (non-BSB) individuals* are personally responsible for their own conduct and for their own professional work, whether they are acting in a self-employed or employed capacity (in the case of *BSB authorised individuals*)or as an *employee* or *manager* of a *BSB authorised body* (in the case of *authorised (non-BSB) individuals*).

**gC65** Nothing in Rule C20 is intended to prevent you from delegating or outsourcing to any other person discrete tasks (for example, research) which such other person is well-equipped to provide. However, where such tasks are delegated or outsourced, you remain personally responsible for such work. Further, in circumstances where such tasks are being outsourced, Rule C87 which deals with outsourcing, must be complied with.

**gC66** You are responsible for the service provided by all those who represent you in your dealings with your *client*, including your clerks or any other *employees* or agents.

**gC67** Nothing in this rule or guidance prevents a *BSB authorised body* from contracting on the basis that any civil liability for the services provided by a *BSB regulated individual* lies with the *BSB authorised body* and the *BSB regulated individual* is not to be liable. However, any such stipulation as to civil liability does not affect the regulatory obligations of the *BSB regulated individual* including (but not limited to) that of being personally responsible under Rule rC20 for the professional judgments made.

**gC68** See, further, guidance to Rule C19, as regards work by *pupils* and *devils* Rule C15, gC124 and Rule C85 (on outsourcing).

## R Rules

### Accepting instructions

**rC21** You must not accept *instructions* to act in a particular matter if:

.1 due to any existing or previous *instructions* you are not able to fulfil your obligation to act in the best interests of the prospective *client*; or

.2 there is a conflict of interest between your own personal interests and the interests of the prospective *client* in respect of the particular matter; or

.3 there is a conflict of interest between the prospective *client* and one or more of your former or existing *clients* in respect of the particular matter unless all of the *clients* who have an interest in the particular matter give their informed consent to your acting in such circumstances; or

.4 there is a real risk that information confidential to another former or existing *client*, or any other person to whom you owe duties of confidence, may be relevant to the matter, such that if, obliged to maintain confidentiality, you could not act in the best interests of the prospective *client*, and the former or existing *client* or person to whom you owe that duty does not give informed consent to disclosure of that confidential information; or

.5 your instructions seek to limit your ordinary authority or discretion in the conduct of proceedings in *court*; or

.6 your instructions require you to act other than in accordance with law or with the provisions of this *Handbook*; or

.7   you are not authorised and/or otherwise accredited to perform the work required by the relevant *instruction*; or

.8   you are not competent to handle the particular matter or otherwise do not have enough experience to handle the matter; or

.9   you do not have enough time to deal with the particular matter, unless the circumstances are such that it would nevertheless be in the *client's* best interests for you to accept; or

.10   there is a real prospect that you are not going to be able to maintain your independence.

## G   Guidance

### Guidance on Rule C21

**gC69**   Rules C21.2, C21.3 and C21.4 are intended to reflect the law on conflict of interests and confidentiality and what is required of you by your duty to act in the *client's* best interests (CD2), independently (CD4), and maintaining *client* confidentiality (CD6). You are prohibited from acting where there is a conflict of interest between your own personal interests and the interests of a prospective *client*. However, where there is a conflict of interest between an existing *client* or *clients* and a prospective *client* or *clients* or two or more prospective *clients*, you may be entitled to accept instructions or to continue to act on a particular matter where you have fully disclosed to the relevant *clients* and prospective *clients* (as appropriate) the extent and nature of the conflict; they have each provided their informed consent to you acting; and you are able to act in the best interests of each *client* and independently as required by CD2 and CD4.

**gC70**   Examples of where you may be required to refuse to accept *instructions* in accordance with Rule C21.7 include:

.1   where the *instructions* relate to the provision of litigation services and you have not been authorised to *conduct litigation* in accordance with the requirements of this *Handbook*; and

.2   where the matter involves *criminal advocacy* and you are not (or, where you are a *BSB authorised body*, none of your *managers* or *employees* are) accredited at the correct *QASA level* to undertake such work in accordance with the Quality Assurance Scheme for Advocates Rules set out at 2.C3; and

.3   where the matter would require you to conduct correspondence with parties other than your *client* (in the form of letters, faxes, emails or the like), you do not have adequate systems, experience or resources for managing appropriately such correspondence and/or you do not have adequate insurance in place in accordance with Rule C75 which covers, amongst other things, any loss suffered by the *client* as a result of the conduct of such correspondence.

**gC71**   Competency and experience under Rule C21.8 includes your ability to work with vulnerable *clients*.

**gC72**   Rule C21.9 recognises that there may be exceptional circumstances when *instructions* are delivered so late that no suitable, competent advocate would have adequate time to prepare. In those cases you are not required to refuse *instructions* as it will be in the *client's* best interests that you accept. Indeed, if you are obliged under the cab rank rule to accept the *instructions,* you must do so.

**gC73**   Rule C21.10 is an aspect of your broader obligation to maintain your independence (CD4). Your ability to perform your duty to the *court* (CD1) and act in the best interests of your *client* (CD2) may be put at risk if you act in circumstances where your independence is compromised. Examples of when you may not be able to maintain your independence include appearing as an advocate in a matter in which you are likely to be called as a witness (unless the matter on which you are likely to be called as a witness is peripheral or minor in the context of the litigation as a whole and is unlikely to lead to your involvement in the matter being challenged at a later date). However, if you are planning to withdraw from a case because it appears that you are likely to be a witness on a material question of fact, you should only withdraw if you can do so without jeopardising the *client's* interests.

**gC74**   Where the *instructions* relate to public access or licensed access work and you are a self-employed barrister you will also need to have regard to the relevant rules at 2.D2. If you are a *BSB authorised body*, you should have regard to the guidance to Rule S28.

## R   Rules

### Defining terms or basis on which instructions are accepted

**rC22**   Where you first accept *instructions* to act in a matter:

.1   you must, subject to Rule C23, confirm in writing acceptance of the *instructions* and the terms and/or basis on which you will be acting, including the basis of charging;

.2   where your instructions are from a *professional client*, the confirmation required by rC22.1 must be sent to the *professional client*;

.3   where your instructions are from a *client*, the confirmation required by rC22.1 must be sent to the *client*.

.4   if you are a *BSB authorised body*, you must ensure that the terms under which you accept instructions from *clients* include consent from clients to disclose and give control of files to the *Bar Standards Board* or its agent in circumstances where the conditions in rS113.5 are met.

**rC23**   In the event that, following your acceptance of the *instructions* in accordance with Rule C22, the scope of the *instructions* is varied by the relevant *client* (including where the *client* instructs you on additional aspects relating to the same matter), you are not required to confirm again in writing acceptance of the instructions or the terms and/or basis upon which you will be acting. In these circumstances, you will be deemed to have accepted the instructions when you begin the work, on the same terms or basis as before, unless otherwise specified.

**rC24**   You must comply with the requirements set out in Rules C22 and C23 before doing the work unless that is not reasonably practicable, in which case you should do so as soon as reasonably practicable.

## G   Guidance

### Guidance to Rules C22 to C24

**gC75**   Compliance with the requirement in Rule C22 to set out the terms and/or basis upon which you will be acting may be achieved by including a reference or link to the relevant terms in your written communication of acceptance. You may, for example, refer the *client* or *professional client* (as the case may be) to the terms of service set out on your website or to standard terms of service set out on the *Bar Council's* website (in which regard, please also refer to the guidance on the use of the standard terms of service which can be found here http://www.barcouncil.org.uk/media/185511/contractualterms.pdf). Where you agree to do your work on terms and conditions that have been proposed to you by the *client* or by the *professional client*, you should confirm in writing that that is the basis on which your work is done. Where there are competing sets of terms and conditions, which terms have been agreed and are the basis of your retainer will be a matter to be determined in accordance with the law of contract.

**gC76**   Your obligation under Rule C23 is to ensure that the basis on which you act has been defined, which does not necessarily mean governed by your own contractual terms. In circumstances where Rule

C23 applies, you should take particular care to ensure that the *client* is clear about the basis for charging for any variation to the work where it may be unclear. You must also ensure that you comply with the requirements of the Provision of Services Regulations 2009 http://www.legislation.gov.uk/ukdsi/2009/9780111486276/contents. See further Rule C19 (not misleading *clients* or prospective *clients*) and the guidance to that rule at gC52 to gC62.

**gC77**   If you are a *self-employed barrister* a clerk may confirm on your behalf your acceptance of *instructions* in accordance with Rules C22 and C23 above.

**gC78**   When accepting *instructions*, you must also ensure that you comply with the *complaints* handling rules set out in Section 2.D.

**gC79**   When accepting instructions in accordance with Rule C22, confirmation by email will satisfy any requirement for written acceptance.

**gC80**   You may have been instructed in relation to a discrete and finite task, such as to provide an opinion on a particular issue, or to provide ongoing services, for example, to conduct particular litigation. Your confirmation of acceptance of instructions under Rule C22 should make clear the scope of the *instructions* you are accepting, whether by cross-referring to the *instructions*, where these are in writing or by summarising your understanding of the scope of work you are instructed to undertake.

**gC81**   Disputes about costs are one of the most frequent complaints. The provision of clear information before work starts is the best way of avoiding such complaints. *The Legal Ombudsman* has produced a useful guide "An Ombudsman's view of good costs service" which can be found here http://www.legalombudsman.org.uk/downloads/documents/publications/Ombudsman-view-good-costs-service.pdf.

**gC82**   Where the *instructions* relate to public access or licensed access work and you are a self-employed barrister, you will also need to have regard to the relevant rules at 2.D2. If you are a *BSB authorised body*, you should have regard to the guidance to Rule S23.

## R    Rules

### Returning instructions

**rC25**   Where you have accepted *instructions* to act but one or more of the circumstances set out in Rules C21.1 to C21.10 above then arises, you must cease to act and return your *instructions* promptly. In addition, you must cease to act and return your *instructions* if:

.1    in a case funded by the *Legal Aid Agency* as part of Criminal Legal Aid or Civil Legal Aid it has become apparent to you that this funding has been wrongly obtained by false or inaccurate information and action to remedy the situation is not immediately taken by your *client*; or

.2    the *client* refuses to authorise you to make some disclosure to the *court* which your duty to the *court* requires you to make; or

.3    you become aware during the course of a case of the existence of a document which should have been but has not been disclosed, and the *client* fails to disclose it or fails to permit you to disclose it, contrary to your advice.

**rC26**   You may cease to act on a matter on which you are instructed and return your *instructions* if:

.1    your professional conduct is being called into question; or

.2    the *client* consents; or

.3    you are a *self-employed barrister* and:

.a despite all reasonable efforts to prevent it, a hearing becomes fixed for a date on which you have already entered in your professional diary that you will not be available; or

.b illness, injury, pregnancy, childbirth, a bereavement or a similar matter makes you unable reasonably to perform the services required in the *instructions*; or

.c you are unavoidably required to attend on jury service;

.4 you are a *BSB authorised body* and the only appropriate *authorised individual(s)* are unable to continue acting on the particular matter due to one or more of the grounds referred to at Rules C26.3.a to C26.3.c above occurring;

.5 you do not receive payment when due in accordance with terms agreed, subject to Rule C26.7 (if you are conducting litigation) and in any other case subject to your giving reasonable notice requiring the non-payment to be remedied and making it clear to the *client* in that notice that failure to remedy the non-payment may result in you ceasing to act and returning your *instructions* in respect of the particular matter; or

.6 you become aware of confidential or privileged information or documents of another person which relate to the matter on which you are instructed; or

.7 if you are conducting litigation, and your *client* does not consent to your ceasing to act, your application to come off the record has been granted; or

.8 there is some other substantial reason for doing so (subject to Rules C27 to C29 below).

## G Guidance

### Guidance on Rule C26

**gC83** In deciding whether to cease to act and to return existing instructions in accordance with Rule C26, you should, where possible and subject to your overriding duty to the *court*, ensure that the *client* is not adversely affected because there is not enough time to engage other adequate legal assistance.

**gC84** If you are working on a referral basis and your *professional client* withdraws, you are no longer instructed and cannot continue to act unless appointed by the *court*, or you otherwise receive new instructions. You will not be bound by the cab rank rule if appointed by the court. For these purposes working on a "referral basis" means where a *professional client* instructs a *BSB authorised individual* to provide *legal services* on behalf of one of that *professional client's* own clients

**gC85** You should not rely on Rule C26.3 to break an engagement to supply legal services so that you can attend or fulfil a non-professional engagement of any kind other than those indicated in Rule C26.3.

**gC86** When considering whether or not you are required to return instructions in accordance with Rule C26.6 you should have regard to relevant case law including: *English & American Insurance Co Ltd & Others -v- Herbert Smith*; ChD 1987; (1987) NLJ 148 and *Ablitt -v- Mills & Reeve (A Firm) and Another*; ChD (Times, 24-Oct-1995).

**gC87** If a fundamental change is made to the basis of your remuneration, you should treat such a change as though your original instructions have been withdrawn by the *client* and replaced by an offer of new *instructions* on different terms. Accordingly:

.1 you must decide whether you are obliged by Rule C29 to accept the new *instructions*;

.2 if you are obliged under Rule C29 to accept the new *instructions*, you must do so;

.3   if you are not obliged to accept the new *instructions*, you may decline them;

.4   if you decline to accept the new *instructions* in such circumstances, you are not to be regarded as returning your *instructions*, nor as withdrawing from the matter, nor as ceasing to act, for the purposes of Rules C25 to C26, because the previous *instructions* have been withdrawn by the *client*.

## R | Rules

**rC27**   Notwithstanding the provisions of Rules C25 and C26, you must not:

.1   cease to act or return *instructions* without either:

  .a   obtaining your *client's* consent; or

  .b   clearly explaining to your *client* or your *professional client* the reasons for doing so; or

.2   return instructions to another person without the consent of your *client* or your *professional client*.

### Requirement not to discriminate

**rC28**   You must not withhold your services or permit your services to be withheld:

.1   on the ground that the nature of the case is objectionable to you or to any section of *the public*;

.2   on the ground that the conduct, opinions or beliefs of the prospective *client* are unacceptable to you or to any section of *the public*;

.3   on any ground relating to the source of any financial support which may properly be given to the prospective *client* for the proceedings in question.

## G | Guidance

### Guidance on Rule C28

**gC88**   As a matter of general law you have an obligation not to discriminate unlawfully as to those to whom you make your services available on any of the statutorily prohibited grounds such as gender or race. See https://www.barstandardsboard.org.uk/about-bar-standards-board/equality-and-diversity/equality-and-diversity-rules-of-the-bsb-handbook/ and https://www.barstandardsboard.org.uk/media/1562168/bsb_equality_rules_handbook_corrected.pdf for guidance as to your obligations in respect of equality and diversity. This rule of conduct is concerned with a broader obligation not to withhold your services on grounds that are inherently inconsistent with your role in upholding access to justice and the rule of law and therefore in this rule "discriminate" is used in this broader sense. This obligation applies whether or not the *client* is a member of any protected group for the purposes of the Equality Act 2010. For example, you must not withhold services on the ground that any financial support which may properly be given to the prospective *client* for the proceedings in question will be available as part of Criminal Legal Aid and Civil Legal Aid.

## R    Rules

### The 'cab-rank' rule

**rC29**   If you receive *instructions* from a *professional client*, and you are:

.1   a *self-employed barrister* instructed by a *professional client*; or

.2   an *authorised individual* working within a *BSB authorised body*; or

.3   a *BSB authorised body* and the *instructions* seek the services of a named *authorised individual* working for you,

and the *instructions* are appropriate taking into account the experience, seniority and/or field of practice of yourself or (as appropriate) of the named *authorised individual* you must, subject to Rule C30 below, accept the *instructions* addressed specifically to you, irrespective of:

.a   the identity of the *client*;

.b   the nature of the case to which the *instructions* relate;

.c   whether the *client* is paying privately or is publicly funded; and

.d   any belief or opinion which you may have formed as to the character, reputation, cause, conduct, guilt or innocence of the *client*.

**rC30**   The cab rank Rule C29 does not apply if:

.1   you are required to refuse to accept the *instructions* pursuant to Rule C21; or

.2   accepting the *instructions* would require you or the named *authorised individual* to do something other than in the course of their ordinary working time or to cancel a commitment already in their diary; or

.3   the potential liability for professional negligence in respect of the particular matter could exceed the level of professional indemnity insurance which is reasonably available and likely to be available in the market for you to accept; or

.4   you are a Queen's Counsel, and the acceptance of the *instructions* would require you to act without a junior in circumstances where you reasonably consider that the interests of the *client* require that a junior should also be instructed; or

.5   accepting the *instructions* would require you to do any *foreign work*; or

.6   accepting the *instructions* would require you to act for a *foreign lawyer* (other than a *European lawyer*, a lawyer from a country that is a member of EFTA, a *solicitor* or *barrister* of Northern Ireland or a *solicitor* or advocate under the law of Scotland); or

.7   the *professional client*:

.a   is not accepting liability for your fees; or

.b   represents, in your reasonable opinion, an unacceptable credit risk; or

.c   is instructing you as a lay *client* and not in their capacity as a professional *client*; or

.8   you have not been offered a proper fee for your services (except that you shall not be entitled to refuse to accept *instructions* on this ground if you have not made or responded to any fee proposal within a reasonable time after receiving the *instructions*); or

.9   except where you are to be paid directly by (i) the *Legal Aid Agency* as part of the Community Legal Service or the Criminal Defence Service or (ii) the Crown Prosecution Service:

   .a   your fees have not been agreed (except that you shall not be entitled to refuse to accept *instructions* on this ground if you have not taken reasonable steps to agree fees within a reasonable time after receiving the *instructions*);

   .b   having required your fees to be paid before you accept the *instructions*, those fees have not been paid;

   .c   accepting the *instructions* would require you to act other than on (A) the Standard Contractual Terms for the Supply of Legal Services by Barristers to Authorised Persons 2012 as published on the *Bar Council's* website; or (B) if you publish standard terms of work, on those standard terms of work.

## G   Guidance

### Guidance on Rule C29 and C30

**gC89**   Rule C30 means that you would not be required to accept *instructions* to, for example, *conduct litigation* or attend a police station in circumstances where you do not normally undertake such work or, in the case of litigation, are not authorised to undertake such work.

**gC90**   In determining whether or not a fee is proper for the purposes of Rule C30.8, regard shall be had to the following:

   .1   the complexity length and difficulty of the case;

   .2   your ability, experience and seniority; and

   .3   the expenses which you will incur.

**gC91**   Further, you may refuse to accept instructions on the basis that the fee is not proper if the instructions are on the basis that you will do the work under a *conditional fee agreement* or damages based agreement.

**gC91a**   Examples of when you might reasonably conclude (subject to the following paragraph) that a *professional client* represents an unacceptable credit risk for the purposes of Rule C30.7.b include:

   .1   Where they are included on the *Bar Council's* List of Defaulting Solicitors;

   .2   Where to your knowledge a *barrister* has obtained a judgment against a *professional client*, which remains unpaid;

   .3   Where a firm or sole practitioner is subject to insolvency proceedings, an individual voluntary arrangement or partnership voluntary arrangement; or

   .4   Where there is evidence of other unsatisfied judgments that reasonably call into question the *professional client's* ability to pay your fees.

   Even where you consider that there is a serious credit risk, you should not conclude that the *professional client* represents an unacceptable credit risk without first considering alternatives. This will include considering whether the credit risk could be mitigated in other ways, for example by seeking payment of the fee in advance or payment into a third party payment service as permitted by rC74, rC75 and associated guidance.

## Quality Assurance Scheme for Advocates Rules

**R** | **Rules**

### Scope of QASA

**rC31**   Subject to Rule C32, you must not undertake *criminal advocacy* unless you have *provisional accreditation* or *full accreditation* in accordance with these *QASA Rules* and with the *QASA Handbook*.

**rC32**   *Barristers* who do not have *provisional accreditation* or *full accreditation* under the *QASA* are permitted to undertake *criminal advocacy*:

   .1   in hearings which primarily involve advocacy which is outside of the definition of *criminal advocacy*; or

   .2   if they have been instructed specifically as a result of their specialism in work outside of the definition of *criminal advocacy*.

**rC33**   You shall only undertake *criminal advocacy* in hearings which you are satisfied fall within the *QASA level* at which you are accredited, or any *QASA level* below the same, unless you are satisfied that you are competent to accept instructions for a case at a higher *QASA level* strictly in accordance with the criteria prescribed in the *QASA Handbook*.

### Provisional accreditation

**rC34**   If you are granted *provisional accreditation*, you must apply to convert this to *full accreditation* within 12 or 24 months of the date on which your *provisional accreditation* was granted.

### Full accreditation

**rC35**   If you are granted *full accreditation*, it will be valid for 5 years from the date on which it was granted.

### General provisions relating to applications for registration, progression or re-accreditation

**rC36**   You may apply for *registration, progression* or *re-accreditation* under these *QASA Rules*. In support of an application you shall submit such information as may be prescribed by the *QASA*. This will include:

   .1   completing the relevant application form supplied by the *Bar Standards Board* and submitting it to the *Bar Standards Board*;

   .2   submitting such information in support of the application as may be prescribed by the *QASA*. This will include all of the *criminal advocacy evaluation forms* that you have obtained; and

   .3   paying the appropriate fee in the amount determined in accordance with the *Bar Standards Board's* published fees policy.

**rC37**   An application will only have been made once the *Bar Standards Board* has received the application form completed in full, together with all information required in support of the application and confirmation from you in the form of a declaration that the information contained within, or submitted in support of, the application is full and accurate.

**rC38** You are personally responsible for the contents of your application and any information submitted to the *Bar Standards Board* by you or on your behalf, and you must not submit (or cause or permit to be submitted on your behalf) information to the *Bar Standards Board* which you do not believe is full and accurate.

**rC39** On receipt of an application, the *Bar Standards Board* shall decide whether to grant or refuse the application, and shall notify you accordingly, giving reasons for any decision to refuse the application. This decision will take effect when it has been communicated to the *barrister* concerned.

**rC40** Before reaching a decision on the application, the *Bar Standards Board* may appoint an *independent assessor* to conduct an assessment of your competence to conduct *criminal advocacy* at the relevant *QASA level*.

## Registration for QASA

**rC41** In order to be accredited under *QASA barrister*s must first apply for *registration*. In support of an application you shall submit such information as may be prescribed by the *QASA*.

QASA Level 1

.1 If you apply for *registration* at *QASA level* 1 and your application is successful, you will be awarded *full accreditation* at *QASA level* 1.

QASA Levels 2 to 4

.2 If you apply for *registration* at *QASA levels* 2, 3 or 4 and your application is successful, you will be awarded *Provisional accreditation* which will be valid for 24 months.

.3 You must apply to convert your provisional *accreditation* to *full accreditation* within 24 months.

.4 You must be assessed in your first effective criminal trials at your *QASA level* and submit the prescribed number of completed *criminal advocacy evaluation form*s confirming that you are competent in accordance with the competence framework detailed in the *QASA Handbook*.

.5 Your application must include all completed *criminal advocacy* evaluation forms obtained by you in *effective trials*.

.6 If your application is successful you will be awarded *full accreditation*.

.7 Subject to Rule C41.8, if your application for *full accreditation* is unsuccessful, you shall be granted *provisional accreditation* at the *QASA level* below and shall be required to apply to convert this to *full accreditation* at that lower *QASA level* in accordance with Rules C41.3 to C41.5.

.8 If your application for *full accreditation* at *QASA level* 2 is unsuccessful, you shall be granted *accreditation* at *QASA level* 1.

Barristers not undertaking trials

.9 If you do not intend to undertake criminal trials you may apply for *registration* at *QASA level* 2. If your application is successful, you will be awarded *provisional accreditation*. You must be assessed via an *approved assessment organisation* within 24 months.

.10 If your application for *full accreditation* is successful you shall be awarded *full accreditation* and will be permitted to undertake non-trial hearings up to *QASA level* 3 and trials at *QASA level* 1.

.11 Once you have *full accreditation*, if you wish to undertake trials at *QASA level* 2 you must inform the BSB of your intention and comply with Rules C42.2 to Rules C42.5.

Barristers who took silk between 2010 and 2013

.12    If you took silk between 2010 and 2013 inclusive you can register through the modified entry arrangements set out in paragraph 2.38 of the *QASA Handbook* .

## Progression

**rC42**    If you have *full accreditation*, you may apply for *accreditation* at the next higher *QASA level* to your current *QASA level.*

.1    *Progression* to *QASA level* 2

.2    If you wish to progress to *QASA level* 2 you must first obtain *provisional accreditation* at *QASA level* 2 by notifying the *Bar Standards Board* of your intention to progress.

.3    Your *provisional accreditation* will be valid for 24 months. In order to convert this to *full accreditation* you must be assessed in your first effective criminal trials at *QASA level* 2 and submit the prescribed number of completed *criminal advocacy evaluation forms* confirming that you are competent in *QASA level* 2 trials in accordance with the competence framework detailed in the *QASA Handbook* .

.4    Your application must include all completed *criminal advocacy evaluation forms* obtained by you in *effective trials.*

.5    Where your application is successful, you shall be granted *full accreditation* at *QASA level* 2, which is valid for 5 years from the date of issue.

Progression to QASA level 3 and 4

Stage 1

.6    You must first apply for *provisional accreditation* at the next higher *QASA level* to your current *QASA level.* In order to apply for *provisional accreditation*, you must submit the prescribed number of *criminal advocacy evaluation forms* confirming that you are very competent at your current *QASA level* in accordance with the competence framework detailed in the *QASA Handbook* .

.7    Your application must include all completed *criminal advocacy evaluation forms* obtained by you in *effective trials.* These should be obtained within a 12 month period.

.8    If your application is successful you will be awarded *provisional accreditation.*

Stage 2

.9    Your *provisional accreditation* will be valid for 12 months. You must apply to convert your *provisional accreditation* to *full accreditation* before your *provisional accreditation* expires.

.10    You must be assessed in your first effective criminal trials at your new *QASA level* and submit the prescribed number of completed *criminal advocacy evaluation forms* confirming that you are competent in accordance with the competence framework detailed in the *QASA Handbook* .

.11    Your application must include all completed *criminal advocacy evaluation forms* obtained by you in *effective trials.*

.12    If your application is successful you will be awarded *full accreditation.*

.13    If your application for *full accreditation* is unsuccessful, you may continue to conduct *criminal advocacy* at your current *QASA level* until the expiry of your current accreditation.

## Re-accreditation

**rC43**    You must apply for *re-accreditation* at the *QASA level* at which you are accredited within five years from the date on which your *full accreditation* was granted.

**rC44**    You shall submit, in support of an application for *re-accreditation*, evidence to demonstrate your competence to conduct *criminal advocacy* at the *QASA level* at which you are accredited, comprising:

.1    if you are accredited at *QASA level* 1, evidence of the assessed continuing professional development undertaken by you in the field of advocacy in the period since you were accredited at *QASA level* 1 or, if you have previously been re-*accredited* at that *QASA level*, since your most recent *re-accreditation*;

.2    if you are *accredited* at *QASA level* 2, 3 or 4, the number of *criminal advocacy evaluation forms* prescribed by the *QASA*. Your application must include all completed *criminal advocacy evaluation forms* obtained by you in consecutive *effective trials* in the 24 months preceding the application.

**rC45**    If your application is successful you will be awarded *full accreditation* for a period of 5 years.

**rC46**    Subject to Rules C47, if your application for *re-accreditation* is unsuccessful, you shall be granted *provisional accreditation* at the *QASA level* below and shall be required to apply to convert this to *full accreditation* at that lower *QASA level* in accordance with Rules C41.3 to C41.5.

**rC47**    If your application for *re-accreditation* at *QASA level* 2 is unsuccessful, you shall be granted accreditation at *QASA level* 1.

## Lapse of accreditation

**rC48**    Subject to Rule C50, your *provisional accreditation* will lapse if you do not apply for *full accreditation* before it expires.

**rC49**    Subject to Rule C50, your *full accreditation* will lapse if you do not apply for *re-accreditation* within 5 years of the date on which you were awarded *full accreditation*.

**rC50**    If the BSB has received an application within the period of *accreditation*, the accreditation will not lapse whilst a decision is pending.

**rC51**    If your *accreditation* lapses, you may not undertake *criminal advocacy* in accordance with Rule 2.

## Applications for variation

**rC52**    Where your individual circumstances result in you encountering difficulties in obtaining completed *criminal advocacy evaluation forms* within the specified period, then you may apply to the *Bar Standards Board* for an extension of time to comply with the requirements; or

**rC53**    Where your individual circumstances result in you encountering difficulties in obtaining completed *criminal advocacy evaluation forms*, then you may apply to the *Bar Standards Board* for your competence to conduct *criminal advocacy* to be assessed by an *independent assessor*, and you may submit the results of the assessment in support of your application for *registration*, *re-accreditation* or *progression* in the place of one *criminal advocacy* evaluation form.

Managing underperformance

**rC54**    The *Bar Standards Board* may receive *criminal advocacy evaluation forms* raising concerns regarding your competence to conduct *criminal advocacy* at any time.

**rC55** Where concerns regarding your competence to conduct *criminal advocacy* are brought to the attention of the *Bar Standards Board*, either during the course of its consideration of an application brought by you under these Rules, or as a result of concerns raised under Rule C54, it may decide to do one or more of the following:

    .1 appoint an *independent assessor* to conduct an assessment of your *criminal advocacy*;

    .2 recommend that you undertake, at your own cost, such training for such period as it may specify;

    .3 revoke your *accreditation* at your current *QASA level*; and/or

    .4 refer you for consideration of your health or conduct under the Fitness to Practise Rules or the Complaints Rules, as it considers appropriate,

and shall notify you accordingly, giving reasons for its decision.

**rC56** Where your *accreditation* has been revoked, you shall be granted *provisional accreditation* at the *QASA level* below and shall be required to apply to convert this to *full accreditation* in accordance with Rules C41.3 to C41.5.

**rC57** Where you have applied for *registration* or *re-accreditation* at *QASA level* 1, and your application has been refused, you will not be entitled to accept any instructions to conduct *criminal advocacy*, and the *Bar Standards Board* may recommend that you undertake training in accordance with Rule C55.2 before you re-apply for *registration* or *re-accreditation* as appropriate.

**rC58** Where you have undertaken training under Rule C55.2, the *Bar Standards Board* shall, at the end of the specified period, assess whether you have satisfactorily completed the training before reaching a decision in relation to any further steps that it may consider appropriate to take in accordance with Rule C55.2.

## Appeals

**rC59** You may appeal to the *Bar Standards Board* against any decision reached by it under these rules. Appeals must be made in accordance with the published *Bar Standards Board QASA* Appeals Policy.

## Commencement and transitional arrangements

**rC60** Subject to Rule C63, the *QASA Rules* commence on 30 September 2013.

Registration of barristers currently undertaking criminal advocacy

**rC61** *Barristers* currently undertaking *criminal advocacy* are required to apply for *registration* under the *QASA Scheme* in accordance with the phased implementation programme as set out at paragraphs 2.11 to 2.13 of the *QASA Handbook*.

**rC62** The dates for *registration* will depend upon the primary circuit in which you practise. This will be the circuit in which you undertake *criminal advocacy* more frequently than in any other circuit.

    .1 If you primarily practise in the Midland or Western Circuit, you must register for *QASA* from 30 September 2013 and before the first occasion on which you undertake *criminal advocacy* after 7 March 2014.

    .2 If you primarily practise in the South Eastern Circuit, you must register for *QASA* from 10 March 2014 and before the first occasion on which you undertake *criminal advocacy* after 13 June 2014.

    .3 If you primarily practise in the Northern, North Eastern or Wales and Chester Circuit, you must register for *QASA* from 30 June 2014 and before the first occasion on which you undertake *criminal advocacy* after 3 October 2014.

**rC63**    Subject to Rules C63.1, C63.2 and Rule C31 commences for all advocates from 4 October 2014.

.1    Rule C31 will commence for those advocates who primarily practise in the Midland or Western Circuit from 10 March 2014. Any advocate who undertakes *criminal advocacy* in these circuits without *accreditation* must be able to prove to the *Bar Standards Board* that they practise primarily in another circuit.

.2    Rule C31 will commence for those advocates who primarily practise in the South Eastern Circuit from 14 June 2014. Any advocate who undertakes *criminal advocacy* in this circuit without *accreditation* must be able to prove to the *Bar Standards Board* that they practise primarily in the Northern, North Eastern or Wales and Chester Circuit.

## C4. You and your regulator

### O  Outcomes

**oC21**  *BSB regulated persons* are effectively regulated.

**oC22**  The public have confidence in the proper regulation of *persons* regulated by the *Bar Standards Board*.

**oC23**  The *Bar Standards Board* has the information that it needs in order to be able to assess risks and regulate effectively and in accordance with the *regulatory objectives*.

### R  Rules

#### Provision of information to the Bar Standards Board

**rC64**  You must:

.1  promptly provide all such information to the *Bar Standards Board* as it may, for the purpose of its regulatory functions, from time to time require of you, and notify it of any material changes to that information; and

.2  comply in due time with any decision or sentence imposed by the *Bar Standards Board*, a *Disciplinary Tribunal*, the *Visitors*, the High Court, an *interim panel*, a *review panel*, an *appeal panel* or a *Fitness to Practise Panel*.

.3  if you are a *BSB authorised body* or an *owner* or *manager* of a *BSB authorised body* and the conditions outlined in rS113.5 apply, give the B*ar Standards Board* whatever co-operation is necessary, including:

.a  complying with a notice sent by the *Bar Standards Board* or its agent to produce or deliver all documents in your possession or under your control in connection with your activities as a *BSB authorised body* (such notice may require such documents to be produced at a time and place fixed by the *Bar Standards Board* or its agent; and

.b  complying with a notice from the *Bar Standards Board* or its agent to redirect communications, including post, email, fax and telephones.

### G  Guidance

#### Guidance to Rule C64:

**gC92**  Your obligations under Rule C64 include, for example, responding promptly to any request from the *Bar Standards Board* for comments or information relating to any matter whether or not the matter relates to you, or to another *BSB regulated person*.

**gC93**  Information which you are requested to disclose under Rule C64 may include *client* information that is subject to legal privilege. You are not entitled to disclose such information without the consent of the *client*. You may enquire whether your *client* is willing to waive privilege but should be alert to the possibility that you may have a conflict of interest in giving him any advice as to whether he should. The BSB will look at the question of privilege on a case by case basis. It will bear in mind in the exercise of its regulatory functions that a *client* might have been prepared to waive privilege if asked. Observations in R (Morgan Grenfell & Co Ltd) v Special Commissioner [2003] 1 A.C. 563 at [32], referred to in R (Lumsdon) v Legal Services Board [2013] EWHC 28 (Admin) at [73] were made in the context of a different statutory disclosure regime and should not be used as necessarily applicable to disclosure under Rule C64. However, in the meantime, following this guidance should avoid practical difficulties in most cases. For the avoidance of doubt, none of this casts any doubt on a *barrister's* entitlement to withhold from the BSB any material that is subject to the *barrister's* own legal privilege (such as legal advice given to the *barrister* about their own position).

## R    Rules

### Duty to report certain matters to the Bar Standards Board

**rC65**    You must report promptly to the *Bar Standards Board* if:

.1    you are charged with an *indictable offence*; in the jurisdiction of England and Wales or with a *criminal offence* of comparable seriousness in any other jurisdiction;

.2    you are convicted of, or accept a caution, for any *criminal offence*, in any jurisdiction, other than a *minor criminal offence*;

.3    you (or an entity of which you are a *manager*) to your knowledge are the subject of any disciplinary or other regulatory or enforcement action by another *Approved Regulator* or other regulator, including being the subject of disciplinary proceedings;

.4    you are a *manager* of an *non-BSB authorised body* which is the subject of an intervention by the *approved regulator* of that body;

.5    you are a *registered European lawyer* and:

.a    to your knowledge any investigation into your conduct is commenced by your *home regulator*; or

.b    any finding of professional misconduct is made by your *home regulator*; or

.c    your authorisation in your *home state* to pursue professional activities under your *home professional title* is withdrawn or *suspended*; or

.d    you are charged with a disciplinary offence.

.6    any of the following occur:

.a    bankruptcy proceedings are initiated in respect of or against you;

.b    *director's disqualification* proceedings are initiated against you;

.c    a *bankruptcy order* or *director's disqualification order* is made against you;

.d    you have made a composition or arrangement with, or granted a trust deed for, your creditors;

.e    winding up proceedings are initiated in respect of or against you;

.f    you have had an administrator, administrative receiver, receiver or liquidator appointed in respect of you;

.g    administration proceedings are initiated in respect of or against you;

.7    you have committed serious misconduct;

.8    you become authorised to *practise* by another *approved regulator*.

## G Guidance

### Guidance to Rule C65

**gC94** In circumstances where you have committed serious misconduct you should take all reasonable steps to mitigate the effects of such serious misconduct.

**gC94.1** For the avoidance of doubt rC65.2 does not oblige you to disclose cautions or criminal convictions that are "spent" under the Rehabilitation of Offenders Act 1974 unless the Rehabilitation of Offenders Act 1974 (Exceptions) Order 1975 (SI 1975/1023) applies. However, unless the caution or conviction is immediately spent, you must notify the BSB before it becomes spent.

## R Rules

### Reporting serious misconduct by others

**rC66** Subject to your duty to keep the affairs of each *client* confidential and subject also to Rules C67 and C68, you must report to the *Bar Standards Board* if you have reasonable grounds to believe that there has been serious misconduct by a *barrister* or a *registered European lawyer*, a *BSB authorised body*, a *BSB regulated manager* or an *authorised (non-BSB) individual* who is working as a *manager* or an *employee* of a *BSB authorised body*.

**rC67** You must never make, or threaten to make, a report under Rule C66 without a genuine and reasonably held belief that Rule C66 applies.

**rC68** You are not under a duty to report serious misconduct by others if:

.1 you become aware of the facts giving rise to the belief that there has serious misconduct from matters that are in the public domain and the circumstances are such that you reasonably consider it likely that the facts will have come to the attention of the *Bar Standards Board*; or

.2 you are aware that the relevant person that committed the serious misconduct has already reported the serious misconduct to the *Bar Standards Board*; or

.3 the events which led to you becoming aware of that other person's serious misconduct are subject to their legal professional privilege; or

.4 you become aware of such serious misconduct as a result of your work on a Bar Council advice line.

**rC69** You must not victimise anyone for making in good faith a report under Rule C66.

## G Guidance

### Guidance on Rules C65.7 to C68

**gC95** It is in the public interest that the *Bar Standards Board*, as an *Approved Regulator*, is made aware of, and is able to investigate, potential instances of serious misconduct. The purpose of Rules C65.7 to C69, therefore, is to assist the *Bar Standards Board* in undertaking this regulatory function.

**gC96** Serious misconduct includes, without being limited to:

.1 dishonesty (CD3);

.2 assault or harassment (CD3 and/or CD5 and/or CD8);

.3    seeking to gain access without consent to *instructions* or other confidential information relating to the opposing party's case (CD3 and/or CD5); or

.4    seeking to gain access without consent to confidential information relating to another member of *chambers*, member of staff or *pupil* (CD3 and/or CD5);

.5    encouraging a witness to give evidence which is untruthful or misleading (CD1 and/or CD3);

.6    knowingly or recklessly misleading, or attempting to mislead, the *court* or an opponent (CD1 and/or CD3); or

.7    being drunk or under the influence of drugs in *court* (CD2 and/or CD7); or

.8    failure by a *barrister* to report promptly to the *Bar Standards Board* pursuant to rC66 above;

.9    a breach by a *barrister* of rC70 below;

.10    conduct that poses a serious risk to the public.

**gC97**    If you believe (or suspect) that there has been serious misconduct, then the first step is to carefully consider all of the circumstances. The circumstances include:

.1    whether that person's *instructions* or other confidential matters might have a bearing on the assessment of their conduct;

.2    whether that person has been offered an opportunity to explain their conduct, and if not, why not;

.3    any explanation which has been or could be offered for that person's conduct;

.4    whether the matter has been raised, or will be raised, in the litigation in which it occurred, and if not, why not.

**gC98**    Having considered all of the circumstances, the duty to report arises if you have reasonable grounds to believe there has been serious misconduct. This will be so where, having given due consideration to the circumstances, including the matters identified at Guidance C97, you have material before you which as it stands establishes a reasonably credible case of serious misconduct. Your duty under Rule C66 is then to report the potential instance of serious misconduct so that the *Bar Standards Board* can investigate whether or not there has in fact been misconduct.

**gC99**    Circumstances which may give rise to the exception from the general requirement to report serious misconduct set out in Rule C68.1 include for example where misconduct has been widely reported in the national media. In these circumstances it would not be in the public interest for every *BSB regulated person* to have an obligation to report such serious misconduct.

**gC100**    In Rule C68.4 "work on the *Bar Council* advice line" means:

.1    dealing with queries from *BSB regulated persons* who contact an advice line operated by the *Bar Council* for the purposes of providing advice to those persons; and

.2    either providing advice to *BSB regulated persons* in the course of working for an advice line or to any individual working for an advice line where (i) you are identified on the list of *BSB regulated persons* maintained by the *Bar Council* as being permitted to provide such advice (the "approved list"); and (ii) the advice which you are being asked to provide to the individual working for an advice line arises from a query which originated from their work for that service; and

.3    providing advice to *BSB regulated persons* where any individual working for an advice line arranges for you to give such advice and you are on the approved list.

.4    for the purposes of Rule C68, the relevant advice lines are:

–    the Ethical Queries Helpline;

–    the Equality and Diversity Helpline;

–    the Remuneration Helpline; and

–    the Pupillage Helpline.

**gC101**    Rule C68.4 has been carved out of the general requirement to report serious misconduct of others because it is not in the public interest that the duty to report misconduct should constrain *BSB authorised persons* appointed by or on behalf of the *Bar Council* to offer ethical advice to others from doing so or inhibit BSB regulated persons needing advice from seeking it. Consequently, *BSB authorised persons* appointed by or on behalf of the *Bar Council* to offer ethical advice to *BSB regulated persons* through a specified advice service will not be under a duty to report information received by them in confidence from persons seeking such advice, subject only to the requirements of the general law. However, in circumstances where Rule C68.4 applies, the relevant *BSB authorised person* will still be expected to encourage the relevant *BSB regulated person* who has committed serious misconduct to disclose such serious misconduct to the *Bar Standards Board* in accordance with Rule C65.7.

**gC102**    Misconduct which falls short of serious misconduct should, where applicable, be reported to your HOLP so that they can keep a record of non-compliance in accordance with Rule rC96.4.

## R    Rules

### Access to premises

**rC70**    You must permit the *Bar Council*, or the *Bar Standards Board*, or any person appointed by them, reasonable access, on request, to inspect:

.1    any premises from which you provide, or are believed to provide, *legal services* ; and

.2    any documents or records relating to those premises and your *practice*, or *BSB authorised body*,

and the *Bar Council*, *Bar Standards Board*, or any person appointed by them, shall be entitled to take copies of such documents or records as may be required by them for the purposes of their functions and, if you are a *BSB authorised body*, may enter your premises and operate from those premises for the purpose of taking such action as is necessary to protect the interests of clients..

### Co-operation with the Legal Ombudsman

**rC71**    You must give the *Legal Ombudsman* all reasonable assistance requested of you, in connection with the investigation, consideration, and determination, of *complaints* made under the Ombudsman scheme.

### Ceasing to practise

**rC72**    Once you are aware that you (if you are a *self-employed barrister* or a *BSB authorised body*) or the *BSB authorised body* within which you work (if you are an authorised individual or *manager* of such *BSB authorised body*) will cease to practise, you shall effect the orderly wind-down of activities, including:

.1    informing the *Bar Standards Board* and providing them with a contact address;

.2    notifying those *clients* for whom you have current matters and liaising with them in respect of the arrangements that they would like to be put in place in respect of those matters;

.3    providing such information to the *Bar Standards Board* in respect of your practice and your proposed arrangements in respect of the winding down of your activities as the *Bar Standards Board* may require.

## C5. You and your practice

### O Outcomes

**oC24** Your *practice* is run competently in a way that achieves compliance with the Core Duties and your other obligations under this *Handbook*. Your *employees*, *pupils* and trainees understand, and do, what is required of them in order that you meet your obligations under this *Handbook*.

**oC25** *Clients* are clear about the extent to which your services are regulated and by whom, and who is responsible for providing those services.

### C5.1 General

### R Rules

**Client money**

**rC73** Except where you are acting in your capacity as a *manager* of an *authorised (non-BSB) body*, you must not receive, control or handle *client money* apart from what the client pays you for your services.

**rC74** If you make use of a third party payment service for making payments to or from or on behalf of your *client* you must:

.1 Ensure that the service you use will not result in your receiving, controlling or handling *client money;* and

.2 Only use the service for payments to or from or on behalf of your *client* that are made in respect of legal services, such as fees, disbursements or settlement monies; and

.3 Take reasonable steps to check that making use of the service is consistent with your duty to act competently and in your *client's* best interests.

**rC75** The *Bar Standards Board* may give notice under this rule that (effective from the date of that notice) you may only use third party payment services approved by the *Bar Standards Board* or which satisfy criteria set by the *Bar Standards Board*

### G Guidance

**Guidance on Rules C73 and C74**

**gC103** The prohibition in Rule C73 applies to you and to anyone acting on your behalf, including any "ProcureCo" being a company established as a vehicle to enable the provision of *legal services* but does not in itself supply or provide those *legal services*. Rule C73 prohibits you from holding *client money* or other *client* assets yourself, or through any agent, third party or nominee.

**gC104** Receiving, controlling or handling *client money* includes entering into any arrangement which gives you de facto control over the use and/or destination of funds provided by or for the benefit of your *client* or intended by another party to be transmitted to your *client*, whether or not those funds are beneficially owned by your client and whether or not held in an account of yours.

**gC105** The circumstances in which you will have de facto control within the meaning of Rule C73 include when you can cause money to be transferred from a balance standing to the credit of your *client* without that *client's* consent to such a withdrawal. For large withdrawals, explicit consent should usually be required. However, the *client's* consent may be deemed to be given if:

.1    the *client* has given informed consent to an arrangement which enables withdrawals to be made after the *client* has received an invoice; and

.2    the *client* has not objected to the withdrawal within a pre-agreed reasonable period (which should not normally be less than one week from receipt of the invoice).

**gC106**    A fixed fee paid in advance is not *client money* for the purposes of Rule C73.

**gC107**    If you have decided in principle to take a particular case you may request an 'upfront' fixed fee from your prospective *client* before finally agreeing to work on their behalf. This should only be done having regard to the following principles:

- You should take care to estimate accurately the likely time commitment and only take payment when you are satisfied that:

  – it is a reasonable payment for the work being done; and
  – in the case of public access work, that it is suitable for you to undertake.

- If the amount of work required is unclear, you should consider staged payments rather than a fixed fee in advance.

- You should never accept an upfront fee in advance of considering whether it is appropriate for you to take the case and considering whether you will be able to undertake the work within a reasonable timescale.

- If the *client* can reasonably be expected to understand such an arrangement, you may agree that when the work has been done, you will pay the *client* any difference between that fixed fee and (if lower) the fee which has actually been earned based on the time spent, provided that it is clear that you will not hold the difference between the fixed fee and the fee which has been earned on trust for the *client*. That difference will not be *client money* if you can demonstrate that this was expressly agreed in writing, on clear terms understood by the *client*, and before payment of the fixed fee. You should also consider carefully whether such an arrangement is in the *client's* interest, taking into account the nature of the instructions, the *client* and whether the *client* fully understands the implications. Any abuse of an agreement to pay a fixed fee subject to reimbursement, the effect of which is that you receive more money than is reasonable for the case at the outset, will be considered to be holding *client money* and a breach of rC73. For this reason, you should take extreme care if contracting with a *client* in this way.

- In any case, rC22 requires you to confirm in writing the acceptance of any instructions and the terms or basis on which you are acting, including the basis of charging.

**gC108**    Acting in the following ways may demonstrate compliance with Rules C73, C74 and C75:

**gC109**    Checking that any third party payment service you may use is not structured in such a way that the service provider is holding, as your agent, money to which the *client* is beneficially entitled. If this is so you will be in breach of Rule C73.

**gC110**    Considering whether your *client* will be safe in using the third party payment service as a means of transmitting or receiving funds. The steps you should take in order to satisfy yourself will depend on what would be expected in all the circumstances of a reasonably competent legal adviser acting in their *client's* best interests. However, you are unlikely to demonstrate that you have acted competently and in your *client's* best interests if you have not:

.1     ensured that the payment service is authorised or regulated as a payment service by the *Financial Conduct Authority (FCA)* and taken reasonable steps to satisfy yourself that it is in good standing with the FCA;

.2     if the payment service is classified as a small payment institution, ensured that it has arrangements to safeguard *clients'* funds or adequate insurance arrangements;

.3     ensured that the payment service segregates *client* money from its own funds;

.4     satisfied yourself that the terms of the service are such as to ensure that any money paid in by or on behalf of the *client* can only be paid out with the *client's* consent;

.5     informed your *client* that moneys held by the payment service provider are not covered by the *Financial Services Compensation Scheme.*

**gC111**   Unless you are reasonably satisfied that it is safe for your client to use the third party payment service (see rC74.3, gC109 and gC110 above), advising your *client* against using the third party payment service and not making use of it yourself.

**gC112**   This *Handbook* applies in full whether or not you are practising in an association. You are particularly reminded of the need to ensure that, notwithstanding any such association, you continue to comply with Rules C8, C9, C10, C12, C15, C19, C20, C28, C73, C75, C79, C82 and C86 (and, where relevant C80, C81, C83, C74 and C110).

## R   Rules

### Insurance

**rC76**   You must:

.1     ensure that you have adequate insurance (taking into account the nature of your practice) which covers all the *legal services* you supply to *the public;* and

.2     if you are a *BSB authorised person* or a *manager* of a *BSB authorised body,* then in the event that the *Bar Standards Board,* by any notice it may from time to time issue under this Rule C76, stipulates a minimum level of insurance and/or minimum terms for the insurance which must be taken out by *BSB authorised persons,* you must ensure that you have or put in place within the time specified in such notice, insurance meeting such requirements as apply to you.

**rC77**   Where you are acting as a *self-employed barrister,* you must be a member *of BMIF,* unless:

.1     you are a *pupil* who is covered by his *pupil supervisor's* insurance; or

.2     you were called to the *Bar* under Rule Q9498, in which case you must either be insured with *BMIF* or be covered by insurance against claims for professional negligence arising out of the supply of your services in England and Wales in such amount and on such terms as are currently required by the *Bar Standards Board,* and have delivered to the *Bar Standards Board* a copy of the current insurance policy, or the current certificate of insurance, issued by the insurer.

**rC78**   If you are a member *of BMIF,* you must:

.1    pay promptly the insurance premium required by *BMIF*; and

.2    supply promptly such information as *BMIF* may from time to time require pursuant to its rules.

## **G**    Guidance

### Guidance on Rules C75 to C77

**gC113**    Where you are working in a *BSB authorised body*, you will satisfy the requirements of Rule rC76.1 so long as the *BSB authorised body* has taken out insurance, which covers your activities. A *BSB authorised body* will have to confirm each year that it has reviewed the adequacy of its insurance cover on the basis of a risk analysis and that they have complied with this rule.

**gC114**    Any notice issued under Rule rC75 will be posted on the *Bar Standards Board's* website and may also be publicised by such other means as the Bar Standards Board may judge appropriate.

The *Bar Standards Board's* requirements in respect of professional indemnity insurance, including the minimum terms, are concerned with ensuring consumer protection, specifically that there is adequate cover for liabilities which *BSB regulated persons* may incur to their *clients* or other parties to whom they may owe duties when performing their *legal services*. This includes claims for contribution which third parties, such as instructing *solicitors*, may make on the basis that the *BSB regulated person* has such a liability to a mutual *client*. However, Rule C76.1 of the *Handbook* does not require *BSB regulated persons* to carry insurance for other types of liability, which do not relate to their liabilities towards consumers, such as a contractual liability to instructing *solicitors* in respect of losses incurred by the *solicitor* that are not based on any liability the *solicitor* has in turn incurred to the *client*. Nor are the minimum terms concerned with the latter type of liability and whether and on what terms to seek to insure against such exposure is a commercial judgment for *BSB regulated persons* to make. You should however ensure that you are aware of and comply with any general legal requirements for you to carry other types of insurance than professional indemnity cover.

**gC115**    Where you are working in an *authorised (non-BSB) body*, the rules of the *approved regulator* of that body will determine what insurance the *authorised (non-BSB) body* must have.

**gC116**    Where you are working as an *employed barrister (non-authorised body)*, the rule does not require you to have your own insurance if you provide *legal services* only to your *employer*. If you supply *legal services* to other people (to the extent permitted by the *Scope of Practice and Authorisation, ~~and Licensing Rules~~* set out at Section S.B you should consider whether you need insurance yourself having regard to the arrangements made by your *employer* for insuring against claims made in respect of your services. If your *employer* already has adequate insurance for this purpose, you need not take out any insurance of your own. You should ensure that your *employer's* policy covers you, for example, for any pro-bono work you may do.

**gC117**    Where you are a *registered European lawyer*, the rule does not require you to have your own insurance if:

.1    you provide to the *Bar Standards Board* evidence to show that you are covered by insurance taken out or a guarantee provided in accordance with the rules of your *home State*; and

.2    the *Bar Standards Board* is satisfied that such insurance or guarantee is fully equivalent in terms of conditions and extent of cover to the cover required pursuant to Rule C76. However, where the *Bar Standards Board* is satisfied that the equivalence is only partial, the *Bar Standards Board* may require you to arrange additional insurance or an additional guarantee to cover the elements which are not already covered by the insurance or guarantee contracted by you in accordance with the rules of your *home state*

## R | Rules

### Associations with others

**rC79**    You may not do anything, practising in *an association*, which you are otherwise prohibited from doing.

**rC80**    Where you are in *an association* on more than a one-off basis, you must notify the *Bar Standards Board* that you are in *an association*, and provide such details of that association as are required by the *Bar Standards Board*.

**rC81**    If you have a material commercial interest in an organisation to which you plan to refer a *client*, you must:

.1    tell the *client* in writing about your interest in that organisation before you refer the *client*; and

.2    keep a record of your referrals to any such organisation for review by the *Bar Standards Board* on request.

**rC82**    If you have a material commercial interest in an organisation which is proposing to refer a matter to you, you must:

.1    tell the *client* in writing about your interest in that organisation before you accept such *instructions*;

.2    make a clear agreement with that organisation or other public statement about how relevant issues, such as conflicts of interest, will be dealt with; and

.3    keep a record of referrals received from any such organisation for review by the *Bar Standards Board* on reasonable request.

**rC83**    If you refer a *client* to a third party which is not a *BSB authorised person* or an *authorised (non-BSB) person*, you must take reasonable steps to ensure that the *client* is not wrongly led to believe that the third party is subject to regulation by the *Bar Standards Board* or by another *approved regulator*.

**rC84**    You must not have a material commercial interest in any organisation which gives the impression of being, or may be reasonably perceived as being, subject to the regulation of the *Bar Standards Board* or of another *approved regulator*, in circumstances where it is not so regulated.

**rC85**    A material commercial interest for the purposes of Rules C78 to C84 is an interest which an objective observer with knowledge of the salient facts would reasonably consider might potentially influence your judgment.

## G | Guidance

### Guidance on Rules C78 to C84 and CD5

**gC118**    You may not use an association with the purpose of, or in order to evade rules which would otherwise apply to you. You may not do anything, practising in *an association*, which you are individually prohibited from doing.

**gC119**    You will bring yourself and your profession into disrepute (CD5) if you are personally involved in arrangements which breach the restrictions imposed by the Legal Services Act 2007 on those who can provide reserved legal activities. For example, you must not remain a member of any "ProcureCo" arrangement where you know or are reckless as to whether the ProcureCo is itself carrying on reserved legal activities without a licence or where you have failed to take reasonable steps to ensure this is not so before joining or continuing your involvement with the Procureco.

**gC120**    The purpose of Rules C78 to C84 is to ensure that *clients* and members of *the public* are not confused by any such association. In particular, the public should be clear who is responsible for doing work, and about the extent to which that person is regulated in doing it: see Rules C77 and C80.

**gC121** This *Handbook* applies in full whether or not you are practising in an association. You are particularly reminded of the need to ensure that, notwithstanding any such association, you continue to comply with Rules C8, C9, C10, C12, C15, C19, C20, C28, C73, C75, C79, C82 and C86 (and, where relevant C80, C81, C83, C74 and C110) .

**gC122** References to "organisation" in Rules C81 and C82 include *BSB authorised bodies* and *authorised (non-BSB) bodies*, as well as non-authorised bodies. So, if you have an interest, as owner, or manager, in any such body, your relationship with any such organisation is caught by these rules.

**gC123** These rules do not permit you to accept *instructions* from a third party in any case where that would give rise to a potential conflict of interest contrary to CD2 or any relevant part of Rule C79.

**gC124** You should only refer a *client* to an organisation in which you have a material commercial interest if it is in the *client's* best interest to be referred to that organisation. This is one aspect of what is required of you by CD2. Your obligations of honesty and integrity, in CD3, require you to be open with *clients* about any interest you have in, or arrangement you have with, any organisation to which you properly refer the *client*, or from which the *client* is referred to you. It is inherently unlikely that a general referral arrangement obliging you (whether or not you have an interest in such organisation) to refer to that organisation, without the option to refer elsewhere if the *client's* circumstances make that more appropriate, could be justified as being in the best interests of each individual *client* (CD2) and it may well also be contrary to your obligations of honesty and integrity (CD3) and compromise your independence (CD4).

**gC125** The *Bar Standards Board* may require you to provide copies of any protocols that you may have in order to ensure compliance with these rules.

**gC126** Your obligations under CD5 require you not to act in an *association* with a person where, merely by being associated with such person, you may reasonably be considered as bringing the profession into disrepute or otherwise diminishing the trust that the public places in you and your profession.

**gC127** Members of *chambers* are not in partnership but are independent of one another and are not responsible for the conduct of other members. However, each individual member of *chambers* is responsible for his own conduct and the constitution of *chambers* enables, or should enable, each individual member of *chambers* to take steps to terminate another person's membership in specified circumstances. Rule C87 does not require you to sever connection with a member of *chambers* solely because to your knowledge he or she is found to breach this *Handbook*, provided that he or she is not disbarred and complies with such sanctions as may be imposed for such breach; however, your *chambers* constitution should be drafted so as to allow you to exclude from *chambers* a member whose conduct is reasonably considered such as to diminish the trust the public places in you and your profession and you should take such steps as are reasonably available to you under your constitution to exclude any such member.

**R** | **Rules**

## Outsourcing

**rC86** Where you outsource to a third party any support services that are critical to the delivery of any *legal services* in respect of which you are instructed:

.1 any outsourcing does not alter your obligations to your *client*;

.2 you remain responsible for compliance with your obligations under this *Handbook* in respect of the *legal services*;

.3    you must ensure that such outsourcing is subject to contractual arrangements which ensure that such third party:

.a    is subject to confidentiality obligations similar to the confidentiality obligations placed on you in accordance with this *Handbook*;

.b    complies with any other obligations set out in this Code of Conduct which may be relevant to or affected by such outsourcing;

.c    processes any personal data in accordance with your *instructions* and, for the avoidance of doubt, as though it were a data controller under the Data Protection Act; and

.d    is required to allow the *Bar Standards Board* or its agent to obtain information from, inspect the records (including electronic records) of, or enter the premises of such third party in relation to the outsourced activities or functions.

## G    Guidance

### Guidance on Rule C85

**gC128**    Rule C86 applies to the outsourcing of clerking services.

**gC129**    Rule C86 does not apply where the *client* enters into a separate agreement with the third party for the services in question.

**gC130**    Rule C86 does not apply where you are instructing a *pupil* or a *devil* to undertake work on your behalf. Instead rC15 will apply in those circumstances.

**gC131**    Notwithstanding Rule C86.3.c you are still likely to remain the data controller of the personal data in question. Therefore, Rule C86.3.c does not relieve you of your obligations to comply with the Data Protection Act in respect of such data.

## C5.2    Administration and conduct of self-employed practice

## R    Rules

**rC87**    You must take reasonable steps to ensure that:

.1    your practice is efficiently and properly administered having regard to the nature of your practice; and

.2    proper records of your practice are kept.

## G    Guidance

### Guidance on Rule C87.2

**gC132**    The *Supervision Team* of the *Bar Standards Board* reviews the key controls that are in place in *chambers* and *BSB authorised bodies* to manage the risks in relation to key processes. These key processes are shown in guidance that is published on the Supervision section of the *Bar Standards Board's* website: https://www.barstandardsboard.org.uk/regulatory-requirements/for-barristers/supervision/. You should retain relevant policies, procedures, monitoring reports and other records of your practice so that they are available to view if a Supervision visit is arranged.

When deciding how long records need to be kept, you will need to take into consideration various requirements, such as those of this *Handbook* (see, for example, Rules C108, C129 and C141), the Data Protection Act and HM Revenue and Customs. You may want to consider drawing up a Records Keeping policy to ensure that you have identified the specific compliance and other needs of your *practice*.

## **R    Rules**

**rC88**    You must:

.1    ensure that adequate records supporting the fees charged or claimed in a case are kept at least until the later of the following:

.a    your fees have been paid; and

.b    any determination or assessment of costs in the case has been completed and the time for lodging an appeal against that assessment or determination has expired without any such appeal being lodged, or any such appeal has been finally determined;

.2    provide your *client* with such records or details of the work you have done as may reasonably be required for the purposes of verifying your charges.

## C5.3    Administration of chambers

## **R    Rules**

**rC89**    Taking into account the provisions of Rule C90, you must take reasonable steps to ensure that:

.1    your *chambers* is administered competently and efficiently;

.2    your *chambers* has appointed an individual or individuals to liaise with the *Bar Standards Board* in respect of any regulatory requirements and has notified the *Bar Standards Board*;

.3    your *chambers* does not employ any person who has been disqualified from being employed by an authorised person or a *licensed body* by another *approved regulator* pursuant to its or their powers as such and such disqualification is continuing in force;

.4    proper arrangements are made in your *chambers* for dealing with *pupils* and pupillage;

.5    proper arrangements are made in *chambers* for the management of conflicts of interest and for ensuring the confidentiality of *clients*' affairs;

.6    all non-authorised persons working in your *chambers* (irrespective of the identity of their *employer*):

.a    are competent to carry out their duties;

.b    carry out their duties in a correct and efficient manner;

.c    are made clearly aware of such provisions of this *Handbook* as may affect or be relevant to the performance of their duties;

.d    do nothing which causes or substantially contributes to a breach of this *Handbook* by any *BSB authorised individual* or *authorised (non-BSB) individual* within *Chambers*, and all *complaints* against them are dealt with in accordance with the *complaints rules*;

.7 all *registered European lawyers* and all *foreign lawyers* in your *chambers* comply with this *Handbook* insofar as applicable to them;

.8 appropriate risk management procedures are in place and are being complied with; and

.9 there are systems in place to check that:

.a all persons practising from your *chambers* whether they are members of the *chambers* or not have insurance in place in accordance with Rules C75 to C77 above (other than any *pupil* who is covered under his *pupil supervisor's* insurance); and

.b every *BSB authorised individual* practising from your *chambers* has a current *practising certificate* and every other *authorised (non-BSB) individual* providing *reserved legal activities* is currently authorised by their *Approved Regulator.*

**rC90** For the purposes of Rule C89 the steps which it is reasonable for you to take will depend on all the circumstances, which include, but are not limited to:

.1 the arrangements in place in your *chambers* for the management of *chambers*;

.2 any role which you play in those arrangements; and

.3 the independence of individual members of *chambers* from one another.

## **G** Guidance

### Guidance on Rule C88 and C89

**gC133** Your duty under Rule C89.4 to have proper arrangements in place for dealing with pupils includes ensuring:

.1 that all *pupillage* vacancies are advertised in the manner prescribed by the *Pupillage* Funding and Advertising Rules (rC113 to rC118);

.2 that arrangements are made for the funding of *pupils* by *chambers* which comply with the *Pupillage* Funding and Advertising Rules (rC113 to rC118);

**gC134** Your duty under Rule C89.5 to have proper arrangements in place for ensuring the confidentiality of each *client's* affairs includes:

.1 putting in place and enforcing adequate procedures for the purpose of protecting confidential information;

.2 complying with data protection obligations imposed by law;

.3 taking reasonable steps to ensure that anyone who has access to such information or data in the course of their work for you complies with these obligations; and

.4 taking into account any further guidance on confidentiality which is available on the *Bar Standards Board's* website and which can be accessed here https://www.barstandardsboard.org.uk/code-guidance/confidentiality-guidance/.

**gC135** In order to ensure compliance with Rule C89.6.d, you may want to consider incorporating an obligation along these lines in all new employment contracts entered into after the date of this *Handbook.*

**gC136** For further guidance on what may constitute appropriate risk management procedures in accordance with Rule C89.8 please refer to the further guidance published by the *Bar Standards Board* which can be accessed here https://www.barstandardsboard.org.uk/regulatory-requirements/for-barristers/supervision/.

**gC137** Rule C90.3 means that you should consider, in particular, the obligation of each individual members of *chambers* to act in the best interests of his or her own *client* (CD2) and to preserve the confidentiality of his or her own *client's* affairs (CD6), in circumstances where other members of *chambers* are free (and, indeed, may be obliged by the cab rank rule (rC29) to act for *clients* with conflicting interests.

## 5.4   Administration of BSB authorised bodies

### Duties of the BSB authorised body, authorised (non-BSB) individuals and BSB regulated managers

**R  Rules**

**rC91** If you are a *BSB authorised body*, you must ensure that (or, if you are a *BSB regulated individual* working within such *BSB authorised body*, you must use reasonable endeavours (taking into account the provisions of Rule rC95) to procure that the *BSB authorised body* ensures that):

.1   the *BSB authorised body* has at all times a person appointed by it to act as its *HOLP,* who shall be a *manager;*

.2   the *BSB authorised body* has at all times a person appointed by it to act as its *HOFA*; and

.3   subject to rC92, the *BSB authorised body* does not appoint any individual to act as a *HOLP* or a *HOFA*, or to be a *manager* or *employee* of that *BSB authorised body*, in circumstances where that individual has been disqualified from being appointed to act as a *HOLP* or a *HOFA* or from being a *manager* or employed by an *authorised person* (as appropriate) by the *Bar Standards Board* or another *Approved Regulator* pursuant to its or their powers as such and such disqualification is continuing in force.

**rC92** Rule rC91.3 shall not apply where the *BSB authorised body* obtains the express written consent of the *Bar Standards Board* to the appointment of a person who has been disqualified before he is appointed.

**rC93** If you are a *manager* or *employee*, you must not do anything to cause (or substantially to contribute to) a breach by the *BSB authorised body* or by any *BSB authorised individual* in it of their duties under this *Handbook*.

**rC94** If you are a *BSB authorised body*, you must at all times have (or, if you are a *BSB regulated individual* working in such *BSB authorised body*, you must use reasonable endeavours (taking into account the provisions of Rule rC95 to procure that the *BSB authorised body* shall have) suitable arrangements to ensure that:

.1   the *managers* and other *BSB regulated individuals* working as *employees* of the *BSB authorised body* comply with the *Bar Standards Board's* regulatory arrangements as they apply to them, as required under section 176 of the *LSA*;

.2   all *employees*:

   .a   are competent to carry out their duties;

   .b   carry out their duties in a correct and efficient manner;

   .c   are made clearly aware of such provisions of this *Handbook* as may affect or be relevant to the performance of their duties;

   .d   do nothing which causes or substantially contributes to, a breach of this *Handbook* by the *BSB authorised body* or any of the *BSB regulated individuals* employed by it; and

   .e   co-operates with the *Bar Standards Board* in the exercise of its regulatory functions, in particular in relation to any notice issued under rC22, rC64 or rC70;

.3   the *BSB authorised body* is administered in a correct and efficient manner, is properly staffed and keeps proper records of its practice;

.4   *pupils* and *pupillages* are dealt with properly;

.5   conflicts of interest are managed appropriately and that the confidentiality of *clients'* affairs is maintained at all times;

.6   all *registered European lawyers* and all *foreign lawyers* employed by or working for you comply with this *Handbook* insofar as it applies to them;

.7   every *BSB authorised individual* employed by, or working for, the *BSB authorised body* has a current *practising certificate* (except where a *barrister* is working as an *unregistered barrister*, in which case there must be appropriate systems to ensure that they are complying with the provisions of this *Handbook* which apply to *unregistered barristers*) and every other *authorised (non-BSB) individual* providing *reserved legal activities* is currently authorised by their *Approved Regulator*; and

.8   adequate records supporting the fees charged or claimed in a case are kept at least until the later of the following:

   .a   your fees have been paid; and

   .b   any determination or assessment of costs in the case has been completed and the time for lodging an appeal against that assessment or determination has expired without any such appeal being lodged, or any such appeal has been finally determined;

.9   your *client* is provided with such records or details of the work you have done as may reasonably be required for the purpose of verifying your charges;

.10   appropriate procedures are in place requiring all *managers* and *employees* to work with the *HOLP* with a view to ensuring that the *HOLP* is able to comply with his obligations under Rule rC96;

.11   appropriate risk management procedures are in place and are being complied with; and

.12   appropriate financial management procedures are in place and are being complied with.

**rC95**   For the purposes of Rule rC91 and rC94 the steps which it is reasonable for you to take will depend on all the circumstances, which include, but are not limited to:

.1   the arrangements in place in your *BSB authorised body* for the management of it; and

.2    any role which you play in those arrangements.

## G  Guidance

### Guidance to Rules rC91 to rC94

gC138    ~~Section 90 of the *LSA* places obligations on *non-authorised individuals* who are *employees* and *managers* of *licensed bodies*, as well as on *non-authorised individuals* who hold an ownership interest in such a *licensed body* (whether by means of a shareholding or voting powers in respect of the same) to do nothing which causes, or substantially contributes to a breach by the *licensed body* or by its *employees* or *managers*, of this *Handbook*. Rule C91 extends this obligation to *BSB legal services bodies*.~~

gC139    Your duty under Rule rC94.4 to have proper arrangements for dealing with pupils includes ensuring:

.1    that all pupillage vacancies are advertised in the manner prescribed by the Pupillage Funding and Advertising Rules (rC113 to rC118);

.2    that arrangements are made for the funding of *pupils* by *chambers* which comply with the Pupillage Funding and Advertising Rules (rC113 to rC118).

### Duties of the HOLP/HOFA

## R  Rules

rC96    If you are a *HOLP*, in addition to complying with the more general duties placed on the *BSB authorised body* and on the *BSB regulated individuals* employed by it, you must:

.1    take all reasonable steps to ensure compliance with the terms of your *BSB authorised body's* authorisation;

.2    take all reasonable steps to ensure that the *BSB authorised body* and its *employees* and *managers* comply with the duties imposed by section 176 of the *LSA*;

.3    ~~take all reasonable steps to ensure that *non-authorised individuals* subject to the duty imposed by section 90 of the *LSA* comply with that duty;~~

.4    keep a record of all incidents of non-compliance with the Core Duties and this *Handbook* of which you become aware and to report such incidents to the Bar Standards Board as soon as reasonably practicable (where such failures are material in nature) or otherwise on request by the *Bar Standards Board* or during the next monitoring visit or review by the *Bar Standards Board*.

rC97    If you are a *HOFA*, in addition to complying with the more general duties placed on the *BSB authorised body* and its *BSB regulated individuals*, you must ensure compliance with Rules rC73 and rC74.

### New managers/HOLP/HOFA

rC98    A BSB *authorised body* must not take on a new *manager*, *HOLP* or *HOFA* without first submitting an application to the *Bar Standards Board* for approval in accordance with the requirements of Section S.D.

# D. RULES APPLYING TO PARTICULAR GROUPS OF REGULATED PERSONS

## D1. Self-employed barristers, chambers and BSB authorised bodies

### O   Outcomes

**oC26**   *Clients* know that they can make a *complaint* if dissatisfied, and know how to do so.

**oC27**   *Complaints* are dealt with promptly and the *client* is kept informed about the process.

**oC28**   *Self-employed barristers*, *chambers* and *BSB authorised bodies* run their practices without *discrimination*.

**oC29**   *Pupils* are treated fairly and all vacancies for *pupillages* are advertised openly.

### D1.1   Complaints rules

### R   Rules

**Provision of information to clients**

**rC99**   You must notify *clients* in writing when you are *instructed*, or, if that is if not practicable, at the next appropriate opportunity:

    .1   of their right to make a *complaint*, including their right to complain to the *Legal Ombudsman* (if they have such a right), how, and to whom, they can complain, and of any time limits for making a *complaint*;

    .2   if you are doing referral work, that the lay *client* may complain directly to *chambers* or the *BSB authorised body* without going through *solicitors*.

**rC100**   If you are doing public access, or licensed access work using an *intermediary*, the *intermediary* must similarly be informed.

**rC101**   If you are doing referral work, you do not need to give a *professional client* the information set out in Rules C99.1 and C99.2, in a separate, specific letter. It is enough to provide it in the ordinary terms of reference letter (or equivalent letter) which you send when you accept *instructions* in accordance with Rule C21.

| SECTION D: RULES APPLYING TO PARTICULAR GROUPS OF REGULATED PERSONS |
| --- |
| D1: Self-employed barristers, chambers and BSB authorised bodies |

**PART 2**

**rC102**  If you do not send a letter of engagement to a lay *client* in which this information can be included, a specific letter must be sent to him giving him the information set out at Rules C99.1 and C99.2.

**rC103**  *Chambers'* websites and literature must display information about the *chambers'* complaints procedure. A *BSB's authorised body's* website and literature must carry information about that *BSB authorised body's* Complaints Procedure.

## Response to complaints

**rC104**  All *complaints* must be acknowledged promptly. When you acknowledge a *complaint*, you must give the complainant:

.1    the name of the person who will deal with the *complaint* and a description of that person's role in *chambers* or in the *BSB authorised body* (as appropriate);

.2    a copy of the *chambers'* complaints procedure or the *BSB authorised body's* Complaints Procedure (as appropriate);

.3    the date by which the complainant will next hear from *chambers* or the *BSB authorised body* (as appropriate).

**rC105**  When *chambers* or *BSB authorised body* (as appropriate) has dealt with the *complaint*, complainants must be told in writing of their right to complain to the *Legal Ombudsman* (where applicable), of the time limit for doing so, and how to contact him.

## Documents and record keeping

**rC106**  All communications and documents relating to *complaints* must be kept confidential. They must be disclosed only so far as is necessary for:

.1    the investigation and resolution of the *complaint*;

.2    internal review in order to improve *chambers'* or the *BSB authorised body's* (as appropriate) handling of complaints;

.3    complying with requests from the *Bar Standards Board* in the exercise of its monitoring and/or auditing functions.

**rC107**  The disclosure to the *Bar Standards Board* of internal documents relating to the handling of the *complaint* (such as the minutes of any meeting held to discuss a particular *complaint*) for the further resolution or investigation of the *complaint* is not required.

**rC108**  A record must be kept of each *complaint*, of all steps taken in response to it, and of the outcome of the *complaint*. Copies of all correspondence, including electronic mail, and all other documents generated in response to the *complaint* must also be kept. The records and copies should be kept for 6 years from resolution of the *complaint*.

**rC109**  The person responsible for the administration of the procedure must report at least annually to either:

.1    the *HOLP*; or

.2    the appropriate member/committee of *chambers*,

on the number of *complaints* received, on the subject areas of the *complaints* and on the outcomes. The *complaints* should be reviewed for trends and possible *training* issues.

## D1.2  Equality and diversity

**R**  **Rules**

**rC110**  You must take reasonable steps to ensure that in relation to your *chambers* or *BSB authorised body*:

.1  there is in force a written statement of policy on equality and diversity; and

.2  there is in force a written plan implementing that policy;

.3  the following requirements are complied with:

Equality and Diversity Officer

.a  *chambers* or *BSB authorised body* has at least one *Equality and Diversity Officer*;

Training

.b  except in unforeseen and exceptional circumstances, the person with lead responsibility for any *selection panel* and at least one member of any *selection panel* (who may be the same person) has received recent and appropriate *training* in fair recruitment and selection processes;

.c  From July 2014, save in exceptional circumstances, every member of all selection panels must be trained in fair recruitment and selection processes;

Fair and objective criteria

.d  recruitment and selection processes use objective and fair criteria;

Equality monitoring

.e  your *chambers* or *BSB authorised body*:

.i  conducts a *regular review* of its policy on equality and diversity and of its implementation in order to ensure that it complies with the requirements of this Rule C110; and

.ii  takes any appropriate *remedial action* identified in the light of that review;

.f  subject to Rule C110.3.h *chambers* or *BSB authorised body* regularly reviews:

.i  the number and percentages of its *workforce* from different groups; and

.ii  applications to become a member of its *workforce*; and

.iii  in the case of *chambers*, the *allocation of unassigned work*;

.g  the reviews referred to in Rule rC110.3.f above include:

.i  collecting and analysing data broken down by race, disability and gender;

.ii  *investigating* the reasons for any disparities in that data; and

.iii  taking appropriate *remedial action*;

.h  the requirement to collect the information referred to in Rule C110.3.g does not apply to the extent that the people referred to in Rule rC110.3.f.i and Rule rC110.3.f.ii refuse to disclose it.

Fair access to work

.i    if you are a *self-employed barrister*, the affairs of your *chambers* are conducted in a manner which is fair and equitable for all members of *chambers*, *pupils* and/or *employees* (as appropriate). This includes, but is not limited to, the fair distribution of work opportunities among *pupils* and members of *chambers*;

Harassment

.j    *chambers*-or *BSB authorised body* has a written anti-*harassment* policy which, as a minimum:

.i    states that *harassment* will not be tolerated or condoned and that *managers*, *employees*, members of *chambers*, *pupils* and others temporarily in your *chambers or BSB authorised body* such as mini-pupils have a right to complain if it occurs;

.ii    sets out how the policy will be communicated;

.iii    sets out the procedure for dealing with *complaints* of *harassment*;

Parental leave

.k    *chambers*-has a *parental leave* policy which, in the case of a *chambers*, must cover as a minimum:

.i    the right of a member of *chambers* to return to *chambers* after a specified period (which must be at least one year) of parental or adoption leave;

.ii    the extent to which a member of *chambers* is or is not required to contribute to *chambers*' rent and expenses during *parental leave*;

.iii    the method of calculation of any waiver, reduction or reimbursement of *chambers*' rent and expenses during *parental leave*;

.iv    where any element of rent is paid on a flat rate basis, the *chambers* policy must as a minimum provide that *chambers* will offer members taking a period of *parental leave*, or leave following adoption, a minimum of 6 months free of *chambers*' rent;

.v    the procedure for dealing with grievances under the policy;

.vi    *chambers*' commitment to regularly review the effectiveness of the policy;

Flexible working

.l    *chambers* or *BSB authorised body* has a flexible working policy which covers the right of a member of *chambers*, *manager* or *employee* (as the case may be) to take a career break, to work part-time, to work flexible hours, or to work from home, so as to enable them to manage their *family responsibilities* or disability without giving up work;

Reasonable adjustments policy

.m    *chambers* or *BSB authorised body* has a reasonable adjustments policy aimed at supporting disabled *clients*, its *workforce* and others including temporary visitors;

Appointment of Diversity Data Officer

.n    *chambers* or *BSB authorised body* has a Diversity Data Officer;

.o   *chambers* or *BSB authorised body* must provide the name and contact details of the Diversity Data Officer to the *Bar Standards Board* and must notify the *Bar Standards Board* of any change to the identity of the Diversity Data Officer, as soon as reasonably practicable;

Responsibilities of Diversity Data Officer

.p   The Diversity Data Officer shall comply with the requirements in relation to the collection, processing and publication of *diversity data* set out in the paragraphs rC110.3.q to .t below;

Collection and publication of diversity data

.q   The Diversity Data Officer shall invite members of the *workforce* to provide *diversity data* in respect of themselves to the Diversity Data Officer using the model questionnaire in Section 7 of the BSB's Supporting Information on the BSB Handbook Equality Rules (https://www. barstandardsboard.org.uk/media/1596730/bsb_equality_rules_handbook_june_2014.pdf );

.r   The Diversity Data Officer shall ensure that such data is anonymised and that an accurate and updated summary of it is published on *chambers'* or *BSB authorised body's* website every three years. If *chambers or the BSB authorised body* does not have a website, the Diversity Data Officer shall make such data available to the public on request;

.s   The published summary of anonymised data shall:

.i   exclude *diversity data* relating to the characteristics of sexual orientation and religion or belief, unless there is consent from each of the members of the *workforce;* and

   .ii   exclude diversity data in relation to any characteristic where there is a real risk that individuals could be identified, unless all affected individuals consent; and

   .iii   subject to the foregoing, include anonymised data in relation to each characteristic, categorised by reference to the job title and seniority of the *workforce.*

.t   The Diversity Data Officer shall:

.i   ensure that *chambers* or *BSB authorised body* has in place a written policy statement on the collection, publication, retention and destruction of *diversity data* which shall include an explanation that the provision of *diversity data* is voluntary;

   .ii   notify the *workforce* of the contents of the written policy statement; and

   .iii   ask for explicit consent from the *workforce* to the provision and processing of their *diversity data* in accordance with the written policy statement and these rules, in advance of collecting their *diversity data.*

**rC111**   For the purposes of Rule C110 above, the steps which it is reasonable for you to take will depend on all the circumstances, which include, but are not limited to:

.1   the arrangements in place in your *chambers or BSB authorised body* for the management of *chambers* or *the BSB authorised body;* and

.2   any role which you play in those arrangements.

**rC112**   For the purposes Rule C110 above "allocation of unassigned work" includes, but is not limited to work allocated to:

.1   *pupils*;

.2   *barristers* of fewer than four *years' standing*; and

.3   *barristers* returning from *parental leave*;

## G   Guidance

### Guidance to Rule C110 and Rule C111

**gC140**   Rule C110 places a personal obligation on all *self-employed barristers*, however they practise, and on the *managers* of *BSB authorised bodies*, as well as on the entity itself, to take reasonable steps to ensure that they have appropriate policies which are enforced.

**gC141**   In relation to Rule C110, if you are a Head of *chambers* or a *HOLP* it is likely to be reasonable for you to ensure that you have the policies required by Rule C110, that an *Equality and Diversity Officer* is appointed to monitor compliance, and that any breaches are appropriately punished. If you are a member of a *chambers* you are expected to use the means available to you under your constitution to take reasonable steps to ensure there are policies and that they are enforced. If you are a *manager* of a *BSB authorised body*, you are expected to take reasonable steps to ensure that there are policies and that they are enforced.

**gC142**   For the purpose of Rule C110 training means any course of study covering all the following areas:

a)   Fair and effective selection & avoiding unconscious bias

b)   Attraction and advertising

c)   Application processes

d)   Shortlisting skills

e)   Interviewing skills

f)   Assessment and making a selection decision

g)   Monitoring and evaluation

**gC143**   Training may be undertaken in any of the following ways:

a)   Classroom sessions

b)   Online sessions

c)   Private study of relevant materials such as the Bar Council's Fair Recruitment Guide

d)   Completion of CPD covering fair recruitment and selection processes

**gC144**  The purpose of Rule C110.3.d is to ensure that *applicants* with relevant characteristics are not refused *employment* because of such characteristics. In order to ensure compliance with this rule, therefore, it is anticipated that the *Equality and Diversity Officer* will compile and retain data about the relevant characteristics of all *applicants* for the purposes of reviewing the data in order to see whether there are any apparent disparities in recruitment.

**gC145**  For the purpose of Rule C110 "regular review", means as often as is necessary in order to ensure effective monitoring and review takes place. In respect of data on pupils it is likely to be considered reasonable that "regularly" should mean annually. In respect of managers of a *BSB authorised body* or tenants, it is likely to be considered reasonable that "regularly" should mean every three years unless the numbers change to such a degree as to make more frequent monitoring appropriate.

**gC146**  For the purposes of Rule C110, "remedial action" means any action aimed at removing or reducing the disadvantage experienced by particular relevant groups. Remedial action cannot, however, include positive discrimination in favour of members of relevant groups.

**gC147**  Rule C110.3.f.iii places an obligation on *practices* to take reasonable steps to ensure the work opportunities are shared fairly among its *workforce*. In the case of *chambers*, this obligation includes work which has not been allocated by the solicitor to a named *barrister*. It includes fairness in presenting to solicitors names for consideration and fairness in opportunities to attract future named work (for example, fairness in arrangements for marketing). These obligations apply even if individual members of *chambers* incorporate their practices, or use a "ProcureCo" to obtain or distribute work, as long as their relationship between each other remains one of independent service providers competing for the same work while sharing clerking arrangements and costs.

**gC148**  Rule C110.3.k.iv sets out the minimum requirements which must be included in a parental and adoption leave policy if any element of rent is paid on a flat rate. If rent is paid on any other basis, then the policy should be drafted so as not to put any *self-employed barrister* in a worse position than he would have been in if any element of the rent were paid on a flat rate.

**gC149**  For the purposes of Rule C110 above investigation means, considering the reasons for disparities in data such as:

.1  Under or overrepresentation of particular groups e.g. men, women, different ethnic groups or disabled people

.2  Absence of particular groups e.g. men, women, different ethnic groups or disabled people

.3  Success rates of particular groups

.4  In the case of *chambers,* over or under allocation of unassigned work to particular groups

**gC150**  These rules are supplemented by the BSB's Supporting Information on the BSB Handbook Equality Rules ("*the Supporting Information*"): https://www.barstandardsboard.org.uk/media/1562168/bsb_equality_rules_handbook_corrected.pdf. These describe the legal and regulatory requirements relating to equality and diversity and provide guidance on how they should be applied in *chambers* and in *BSB authorised bodies*. If you are a *self-employed barrister*, a *BSB authorised body*, or a *manager* of a *BSB authorised body*, you should seek to comply with the Support Information as well as with the rules as set out above.

**gC151**  *The Supporting Information* is also relevant to all *pupil supervisors* and *authorised training organisations*. These will be expected to show how they comply with the *Supporting Information* as a condition of authorisation.

**gC152**  Although *the Supporting Information* does not apply directly to *BSB authorised persons* working as *employed barristers* (non-authorised bodies) or *employed barristers* (*authorised non-BSB body*), they provide helpful guidance which you are encouraged to take into account in your practice.

## D1.3  Pupillage funding

**R** | **Rules**

### Funding

**rC113**    The members of a set of *chambers* or *the BSB authorised body* must pay to each non-practising *pupil* (as appropriate), by the end of each month of the non-practising six months of his *pupillage* no less than:

    .1    the *specified amount*; and

    .2    such further sum as may be necessary to reimburse expenses reasonably incurred by the *pupil* on:

    .3    travel for the purposes of his *pupillage* during that month; and

    .4    attendance during that month at courses which he is required to attend as part of his *pupillage*.

**rC114**    The members of a set of *chambers*, or the *BSB authorised body*, must pay to each practising *pupil* by the end of each month of the practising six months of his *pupillage* no less than:

    .1    the *specified amount*; plus

    .2    such further sum as may be necessary to reimburse expenses reasonably incurred by the *pupil* on:

        .a    travel for the purposes of his *pupillage* during that month; and

        .b    attendance during that month at courses which he is required to attend as part of his *pupillage*; less

        .c    such amount, if any, as the *pupil* may receive during that month from his *practice* as a *barrister*; and less

        .d    such amounts, if any, as the *pupil* may have received during the preceding months of his practising *pupillage* from his *practice* as a *barrister*, save to the extent that the amount paid to the *pupil* in respect of any such month was less than the total of the sums provided for in sub-paragraphs rC114.2.a and .b above.

**rC115**    The members of a set of *chambers*, or the *BSB authorised body*, may not seek or accept repayment from a *chambers pupil* or an entity *pupil* of any of the sums required to be paid under Rules rC113 and rC114 above, whether before or after he ceases to be a chambers pupil or an entity *pupil*, save in the case of misconduct on his part.

**rC116**    If you are a *self-employed barrister*, you must pay any *chambers pupil* for any work done for you which because of its value to you warrants payment, unless the *pupil* is receiving an award or remuneration which is paid on terms that it is in lieu of payment for any individual item of work.

### Application

**rC117**    The requirements set out in Rules C113 to C116 above:

.1    do not apply in the case of *pupils* who were granted exemption from the *vocational stage* of *training* under Rule Q73;

.2    do not apply in the case of *pupils* who are doing a period of *pupillage* in a set of *chambers*, or in a *BSB authorised body*, as part of a *training* programme offered by another organisation which is authorised by the *Bar Standards Board* to take *pupils*;

.3    do not apply in the case of *pupils* who have completed both the non-practising and the practising six months of *pupillage*;

.4    save as provided in Rule C117.3 above, do not apply in respect of any period after a *pupil* ceases, for whatever reason, to be a *chambers pupil* or an entity *pupil*; and

.5    may be waived in part or in whole by the *Pupillage* Funding Committee of the BSB.

**rC118**    For the purposes of these requirements:

.1    "*chambers pupil*" means, in respect of any set of *chambers*, a *pupil* doing the non-practising or practising six months of *pupillage* with a *pupil supervisor*, or *pupil supervisors*, who is or are a member, or members, of that set of *chambers*;

.2    "entity *pupil*" means, in respect of a *BSB authorised body*, a *pupil* doing the non-practising or practising six months of *pupillage* with a *pupil*-master or *pupil*-masters who are *managers* or *employees* of such *BSB authorised body*;

.3    "non-practising *pupil*" means a *chambers pupil* or an entity *pupil* doing the non-practising six months of *pupillage*;

.4    "practising *pupil*" means a *chambers pupil* or an entity *pupil* doing the practising six months of *pupillage*;

.5    "month" means calendar month starting on the same day of the month as that on which the *pupil* began the non-practising, or practising, six months *pupillage*, as the case may be;

.6    any payment made to a *pupil* by a *barrister* pursuant to Rule C115 above shall constitute an amount received by the *pupil* from his *practice* as a *barrister*; and

.7    the following travel by a *pupil* shall not constitute travel for the purposes of his *pupillage*:

.a    travel between his home and *chambers* or, for an entity *pupil*, his place of work; and

.b    travel for the purposes of his *practice* as a *barrister*.

## D2.   Barristers undertaking public access and licensed access work

**O**   **Outcomes**

**oC30**   *Barristers* undertaking public access or licensed access work have the necessary skills and experience required to do work on that basis.

**oC31**   *Barristers* undertaking public access or licensed access work maintain appropriate records in respect of such work.

**oC32**   *Clients* only instruct via public access when it is in their interests to do so and they fully understand what is expected of them.

### D2.1   Public access rules

**R**   **Rules**

**rC119**   These rules apply to *barristers* instructed by or on behalf of a lay *client* (other than a *licensed access client*) who has not also instructed a *solicitor* or other *professional client* (public access clients). Guidance on public access rules is available on the *Bar Standards Board website* https://www.barstandardsboard.org.uk/regulatory-requirements/bsb-handbook/code-guidance/.

**rC120**   Before accepting any *public access instructions* from or on behalf of a *public access client*, a *barrister* must:

.1   be properly qualified by having been issued with a full *practising certificate*, by having satisfactorily completed the appropriate public access training, and by registering with the *Bar Council* as a public access practitioner;

.2   if a barrister was already registered with the *Bar Council* to undertake public access work on October 4 2013 then he must undertake any additional training required by the *Bar Standards Board* within 24 months of that date or cease to undertake public access work;

.3   take such steps as are reasonably necessary to ascertain whether it would be in the best interests of the *client* or in the interests of justice for *the* public access client to instruct a *solicitor* or other *professional client*; and

.4   take such steps as are reasonably necessary to ensure that the *client* is able to make an informed decision about whether to apply for legal aid or whether to proceed with public access.

**rC121**   A barrister with less than three *years' standing* who has completed the necessary training must:

.1   Have a *barrister* who is a qualified person within Rule S22 and has registered with the *Bar Council* as a public access practitioner readily available to provide guidance to the *barrister*;

.2   Maintain a log of public access cases they have dealt with, including any issues or problems which have arisen;

.3   Seek appropriate feedback from their public access *clients* on the service provided;

.4   Make this log available, on request, to the *Bar Standards Board* for review.

**rC122**   A *barrister* may not accept direct *instructions* from or on behalf of a public access *client* in or in connection with any matter of proceedings in which, in all the circumstances, it would be in the best interests of the public access *client* or in the interests of justice for the public access *client* to instruct a *solicitor* or other *professional client*.

**rC123**   In any case where a *barrister* is not prohibited from accepting *instructions*, the *barrister* must at all times consider the developing circumstances of the case, and whether at any stage it is in the best interests of the public access *client* or in the interests of justice for the public access *client* to instruct a *solicitor* or other *professional client*. If, after accepting direct *instructions* from a public access *client* a *barrister* forms the view that circumstances are such that it would be in the best interests of the public access *client*, or in the interests of justice for the public access *client* to instruct a *solicitor* or other *professional client* the *barrister* must:

.1   inform the public access *client* of his view; and

.2   withdraw from the case in accordance with the provisions of Rules C25 and C26 and associated guidance unless the *client* instructs a *solicitor* or other *professional client* to act in the case.

**rC124**   A *barrister* must have regard to guidance published from time to time by the *Bar Standards Board* in considering whether to accept and in carrying out any *public access instructions*.

**rC125**   A *barrister* who accepts *public access instructions* must forthwith notify his public access *client* in writing, and in clear and readily understandable terms, of:

.1   the work which the *barrister* has agreed to perform;

.2   the fact that in performing his work the *barrister* will be subject to the requirements of Parts 2 and 3 of this *Handbook* and, in particular, Rules C25 and C26;

.3   unless authorised to *conduct litigation* by the *Bar Standards Board*, the fact that the *barrister* cannot be expected to perform the functions of a *solicitor* or other authorised litigator and in particular to fulfil limitation obligations, disclosure obligations and other obligations arising out of or related to the *conduct of litigation*;

.4   the fact that the *barrister* is self-employed, is not a *member* of a firm and does not take on any arranging role;

.5   in any case where the *barrister* has been instructed by an *intermediary*:

.a   the fact that the *barrister* is independent of and has no liability for the *intermediary*; and

.b   the fact that the *intermediary* is the agent of the lay *client* and not the agent of the *barrister*;

.6   the fact that the *barrister* may be prevented from completing the work by reason of his professional duties or conflicting professional obligations, and what the *client* can expect of the *barrister* in such a situation;

.7   the fees which the *barrister* proposes to charge for that work, or the basis on which his fee will be calculated;

.8   the *barrister's* contact arrangements; and

.9   the information about the *barrister's* complaints procedure required by D1.1 of this Part 2.

**rC126**   Save in exceptional circumstances, a *barrister* will have complied with Rule rC124 above if he has written promptly to the public access *client* in the terms of the model letter provided on the *Bar Standards Board* website.

**rC127**   In any case where a *barrister* has been instructed by an *intermediary*, he must give the notice required by Rule C123 above both:

    .1   directly to the public access *client*; and

    .2   to the *intermediary*.

**rC128**   A *barrister* who accepts *public access instructions* must keep a case record which sets out:

    .1   the date of receipt of the *instructions*, the name of the lay *client*, the name of the case, and any requirements of the *client* as to time limits;

    .2   the date on which the *instructions* were accepted;

    .3   the dates of subsequent *instructions*, of the despatch of advices and other written work, of conferences and of telephone conversations;

    .4   when agreed, the fee.

**rC129**   A *barrister* who accepts *public access instructions* must either himself retain or take reasonable steps to ensure that the lay *client* will retain for at least seven years after the date of the last item of work done:

    .1   copies of all *instructions* (including supplemental *instructions*);

    .2   copies of all advices given and documents drafted or approved;

    .3   the originals, copies or a list of all documents enclosed with any *instructions*;

    .4   notes of all conferences and of all advice given on the telephone.

**rC130**   A *barrister* who has accepted *public access instructions* may undertake correspondence where it is ancillary to permitted work, and in accordance with the guidance published by the *Bar Standards Board*.

**rC131**   Save where otherwise agreed:

    .1   a *barrister* shall be entitled to copy all documents received from his lay *client*, and to retain such copies permanently;

    .2   a *barrister* shall return all documents received from his lay *client* on demand, whether or not the *barrister* has been paid for any work done for the lay *client*;

    .3   a *barrister* shall not be required to deliver to his lay *client* any documents drafted by the *barrister* in advance of receiving payment from the lay *client* for all work done for that *client*;

    .4   a *barrister* who has accepted *public access instructions* in any civil matter may take a proof of evidence from his *client* in that matter.

## D2.2   Licensed access rules

**R**   **Rules**

**rC132**   Subject to these rules and to compliance with the Code of Conduct (and to the *Scope of Practice, Authorisation and Licensing Rules*) a barrister in self-employed practice may accept *instructions* from a *licensed access client* in circumstances authorised in relation to that *client* by the Licensed Access Recognition Regulations https://www.barstandardsboard.org.uk/regulatory-requirements/for-barristers/licensed-access-recognition-regulations/) whether that *client* is acting for himself or another.

**rC133**   These rules apply to every matter in which a *barrister* in self-employed *practice* is instructed by a *licensed access client* save that Rules rC134.2, rC136, rC137 and rC139 do not apply to any matter in which a *licensed access client* is deemed to be a *licensed access client* by reason only of paragraph 7 or paragraph 8 of the Licensed Access Recognition Regulations (https://www.barstandardsboard.org.uk/regulatory-requirements/for-barristers/licensed-access-recognition-regulations/).

**rC134**   A *barrister* is only entitled to accept *instructions* from a *licensed access client* if at the time of giving *instructions* the *licensed access client*:

.1   is identified; and

.2   sends the *barrister* a copy of the Licence issued by the *Bar Standards Board*.

**rC135**   A *barrister* must not accept any *instructions* from a *licensed access client*:

.1   unless the *barrister* and his *chambers* are able to provide the services required of them by that *licensed access client*;

.2   if the *barrister* considers it in the interests of the lay *client* or the interests of justice that a *solicitor* or other authorised litigator or some other appropriate *intermediary* (as the case may be) be instructed either together with or in place of the *barrister*.

**rC136**   A *barrister* who accepts *instructions* from a *licensed access client* otherwise than on the terms of the Licensed Access Terms of Work:

.1   must first agree in writing the terms upon which he has agreed to do the work and the basis upon which he is to be paid;

.2   must keep a copy of the agreement in writing with the *licensed access client* setting out the terms upon which he has agreed to do the work and the basis upon which he is to be paid.

**rC137**   A *barrister* who accepts *instructions* from a *licensed access client*:

.1   must promptly send the *licensed access client*:

.2   a statement in writing that the *instructions* have been accepted (as the case may be) (1) on the standard terms previously agreed in writing with that *licensed access client* or (2) on the terms of the Licensed Access Terms of Work (and thereafter if requested a copy of the Licensed Access Terms of Work); or

.3   if he has accepted *instructions* otherwise than on such standard terms or on the terms of the Licensed Access Terms of Work, a copy of the agreement in writing with the *licensed access client* setting out the terms upon which he has agreed to do the work and the basis upon which he is to be paid;

.4    unless he has accepted *instructions* on the terms of the Licensed Access Terms of Work or on terms which incorporate the following particulars must at the same time advise the *licensed access client* in writing of:

.a    the effect of rC21 as it relevantly applies in the circumstances;

.b    unless authorised by the *Bar Standards Board* to *conduct litigation*, the fact that the *barrister* cannot be expected to perform the functions of a *solicitor* or other authorised litigator and in particular to fulfil limitation obligations disclosure obligations and other obligations arising out of or related to the *conduct of litigation*;

.c    the fact that circumstances may require the *client* to retain a *solicitor* or other authorised litigator at short notice and possibly during the case.

rC138    If at any stage a *barrister* who is instructed by a *licensed access client* considers it in the interests of the lay *client* or the interests of justice that a *solicitor* or other authorised litigator or some other appropriate *intermediary* (as the case may be) be instructed either together with or in place of the *barrister*:

.1    the *barrister* must forthwith advise the *licensed access client* in writing to instruct a *solicitor* or other authorised litigator or other appropriate *intermediary* (as the case may be); and

.2    unless a *solicitor* or other authorised litigator or other appropriate *intermediary* (as the case may be) is instructed as soon as reasonably practicable thereafter the *barrister* must cease to act and must return any *instructions*.

rC139    If at any stage a *barrister* who is instructed by a *licensed access client* considers that there are substantial grounds for believing that the *licensed access client* has in some significant respect failed to comply either with the terms of the Licence granted by the *Bar Standards Board* or (where applicable) with the terms of the Licensed Access Terms of Work the *barrister* must forthwith report the facts to the *Bar Standards Board*.

rC140    A *barrister* who accepts *instructions* from a *licensed access client* must keep a case record (whether on card or computer) which sets out:

.1    the date of receipt of the *instructions*, the name of the *licensed access client*, the name of the case, and any requirements of the *licensed access client* as to time limits;

.2    the date on which the *instructions* were accepted;

.3    the dates of subsequent *instructions*, of the despatch of advices and other written work, of conferences and of telephone conversations;

.4    when agreed, the fee.

rC141    A *barrister* who accepts *instructions* from a *licensed access client* must either himself retain or take reasonable steps to ensure that the *licensed access client* will retain for six years after the date of the last item of work done:

.1    copies of *instructions* (including supplemental *instructions*);

.2    copies of all advices given and documents drafted or approved;

.3    a list of all documents enclosed with any *instructions*;

.4    notes of all conferences and of all advice given on the telephone.

## D3. Registered European lawyers

### O Outcomes

**oC33** *Clients* are not confused about the qualifications and status of *registered European lawyers*.

### R Rules

**rC142** If you are a *registered European lawyer* and not a *barrister*, you must not hold yourself out to be a *barrister*.

**rC143** You must in connection with all professional work undertaken in England and Wales as a *registered European lawyer*:

.1 use your *home professional title*;

.2 indicate the name of your *home professional body* or the *court* before which you are entitled to practise in that *Member State*; and

.3 indicate that you are registered with the *Bar Standards Board* as a *European lawyer*.

## D4.  Unregistered barristers

### O  Outcomes

**oC34**   *Client*s who receive *legal services* from *unregistered barristers* are aware that such *unregistered barristers* are not subject to the same regulatory safeguards that would apply if they instructed a *practising barrister*.

### R  Rules

**rC144**   If you are an *unregistered barrister* and you supply *legal services* (other than as provided for in Rule C145) to any inexperienced *client* then, before supplying such services:

.1    you must explain to the *client* that:

.a    (unless you are supplying *legal services* pursuant to Rule S12) you are not acting as a *barrister*;

.b    you are not subject to those parts of the Code of Conduct and other provisions of this *Handbook* which apply only to *BSB authorised persons*;

.c    the *Bar Standards Board* will only consider *complaints* about you which concern the Core Duties or those parts of the Code of Conduct and other provisions of this *Handbook* which apply to you;

.d    (unless you are covered by professional indemnity insurance) you are not covered by professional indemnity insurance;

.e    they have the right to make a *complaint*, how they can complain, to whom, of any time limits for making a *complaint* but that they have no right to complain to the *Legal Ombudsman* about the services you supply;

.2    you must get written confirmation from the *client* that you have given this explanation.

For the purposes of this Rule C144, an inexperienced *client* includes any individual or other person who would, if you were a *BSB authorised person*, have a right to bring a *complaint* pursuant to the Legal Ombudsman Scheme Rules.

### G  Guidance

#### Guidance on Rule C144

**gC153**   For the purposes of determining whether Rule C144 applies, the people who would be entitled to complain to the *Legal Ombudsman* if you were a *BSB authorised person* are:

.1    an individual; or

.2    a business or enterprise that was a micro-enterprise within the meaning of Article 1 and Article 2(1) and (3) of the Annex to Commission Recommendation 2003/361/EC (broadly a business or enterprise with fewer than 10 employees and turnover or assets not exceeding €2 million), when it referred the *complaint* to you; or

.3    a charity with an annual income net of tax of less than £1 million at the time at which the complainant refers the *complaint* to you; or

.4    a club, association or organisation, the affairs of which are managed by its members or a committee of its members, with an annual income net of tax of less than £1 million at the time at which the complainant refers the *complaint* to you; or

.5    a trustee of a trust with an asset value of less than £1 million at the time at which the complainant refers the *complaint* to you; or

.6    a personal representative or beneficiary of the estate of a person who, before he or she died, had not referred the complaint to the *Legal Ombudsman.*

## R  Rules

**rC145**    rC144 does not apply to you if you supply *legal services*:

.1    as an *employee* or *manager* of an *authorised body*;

.2    as an *employee* or *manager* of a body subject to regulation by a professional body or regulator;

.3    as provided for in Section S.B9 (*Legal Advice Centres*);

.4    pursuant to an authorisation that you have obtained from another *approved regulator*; or

.5    in accordance with Rules S13 and S14.

## G  Guidance

### Guidance on Rule C145

**gC154**    Guidance on the disclosures which unregistered barristers should consider making to *clients* covered by Rule C145, and other *clients* who are not inexperienced *clients*, to ensure that they comply with Rule C19 and do not mislead those *clients* is available on BSB website https://www.barstandardsboard. org.uk/regulatory-requirements/bsb-handbook/code-guidance/.

| SECTION D: RULES APPLYING TO PARTICULAR GROUPS OF REGULATED PERSONS | PART 2 |
|---|---|
| D5: Cross-Border activities within the European Union and the European Economic Area | |

## D5.    Cross-border activities within the European Union and the European Economic Area

**O**  Outcomes

**oC35**    *BSB regulated persons* who undertake *cross-border activities* comply with the terms of the *Code of Conduct for European Lawyers*.

**R**  Rules

**rC146**    If you are a *BSB regulated person* undertaking *cross-border activities* then, in addition to complying with the other provisions of this *Handbook* which apply to you, you must also comply with Rules C147 to C158 below.

**G**  Guidance

### Guidance on Rule C146

**gC155**    Where the *cross-border activities* constitute *foreign work* (in other words, limb (a) of the definition of *cross-border activities*), you should note, in particular, Rules C13 and C14 and the associated guidance.

**gC156**    The purpose of this section D5 is to implement those provisions of the *Code of Conduct for European Lawyers* which are not otherwise covered by the *Handbook*. If a provision of the *Code of Conduct for European Lawyers* has not been included here then the equivalent provisions of *Handbook* need to be complied with in respect of all *cross-border activities* (including where they place a higher burden on the *BSB regulated person* than the *Code of Conduct for European Lawyers* itself which is the case, for example, in respect of the handling of *client* money (Rule C73 and C74)).

**R**  Rules

### Incompatible occupations

**rC147**    If you act in legal proceedings or proceedings before public authorities in a *CCBE State* other than the *UK*, you must, in that *CCBE State*, observe the Rules regarding incompatible occupations as they are applied to lawyers of that *CCBE State*.

**rC148**    If you are established in a *CCBE State* other than the *UK* and you wish to participate directly in commercial or other activities not connected with the practice of the law in that *CCBE State*, you must respect the Rules regarding forbidden or incompatible occupations as they are applied to lawyers of that *CCBE State*.

### Fee sharing with non-lawyers

**rC149**    You must not share your fees with a person situated in a *CCBE State* other than the *UK* who is not a lawyer except where otherwise permitted by the terms of this *Handbook* or Rule C150 below.

**rC150**    Rule C149 shall not preclude you from paying a fee, commission or other compensation to a deceased lawyer's heirs or to a retired lawyer in respect of taking over the deceased or retired lawyer's practice.

## Co-operation among lawyers of different member states

**rC151**   If you are approached by a lawyer of a *CCBE State* other than the UK to undertake work which you are not competent to undertake, you must assist that lawyer to obtain the information necessary to find and instruct a lawyer capable of providing the service asked for.

**rC152**   When co-operating with a lawyer of a *CCBE State* other than the UK you must take into account the differences which may exist between your respective legal systems and the professional organisations, competencies and obligations of lawyers in your respective states.

## Correspondence between lawyers in different CCBE states

**rC153**   If you want to send to a lawyer in a *CCBE State* other than the UK a communication which you wish to remain "confidential" or "without prejudice", you must, before sending the communication, clearly express your intention in order to avoid misunderstanding, and ask if the lawyer is able to accept the communication on that basis.

**rC154**   If you are the intended recipient of a communication from a lawyer in another *CCBE State* which is stated to be "confidential" or "without prejudice", but which you are unable to accept on the basis intended by that lawyer, you must inform that lawyer accordingly without delay.

## Responsibility for fees

**rC155**   If in the course of practice you instruct a lawyer of a *CCBE State* other than the UK to provide *legal services* on your behalf, you must pay the fees, costs and outlays which are properly incurred by that lawyer (even where the *client* is insolvent) unless:

.1   you were simply introducing the *client* to him and the lawyer of the *CCBE State* other than the UK has since had a direct contractual relationship with the *client*; or

.2   you have expressly disclaimed that responsibility at the outset, or at a later date you have expressly disclaimed responsibility for any fees incurred after that date; or the lawyer of the *CCBE State* other than the UK is, in the particular matter, practising as a lawyer in England or Wales (whether authorised by the *BSB* or any other *Approved Regulator*).

## Disputes amongst lawyers in different member states

**rC156**   If you consider that a lawyer in a *CCBE State* other than the UK has acted in breach of a rule of professional conduct you must draw the breach to the other lawyer's attention.

**rC157**   If any personal dispute of a professional nature arises between you and a lawyer in a *CCBE State* other than the UK you must first try to settle it in a friendly way.

**rC158**   You must not commence any form of proceedings against a lawyer in a *CCBE State* other than the UK on matters referred to in Rules C156 or C157 without first informing the *Bar Council* and the other lawyer's bar or law society in order to allow them an opportunity to assist in resolving the matter.

Part 3

# Scope of practice, *authorisation and licensing* rules

> **SCOPE OF PRACTICE, *AUTHORISATION AND LICENSING* RULES**
>
> Contents

PART 3

# CONTENTS

# A. APPLICATION

**rS1**    Section 3.B applies to all *BSB regulated persons* and "You" and "Your" should be construed accordingly. It provides that you must not carry on any *reserved legal activity* or practise as a *barrister* unless you are authorised to do so, and explains the different capacities within which you may work if you are so authorised and any limitations on the scope of your *practice*. It also explains the further requirements which you must follow if you intend to work in more than one capacity.

**rS2**    Section 3.C applies to *barristers* and *registered European lawyers* and sets out the basis on which they may apply for a *practising certificate* which will entitle them to practise within England and Wales.

**rS3**    Section 3.D applies to *European lawyers and provides details about how to apply to* become a *registered European lawyer* in England and Wales, thus entitling them to apply for a *practising certificate* in accordance with the provisions of 3.C.

**rS4**    Section 3.E applies to all entities wishing to be regulated by the BSB and sets out the basis upon which entities may be:

.1    authorised to practise as a *BSB authorised body*; ~~or~~

.2    ~~licensed to practise as a *BSB licensed body.*~~

**rS5**    Section 3.F applies to all BSB authorised bodies. It contains the continuing compliance requirements which apply to them.

# B. SCOPE OF PRACTICE

## B1. No practise without authorisation

**rS6**    You must not carry on any *reserved legal activity* unless you are entitled to do so under the *LSA*.

**G**  **Guidance**

### Guidance to Rule S6

**gS1**    You are not entitled to carry on any *reserved legal activity*, whether on your own behalf or acting as a *manager* or *employee*, unless you are either authorised or exempt in respect of that *reserved legal activity*. Where you are a *manager* or *employee* of a *person* who, as part of his *practice*, supplies services to *the public* or to a section of *the public* (with or without a view to profit), which consist of, or include, the carrying on of *reserved legal activities*, that *person* must also be entitled to carry on that *reserved legal activity* under the *LSA*. Authorisation in accordance with this Part 3 permits you to carry on the *reserved legal activities* specified in your authorisation.

**rS7**    You must not permit any third party who is not authorised to provide *reserved legal activities* to provide such *reserved legal activities* on your behalf.

**rS8**    If:

    .1    you are an individual and do not have a *practising certificate*; or

    .2    you are an entity and you have not been authorised ~~or licensed~~ to provide *reserved legal activities* in accordance with Section 3.E,

    then:

        .a    you may not practise as a *barrister* or a *registered European lawyer* or as a *BSB authorised body* (as appropriate); and

        .b    you are not authorised by the *Bar Standards Board* to carry on any *reserved legal activity*.

**rS9**    For the purposes of this *Handbook*, you practise as a *barrister* or a *registered European lawyer*, or a *BSB authorised body* if you are supplying *legal services* and:

    .1    you are an individual and you hold a *practising certificate*; or

    .2    you hold yourself out as a *barrister* or a *registered European lawyer* (as appropriate) or

    .3    you are an entity and you have been authorised ~~or licensed~~ to provide *reserved legal activities* in accordance with Section 3.E; or

    .4    you act as a *manager* of, or have an ownership interest in, an *authorised (non-BSB) body* and as such you are required by the rules of that body's *Approved Regulator* to hold a *practising certificate* issued by the *Bar Council* (as the case may be).

**rS10**   For the purposes of this Section 3.B1 any reference to the supply of *legal services* includes an offer to supply such services.

**rS11**   Rule S9.1 above does not apply to you if you are a *pupil* in the non-practising six months of *pupillage* if and insofar as you accept a noting brief with the permission of your *pupil-supervisor* or head of *chambers* or *HOLP*.

**rS12**   If you are an *unregistered barrister* or *registered European lawyer* but do not hold a *practising certificate* and you supply *legal services* in the manner provided for in Rules S13, S14 and S15 below, then you shall not, by reason of supplying those services:

    .1   be treated for the purposes of this Section B of Part 3 as *practising barrister* or a *registered European lawyer*; or

    .2   be subject to the rules in Part 2 of this *Handbook* or the rules in this Section 3.B which apply to *practising barristers*.

**rS13**   Rule S12 applies to you if and insofar as:

    .1   you are practising as a *foreign lawyer*; and

    .2   you do not:

        (a)   give advice on *English Law*; or

        (b)   supply *legal services* in connection with any proceedings or contemplated proceedings in England and Wales (other than as an expert witness on foreign law).

**rS14**   Rule S12 applies to you if:

    .1   you are authorised and currently permitted to carry on reserved legal activities by another *Approved Regulator*; and

    .2   you hold yourself out as a *barrister* or a *registered European lawyer* (as appropriate) other than as a *manager* or *employee* of a *BSB authorised body*; and

    .3   when supplying *legal services* to any *person* or *employer* for the first time, you inform them clearly in writing at the earliest opportunity that you are not practising as a *barrister* or a *registered European lawyer*.

**rS15**   Rule S12 applies to you provided that:

    .1   you supplied *legal services* prior to 31 March 2012 pursuant to paragraph 206.1 or 206.2 of the 8th Edition of the Code; and

    .2   if you supply any *legal services* in England and Wales, you were called to the *Bar* before 31 July 2000; and

    .3   before 31 March in each year, and promptly after any change in the details previously supplied to the *Bar Council* (acting by the *Bar Standards Board*), you provide in writing to the *Bar Council* (acting by the *Bar Standards Board*), details of the current address(es) with telephone number(s) of the office or premises from which you do so, and:

        (a)   if you are employed, the name, address, telephone number and nature of the *practice* of your *employer*; or

(b)    if you are an *employee* or *manager* of, or you have an ownership interest in, an *authorised body*, the name, address, email address, telephone number and the name of the *authorised body* and its *Approved Regulator*; and

.4    unless you only offer services to your *employer* or to the *authorised body* of which you are a *manager* or an *employee* or which you have an ownership interest in, you are (or, if you are supplying *legal services* to *clients* of your *employer* or *authorised body* of which you are an *owner*, *manager* or an *employee*, your *employer* or such body is) currently insured in accordance with the requirements of Rule C76r and you comply with the requirements of Section 2.D4.

## B2.    Provision of *reserved* legal activities and of legal services

**rS16**    You may only carry on *reserved legal activities* or supply other *legal services* in the following capacities:

.1    as a *self-employed barrister*, subject to the limitations imposed by Section 3.B3;

.2    as a *BSB authorised body*, subject to the limitations imposed by Section 3.B4;

.3    as a *manager* of a *BSB authorised body* or as an *employed barrister* (*BSB authorised body*), subject to the limitations imposed by Section 3.B5;

.4    as a *manager* of an *authorised (non-BSB) body* or as an *employed barrister* (*authorised non-BSB body*), subject to the limitations imposed by Section 3.B6;

.5    as an *employed barrister (non authorised body)*, subject to the limitations imposed by Section 3.B7; or

.6    as a *registered European lawyer* in any of the above capacities, in which case the equivalent limitations that would have applied if you were practising as a *barrister* shall apply to your *practice* as a *registered European lawyer*.

**rS17**    Where you carry on *reserved legal activities* in one of the capacities set out at Rule S16, so as to be subject to regulation by the *Bar Standards Board* in respect of those *reserved legal activities*, any other *legal services* you may supply in that same capacity will also be subject to regulation by the *Bar Standards Board*, even if unreserved.

**rS18**    You may only *practise* or be involved with the supply of *legal services* (whether *reserved legal activities* or otherwise) in more than one of the capacities listed in Rule S16 after:

.1    having obtained an amended *practising certificate* from the *Bar Standards Board* which recognises the capacities in respect of which you are intending to practise; and

.2    having agreed with each *employer* or *authorised body* with which you are involved a protocol that enables you to avoid or resolve any conflict of interests or duties arising from your *practice* and/or involvement in those capacities,

and provided always that you do not work in more than one capacity in relation to the same case or issue for the same *client*, at the same time.

**rS19**    If you are a *pupil* who has completed or been exempted from the non-practising six months of *pupillage*, you may only supply *legal services* to *the public* or exercise any right which you have by reason of being a *barrister*, if you have the permission of your *pupil-supervisor*, or head of *chambers* or *HOLP* (as appropriate).

**rS20**    Subject to Rule S21, if you are a *barrister* of less than three *years' standing*, you may:

.1    only supply *legal services* to *the public* or exercise any *right of audience* by virtue of authorisation by the *Bar Standards Board*; or

.2    only *conduct litigation* by virtue of authorisation by the *Bar Standards Board*,

if your principal place of *practice* (or if you are *practising* in a dual capacity, each of your principal places of *practice*) is either:

.a    a *chambers* or an annex of *chambers* which is also the principal place of *practice* of a relevant qualified *person* who is readily available to provide guidance to you; or

.b    an office of an organisation of which an *employee, partner, manager* or *director* is a relevant qualified *person* who is readily available to provide guidance to you.

**rS21**    If you are an *employed barrister (non-authorised body)* and you are only providing *legal services*, exercising a *right of audience* or conducting litigation for those *persons* listed at Rule S39.1 to rS39.6, then the place of *practice* from which you perform such duties is only required to be an office of an organisation of which an *employee, partner, manager* or *director* is a relevant qualified *person* who is readily available to provide guidance to you if you are of less than one year's standing.

**rS22**    In Rule S20 and Rule S21 above, the references to "qualified *person*" mean the following:

### Supply of legal services to the public – qualified person

.1    Where you are a *barrister* intending to supply *legal services* to the *public*, a *person* shall be a qualified *person* for the purpose of Rule S20 if he:

.a    has been entitled to *practise* and has *practised* as a *barrister* (other than as a *pupil* who has not completed *pupillage* in accordance with the *Bar Training Regulations*) or as a *person* authorised by another *Approved Regulator* for a period (which need not have been as a *person* authorised by the same *Approved Regulator*) for at least six years in the previous eight years; and

.b    for the previous two years has made such *practice* his primary occupation; and

.c    is not acting as a qualified *person* in relation to more than two other people; and

.d    has not been designated by the *Bar Standards Board* as unsuitable to be a qualified *person*.

### The exercise of a right of audience – qualified person

.2    Where:

.a    you are a *barrister* exercising a *right of audience* in England and Wales, a *person* is a qualified *person* for the purpose of Rule S20 if he:

.i    has been entitled to *practise* and has *practised* as a *barrister* (other than as a *pupil* who has not completed *pupillage* in accordance with the *Bar Training Regulations*) or as a *person* authorised by another *Approved Regulator* for a period (which need not have been as a *person* authorised by the same *Approved Regulator*) for at least six years in the previous eight years; and

.ii    for the previous two years:

(1)    has made such *practice* his primary occupation; and

(2)    has been entitled to exercise a *right of audience* before every *court* in relation to all proceedings; and

.iii    is not acting as a qualified *person* in relation to more than two other people; and

.iv    has not been designated by the *Bar Standards Board* as unsuitable to be a qualified *person*; or

.b    you are a *barrister* exercising a *right of audience* in a *Member State* other than the United Kingdom pursuant to the *Establishment Directive*, or in Scotland or Northern Ireland pursuant to the European Communities (Lawyer's Practice) Regulations 2000, a *person* shall be a qualified *person* for the purposes of Rule S20 if he:

.i    has been designated by the *Bar Standards Board* as possessing qualifications and experience in that state or country which are equivalent to the qualifications and experience required by Rule S22.3.a.i and S22.3.a.ii above; and

.ii    is not acting as a qualified *person* in relation to more than two other people; and

.iii    has not been designated by the *Bar Standards Board* as unsuitable to be a qualified *person*.

### The exercise of a right to conduct litigation – qualified person

.3    Where:

.a    you are a *barrister* exercising a *right to conduct litigation* in England and Wales, a *person* is a qualified *person* for the purpose of Rule S20 if he:

.i    has been entitled to *practise* and has *practised* as a *barrister* (other than as a *pupil* who has not completed *pupillage* in accordance with the *Bar Training Regulations*) or as a *person* authorised by another *Approved Regulator* for a period (which need not have been as a *person* authorised by the same *Approved Regulator*) for at least six years in the previous eight years; and

.ii    for the previous two years has made such *practice* his primary occupation; and

.iii    is entitled to *conduct litigation* before every *court* in relation to all proceedings; and

.iv    is not acting as a qualified *person* in relation to more than two other people; and

.v    has not been designated by the *Bar Standards Board* as unsuitable to be a qualified *person*; or

.b    you are a *barrister* exercising a *right to conduct litigation* in a *Member State* other than the United Kingdom pursuant to the *Establishment Directive*, or in Scotland or Northern Ireland pursuant to the European Communities (Lawyer's Practice) Regulations 2000, a *person* is a qualified *person* for the purposes of Rule S20 and S21 if he:

.i    has been designated by the *Bar Standards Board* as having qualifications and experience in that state or country which are equivalent to the qualifications and experience required by Rule S22.3.a.i and S22.3.a.ii above; and

.ii    is not acting as a qualified *person* in relation to more than two other people; and

.iii    has not been designated by the *Bar Standards Board* as unsuitable to be a qualified *person*..

## G  Guidance

### Guidance to Rules S20 and S22

**gS2**    If you are a *practising barrister* of less than three *years' standing* and you are authorised to *conduct litigation*, you will need to work with a qualified *person* who is authorised to do litigation as well as with someone who meets the criteria for being a qualified *person* for the purpose of providing services to *the public* and exercising *rights of audience*. This may be, but is not necessarily, the same *person*.

## B3.  Scope of practice as a self-employed barrister

**rS23**  Rules S24 and S25 below apply to you where you are acting in your capacity as a self-*employed barrister*, whether or not you are acting for a fee.

**rS24**  You may only supply *legal services* if you are appointed or instructed by the *court* or instructed:

.1  by a *professional client* (who may be an *employee* of the *client*); or

.2  by a *licensed access client*, in which case you must comply with the *licensed access rules*; or

.3  by or on behalf of any other *client*, provided that:

.a  the matter is *public access instructions* and:

.i  you are entitled to provide public access work and the *instructions* are relevant to such entitlement; and

.ii  you have notified the *Bar Standards Board* that you are willing to accept *instructions* from lay *clients*; and

.iii  you comply with the *public access rules*; or

.b  the matter relates to the *conduct of litigation* and

.i  you have a litigation extension to your *practising certificate*; and

.ii  you have notified the *Bar Standards Board* that you are willing to accept *instructions* from lay *clients*.

**G**  **Guidance**

### Guidance to Rule S24

**gS3**  References to professional *client* in Rule S24.1 include *foreign lawyers* and references to *client* in Rule S24.3 include *foreign clients*.

**gS4**  If you are instructed by a *foreign lawyer* to provide advocacy services in relation to *court* proceedings in England and Wales, you should advise the *foreign lawyer* of any limitation on the services you can provide. In particular, if *conduct of litigation* will be required, and you are not authorised to *conduct litigation* or have not been instructed to do so, you should advise the *foreign lawyer* to take appropriate steps to instruct a *person* authorised to *conduct litigation* and, if requested, assist the *foreign lawyer* to do so. If it appears to you that the *foreign lawyer* is not taking reasonable steps to instruct someone authorised to *conduct litigation*, then you should consider whether to return your *instructions* under rules C25 and C26.

**rS25**  Subject to Rule S26, you must not in the course of your *practice* undertake the management, administration or general conduct of a *client's* affairs.

**rS26**  Nothing in Rule S25 prevents you from undertaking the management, administration or general conduct of a client's affairs where such work is *foreign work* performed by you at or from an office outside England and Wales which you have established or joined primarily for the purposes of carrying out that particular *foreign work* or *foreign work* in general.

# B4.   Scope of practice as a BSB authorised body

**rS27**   Rules rS28 and rS29 apply to you where you are acting in your capacity as a *BSB authorised body*.

**rS28**   You may only supply *legal services* if you are appointed or instructed by the *court* or instructed:

.1   by a professional *client* (who may be an *employee* of the *client*);

.2   by a *licensed access client*, in which case you must comply with the *licensed access rules*; or

.3   by or on behalf of any other *client*, provided that:

.a   at least one manager or employee is suitably qualified and experienced to undertake public access work; and

.b   you have notified the *Bar Standards Board* that you are willing to accept *instructions* from lay *clients*.

## G   Guidance

### Guidance to Rule rS28

**gS5**   References to professional client in Rule rS28.1 include foreign lawyers and references to client in Rule rS28.3 include foreign clients.

**gS6**   If you are instructed to provide advocacy services in relation to *court* proceedings in England and Wales by a *foreign lawyer* or other professional *client* who does not have a *right* to *conduct litigation* pursuant to Rule rS28.1 and you are not authorised to *conduct litigation* yourself or you are otherwise not instructed to conduct the litigation in the particular matter, then you must:

.1   advise the *foreign lawyer* to take appropriate steps to instruct a *solicitor* or other authorised litigator to conduct the litigation and, if requested, take reasonable steps to assist the *foreign lawyer* to do so;

.2   cease to act and return your *instructions* if it appears to you that the *foreign lawyer* is not taking reasonable steps to instruct a *solicitor* or other authorised litigator to conduct the litigation; and

.3   not appear in *court* unless a *solicitor* or other authorised litigator has been instructed to conduct the litigation.

**gS7**   The public access and licensed access rules do not apply to *BSB authorised bodies* as their circumstances will vary considerably. Nevertheless those rules provide guidance on best practice. In the case of a barrister, "suitably qualified and experienced to undertake public access work" will mean successful completion of the public access training required by the BSB or an exemption for the requirement to do the training. If you are a *BSB authorised body*, you will also need to have regard to relevant provisions in the Code of Conduct (Part 2 of this Handbook), especially C17, C21.vii, C21.viii and C22. You will therefore need to consider whether:

.1    You have the necessary skills and experience to do the work, including, where relevant, the ability to work with a vulnerable client;

.2    The employees who will be dealing with the *client* are either authorised to *conduct litigation* or entitled to do public access work or have had other relevant training and experience;

.3    it would be in the best interests of the client or of the interests of justice for the client to instruct a solicitor or other professional client if you are not able to provide such services;

.4    If the matter involves the *conduct of litigation* and you are not able or instructed to *conduct litigation*, whether the client will be able to undertake the tasks that you cannot perform for him;

.5    The *client* is clear about the services which you will and will not provide and any limitations on what you can do, and what will be expected of him;

.6    If you are not able to act in legal aid cases, the *client* is in a position to take an informed decision as to whether to seek legal aid or proceed with public access.

**gS8**    You will also need to ensure that you keep proper records.

**rS29**    Subject to Rule rS30, you must not in the course of your *practice* undertake the management, administration or general conduct of a *client's* affairs

**rS30**    Nothing in Rule rS29 prevents you from undertaking the management, administration or general conduct of a client's affairs where such work is foreign work performed by you at or from an office outside England and Wales which you have established or joined primarily for the purposes of carrying out that particular foreign work or foreign work in general.

## B5. Scope of practice as a manager of a BSB authorised body or as an employed barrister (BSB authorised body)

**rS31**    Rules rS32 and rS33 below apply to you where you are acting in your capacity as a *manager* of a *BSB authorised body* or as an *employed barrister* (*BSB authorised body*).

**rS32**    You may only supply *legal services* to the following *person*s:

.1    the *BSB authorised body*; or

.2    any *employee, director,* or company secretary of the *BSB authorised body,* in a matter arising out of or relating to that *person*'s *employment*;

.3    any *client* of the *BSB authorised body*;

.4    if you supply *legal services* at a *Legal Advice Centre, clients* of the *Legal Advice Centre*; or

.5    if you supply *legal services* free of charge, members of the public.

**rS33**    Subject to Rule rS34, you must not in the course of your *practice* undertake the management, administration or general conduct of a *client's* affairs.

**rS34**    Nothing in Rule rS33 prevents you from undertaking the management, administration or general conduct of a client's affairs where such work is foreign work performed by you at or from an office outside England and Wales which you have established or joined primarily for the purposes of carrying out that particular foreign work or foreign work in general.

**SECTION B: SCOPE OF PRACTICE**

B6: Scope of practice as a manager of an authorised (non-BSB) body or as an employed barrister (authorised non-BSB body)

PART 3

## B6. Scope of practice as a manager of an authorised (non-BSB) body or as an employed barrister (authorised non-BSB body)

**rS35** Rules S36 and S37 apply to you where you are acting in your capacity as a *manager* of an *authorised (non-BSB) body* or as an *employed barrister* (*authorised non-BSB body*)

**rS36** You may only supply *legal services* to the following *person*s:

.1 the *authorised (non-BSB) body*;

.2 any *employee, director* or company secretary of the *authorised (non-BSB) body* in a matter arising out of or relating to that *person*'s *employment*;

.3 any *client* of the *authorised (non-BSB) body*;

.4 if you provide *legal services* at a *Legal Advice Centre*, *clients* of the *Legal Advice Centre*; or

.5 if you supply *legal services* free of charge, members of the public.

**rS37** You must comply with the rules of the *Approved Regulator* or *licensing authority* of the *authorised (non-BSB) body*.

# B7.  Scope of practice as an employed barrister (non authorised body)

**rS38**    *Rule* S39 *applies to you where you are acting in your capacity as an employed barrister (non authorised body).*

**rS39**    Subject to s. 15(4) of the Legal Services Act 2007, you may only supply *legal services* to the following *person*s:

.1    your *employer*;

.2    any *employee*, *director* or company secretary of your *employer* in a matter arising out of or relating to that *person's employment*;

.3    if your *employer* is a public authority (including the Crown or a Government department or agency or a local authority), another public authority on behalf of which your *employer* has made arrangements under statute or otherwise to supply any *legal services* or to perform any of that other public authority's functions as agent or otherwise;

.4    if you are employed by or in a Government department or agency, any Minister or Officer of the Crown;

.5    if you are employed by a *trade association*, any individual member of the association;

.6    if you are, or are performing the functions of, a *Justices' clerk*, the Justices whom you serve;

.7    if you are employed by the *Legal Aid Agency*, members of the public;

.8    if you are employed by or at a *Legal Advice Centre*, *clients* of the *Legal Advice Centre*;

.9    if you supply *legal services* free of charge, members of the public; or

.10    if your *employer* is a *foreign lawyer* and the *legal services* consist of foreign work, any *client* of your *employer*.

## B8.    Scope of practice of a barrister called to undertake a particular case

**rS40**    If you are called to the *Bar* under rQ98 of the *Bar Training Regulations* (temporary membership of the *Bar*), you may not *practise* as a *barrister* other than to conduct the case or cases specified in the certificate referred to in rQ99.

# B9.  Legal Advice Centres

**rS41**    You may supply *legal services* at a *Legal Advice Centre* on a voluntary or part time basis and, if you do so, you will be treated for the purposes of this *Handbook* as if you were employed by the *Legal Advice Centre*.

**rS42**    If you supply *legal services* at a *Legal Advice Centre* to *clients* of a *Legal Advice Centre* in accordance with Rule S41:

.1    you must not in any circumstances receive either directly or indirectly any fee or reward for the supply of any *legal services* to any *client* of the *Legal Advice Centre* other than a salary paid by the *Legal Advice Centre*;

.2    you must ensure that any fees in respect of *legal services* supplied by you to any *client* of the *Legal Advice Centre* accrue and are paid to the *Legal Advice Centre*, or to the Access to Justice Foundation or other such charity as prescribed by order made by the Lord Chancellor under s.194(8) of the Legal Services Act 2007; and

.3    you must not have any financial interest in the *Legal Advice Centre*.

## G    Guidance

### Guidance to Rules S41 and S42

**gS9**    You may provide *legal services* at a *Legal Advice Centre* on an unpaid basis irrespective of the capacity in which you normally work.

**gS10**    If you are a *self-employed barrister*, you do not need to inform the Bar Standards Board that you are also working for a *Legal Advice Centre*.

**gS11**    Transitional arrangements under the *LSA* allow *Legal Advice Centres* to provide *reserved legal activities* without being authorised. When this transitional period comes to an end, the Rules relating to providing services at *Legal Advice Centres* will be reviewed.

## B10. Barristers authorised by other approved regulators

**rS43**    If you are authorised by another *Approved Regulator* to carry on a *reserved legal activity* and currently permitted to *practise* by that *Approved Regulator*, you must not *practise* as a *barrister* and you are not eligible for a *practising certificate*.

# C. PRACTISING CERTIFICATE RULES

## C1.   Eligibility for practising certificates and litigation extensions

**rS44**   In this Section 3.C, references to "you" and "your" are references to *barristers* and *registered European lawyers* who are intending to apply for authorisation to *practise* as a *barrister* or a *registered European lawyer* (as the case may be) or who are otherwise intending to apply for a *litigation extension* to their existing *practising certificate*.

**rS45**   You are eligible for a *practising certificate* if:

.1   you are a *barrister* or *registered European lawyer* and you are not currently *suspended* from *practice* and have not been disbarred; and

.2   you meet the requirements of Rules S46.1, S46.2, S46.3 or S46.4; and

.3   [either:

.a   within the last 5 years either (i) you have held a *practising certificate*; or (ii) you have satisfactorily completed (or have been exempted from the requirement to complete) either the non-practising period of 6 months of pupilage or 12 months of pupilage; or

.b   if not, you have complied with such training requirements as may be imposed by the *Bar Standards Board*.][1]

**rS46**   You are eligible for:

.1   a *full practising certificate* if either:

.a   you have satisfactorily completed 12 months *pupillage*; or

.b   you have been exempted from the requirement to complete 12 months of *pupillage*; or

.c   on 30 July 2000, you were entitled to exercise full *rights of audience* by reason of being a *barrister*; or

.d   you were called to the *Bar* before 1 January 2002 and:

.i   you notified the *Bar Council* that you wished to exercise a *right of audience* before every *court* and in relation to all proceedings; and

---

1. Rule rS45.3 does not come into effect until 1 April 2015

.ii  you have complied with such training requirements as the *Bar Council* or the *Bar Standards Board* may require or you have been informed by the *Bar Council* or the *Bar Standards Board* that you do not need to comply with any such further requirements;

in each case, before 31 March 2012;

.2  a *provisional practising certificate* if you have satisfactorily completed (or have been exempted from the requirement to complete) the non-practising period of 6 months of *pupillage* and at the time when you apply for a *practising certificate* you are registered as a *Pupil*;

.3  a *limited practising certificate* if you were called to the *Bar* before 1 January 2002 but you are not otherwise eligible for a *full practising certificate* in accordance with Rule S46.1 above; or

.4  a *registered European lawyer's practising certificate* if you are a *registered European lawyer*.

**rS47**    You are eligible for a litigation extension:

.1  where you have or are due to be granted a *practising certificate* (other than a *provisional practising certificate*); and

.2  where you are:

.a  more than three *years' standing*; or

.b  less than three *years' standing*, but your principal place of *practice* (or if you are *practising* in a dual capacity, each of your principal places of *practice*) is either:

.i  a *chambers* or an annex of *chambers* which is also the principal place of *practice* of a qualified *person* (as that term is defined in Rule S22.3) who is readily available to provide guidance to you; or

.ii  an office of an organisation of which an *employee*, *partner*, *manager* or *director* is a qualified *person* (as that term is defined in Rule S22.3) who is readily available to provide guidance to you;

.3  you have the relevant administrative systems in place to be able to provide *legal services* direct to *clients* and to administer the *conduct of litigation*; and

.4  you have the procedural knowledge to enable you to *conduct litigation* competently.

## G    Guidance

### Guidance to Rules S47.3

**gS12**    You should refer to the more detailed guidance published by the *Bar Standards Board* from time to time which can be found at https://www.barstandardsboard.org.uk/regulatory-requirements/for-barristers/authorisation-to-conduct-litigation/. This provides more information about the evidence you may be asked for to show that you have procedural knowledge to enable you to *conduct litigation* competently.

## C2.  Applications for practising certificates and litigation extensions by barristers and registered European lawyers

**rS48**    You may apply for a *practising certificate* by:

.1    completing the relevant application form supplied by the *Bar Council* (acting by the *Bar Standards Board*) and submitting it to the *Bar Council* (acting by the *Bar Standards Board*); and

.2    submitting such information in support of the application as may be prescribed by the *Bar Council* (acting by the *Bar Standards Board*); and

.3    paying (or undertaking to pay in a manner determined by the *Bar Council*) the appropriate *practising certificate fee* in the amount determined in accordance with Rule S50 (subject to any reduction pursuant to Rule S53).

**rS49**    You may apply for a litigation extension to a *practising certificate* (other than a *provisional practising certificate*) by:

.1    completing the relevant application form supplied by the *Bar Council* (acting by the *Bar Standards Board*) and submitting it to the *Bar Council* (acting by the *Bar Standards Board*); and

.2    confirming that you meet the relevant requirements of Rule S47.1;

.3    paying (or undertaking to pay in a manner determined by the *Bar Council*) the *application fee* (if any) and the *litigation extension fee* (if any);

.4    confirming, in such form as the *Bar Standards Board* may require from time to time, that you have the relevant administrative systems in place to be able to provide *legal services* direct to *clients* and to administer the *conduct of litigation* in accordance with Rule S47.3; and

.5    confirming, in such form as the *Bar Standards Board* may require from time to time, that you have the procedural knowledge to enable you to *conduct litigation* competently in accordance with Rule S47.4.

**rS50**    An application will only have been made under either Rule rS48 or rS49 once the *Bar Council* (acting by the *Bar Standards Board*) has received, in respect of the relevant application, the application form in full, together with the *application fee*, *the practising certificate fee*, *the litigation extension fee* (if any, or an undertaking to pay such fees in a manner determined by the *Bar Council*), all the information required in support of the application and confirmation from you, in the form of a declaration, that the information contained in, or submitted in support of, the application is full and accurate.

**rS51**    On receipt of the application, the *Bar Council* (acting by the *Bar Standards Board*) may require, from you or a third party (including, for the avoidance of doubt, any *BSB authorised body*), such additional information, documents or references as it considers appropriate to the consideration of your application.

**rS52**    You are *person*ally responsible for the contents of your application and any information submitted to the *Bar Council* (acting by the *Bar Standards Board*) by you or on your behalf and you must not submit (or cause or permit to be submitted on your behalf) information to the *Bar Council* (acting by the *Bar Standards Board*) which you do not believe is full and accurate.

**rS53**    When applying for a *practising certificate* you may apply to the *Bar Council* for a reduction in the *practising certificate fee payable by you* if your gross fee income or salary is less than such amount as the *Bar Council* may decide from time to time. Such an application must be submitted by completing the form supplied for that purpose by the *Bar Council* which can be found through Barrister Connect.

## C3. Practising certificate fees and litigation extension fees

**rS54**    The *practising certificate fee* shall be the amount or amounts prescribed in the Schedule of *Practising Certificate* Fees issued by the *Bar Council* from time to time, and any reference in these Rules to the "*appropriate practising certificate fee*" or the "*practising certificate fee payable by you*" refers to the *practising certificate fee* payable by you pursuant to that Schedule, having regard , amongst other things, to:

.1    the different annual *practising certificate fees* which may be prescribed by the *Bar Council* for different categories of *barristers*, e.g. for Queen's Counsel and junior counsel, for *barristers* of different levels of seniority, and/or for *barristers practising* in different capacities and/or according to different levels of income (i.e. *self-employed barristers*, *employed barristers*, *managers* or *employees* of authorised bodies or *barristers practising* with dual capacity);

.2    any reductions in the annual *practising certificate fees* which may be permitted by the *Bar Council* in the case of *practising certificates* which are valid for only part of a *practising certificate year*;

.3    any discounts from the annual *practising certificate fee* which may be permitted by the *Bar Council* in the event of payment by specified methods;

.4    any reduction in, or rebate from, the annual *practising certificate fee* which may be permitted by the *Bar Council* on the grounds of low income, change of category or otherwise; and

.5    any surcharge or surcharges to the annual *practising certificate fee* which may be prescribed by the *Bar Council* in the event of an application for renewal of a *practising certificate* being made after the end of the *practising certificate year*.

**rS55**    The *litigation extension fee* shall be the amount or amounts prescribed by the *Bar Council* from time to time, and in these Rules the "*appropriate litigation extension fee*" or the "*litigation extension fee payable by you*" is the *litigation extension fee* payable by you having regard to, among other things:

.1    any reductions in the annual *litigation extension fees* which may be permitted by the *Bar Council* in the case of *litigation extensions* which are valid for only part of a *practising certificate year*;

.2    any discounts from the annual *litigation extension fee* which may be permitted by the *Bar Council* in the event of payment by specified methods;

.3    any reduction in, or rebate from, the annual *litigation extension fee* which may be permitted by the *Bar Council* on the grounds of low income, change of category, or otherwise; and

.4    any surcharge or surcharges to the annual *litigation extension fee* which may be prescribed by the *Bar Council* in the event of an application for a *litigation extension* being made at a time different from the time of your application for a *practising certificate*.

**rS56**    If you have given an undertaking to pay the *practising certificate fee* or *the litigation extension fee*, you must comply with that undertaking in accordance with its terms.

## C4.  Issue of practising certificates and litigation extensions

**rS57**    The *Bar Council* (acting by the *Bar Standards Board*) shall not issue a *practising certificate* to a *barrister* or *registered European lawyer*:

.1    who is not eligible for a *practising certificate*, or for a *practising certificate* of the relevant type; or

.2    who has not applied for a *practising certificate*; or

.3    who has not paid or not otherwise undertaken to pay in a manner determined by the Bar Council, the appropriate *practising certificate fee*; or

.4    who is not insured against claims for professional negligence as provided for in Rule C76.

**rS58**    The *Bar Council* (acting by the *Bar Standards Board*) shall not grant a *litigation extension* to a *barrister* or *registered European lawyer*:

.1    in circumstances where the Bar Council (acting by the Bar Standards Board) is not satisfied that the requirements of *litigation extension* are met; or

.2    who has not applied for a *litigation extension*; or

.3    who has not paid or not otherwise undertaken to pay in a manner determined by the Bar Council, the appropriate *application fee* (if any) and the *litigation extension fee* (if any).

**rS59**    The *Bar Council* (acting by the *Bar Standards Board*) may refuse to issue a *practising certificate* or to grant a *litigation extension*, or may revoke a *practising certificate* or a *litigation extension* in accordance with Section 3.C5, if it is satisfied that the information submitted in support of the application for the *practising certificate* or *litigation extension* (as the case may be) is (or was when submitted) incomplete, inaccurate or incapable of verification, or that the relevant *barrister* or *registered European lawyer*:

.1    does not hold adequate insurance in accordance with Rule C76;

.2    has failed and continues to fail to pay the *appropriate practising certificate fee* or *litigation extension fee* when due;

.3    would be, or is, *practising* in breach of the provisions of Section 3.B; or

.4    has not complied with any of the requirements of the Continuing Professional Development Regulations applicable to him.

**rS60**    When the *Bar Council* (acting by the *Bar Standards Board*) issues a *practising certificate* or a *litigation extension*, it shall:

.1    inform the relevant *barrister* or *registered European lawyer* of that fact; and

.2    in the case of a *practising certificate*, publish that fact, together with the name and *practising address* of the *barrister* and *registered European lawyer* and the other details specified in Rule S61 in the register on the *Bar Standards Board*'s website; or

.3    in the case of a litigation extension:

.a    issue a revised and updated *practising certificate* to incorporate an express reference to such litigation extension in accordance with Rule S66; and

.b    amend the register maintained on the Bar Standards Board's website to show that the relevant *barrister* or *registered European lawyer* (as the case may be) is now authorised to *conduct litigation*.

**rS61**    A *practising certificate* must state:

.1    the name of the *barrister or registered European lawyer* (as the case may be);

.2    the period for which the *practising certificate* is valid;

.3    the *reserved legal activities* which the *barrister or registered European lawyer* (as the case may be) to whom it is issued is thereby authorised to carry on;

.4    the capacity (or capacities) in which the *barrister or registered European lawyer* (as the case may be) practises; and

.5    whether the *barrister or registered European lawyer* (as the case may be) is registered with the *Bar Council* as a *Public Access* practitioner.

**rS62**    A *practising certificate* may be valid for a *practising certificate year* or part thereof and for one month after the end of the *practising certificate year*.

**rS63**    A *full practising certificate* shall authorise a *barrister* to exercise a *right of audience* before every *court* in relation to all proceedings.

**rS64**    A *provisional practising certificate* shall authorise a *pupil* in his second six to exercise a *right of audience* before every *court* in relation to all proceedings.

**rS65**    A *limited practising certificate* shall not authorise a *barrister* to exercise a *right of audience*, save that it shall authorise a *barrister* to exercise any *right of audience* which he had by reason of being a *barrister* and was entitled to exercise on 30 July 2000.

**rS66**    A *practising certificate* shall authorise a *barrister* to *conduct litigation* in relation to every *court* and all proceedings if the *practising certificate* specifies a *litigation extension*.

**rS67**    Every *practising certificate* issued to a *barrister* shall authorise the *barrister*:

.1    to undertake:

.a    *reserved instrument activities*;

.b    *probate activities*;

.c    the *administration of oaths*; and

.d    *immigration work*.

**rS68**    A *registered European lawyer's practising certificate* shall authorise a *registered European lawyer* to carry on the same *reserved legal activities* as a *full practising certificate* issued to a *barrister*, save that:

.1    a *registered European lawyer* is only authorised to exercise a *right of audience* or *conduct litigation* in proceedings which can lawfully only be provided by a *solicitor, barrister* or other qualified *person*, if he acts in conjunction with a *solicitor* or *barrister* authorised to *practise* before the *court*, tribunal or public authority concerned and who could lawfully exercise that right; and

.2    a *registered European lawyer* is not authorised to prepare for remuneration any instrument creating or transferring an interest in land unless he has a *home professional title* obtained in Denmark, the Republic of Ireland, Finland, Sweden, Iceland, Liechtenstein, Norway, the Czech Republic, Cyprus, Hungary or Slovakia.

## C5. Amendment and revocation of practising certificates and litigation extensions

**rS69** You must inform the *Bar Council* (acting by the *Bar Standards Board*) as soon as reasonably practicable, and in any event within 28 days, if any of the information submitted in support of your *practising certificate* application form or *litigation extension* application form:

.1 was incomplete or inaccurate when the application form was submitted; or

.2 changes before the expiry of your *practising certificate*.

**rS70** If you wish to:

.1 change the capacity in which you *practise* (e.g. if you change from being an *employed barrister* or a *manager* or *employee* of a *BSB authorised body* or an *authorised (non-BSB) body* to a *self-employed barrister*, or vice versa, or if you commence or cease *practice* in a dual capacity); or

.2 cease to be authorised to *conduct litigation*,

before the expiry of your *practising certificate*, you must:

.a notify the *Bar Council* (acting by the *Bar Standards Board*) of such requested amendment to your *practising certificate*; and

.b submit to the *Bar Council* (acting by the *Bar Standards Board*) such further information as the *Bar Council* (acting by the *Bar Standards Board*) may reasonably require in order for them to be able to determine whether or not to grant such proposed amendment to your *practising certificate*; and

.c within 14 days of demand by the *Bar Council* pay to the *Bar Council* the amount (if any) by which the *annual practising certificate fee* which would apply to you in respect of your amended *practising certificate* exceeds the *annual practising certificate fee* which you have already paid (or undertaken to pay) to the *Bar Council*. In the event that the revised annual *practising certificate fee* is less than the amount originally paid to the *Bar Council* (acting by the *Bar Standards Board*) or in circumstances where you wish to cease to be authorised to *conduct litigation*, the *Bar Council* (acting by the *Bar Standards Board*) is not under any obligation to refund any part of the annual *practising certificate fee* or *litigation extension fee* already paid although it may in its absolute discretion elect to do so in the circumstances contemplated by the Schedule of *Practising Certificate* Fees issued by the *Bar Council* from time to time.

**rS71** The *Bar Council* (acting by the *Bar Standards Board*) may amend a *practising certificate* if it is satisfied that any of the information contained in the relevant application form was inaccurate or incomplete or has changed, but may not amend a *practising certificate* (except in response to a request from the *barrister or a registered European lawyer*) without first:

.1 giving written notice to the *barrister or registered European lawyer* of the grounds on which the *practising certificate* may be amended; and

.2 giving the *barrister or registered European lawyer* a reasonable opportunity to make representations.

**rS72** The *Bar Council* (acting by the *Bar Standards Board*) shall endorse a *practising certificate* to reflect any qualification restriction or condition imposed on the *barrister* or *registered European lawyer* by the *Bar Council* (acting by the *Bar Standards Board*) or by a *Disciplinary Tribunal, Interim Suspension or Disqualification Panel, Fitness to Practise Panel,* the *Visitors to the Inns of Court* or the High Court.

**rS73** The *Bar Council* (acting by the *Bar Standards Board*):

.1 shall revoke a *practising certificate*:

.a if the *barrister* becomes authorised to practise by another *approved regulator*;

.b if the *barrister or registered European lawyer* is disbarred or *suspended* from *practice* as a *barrister* or *registered European lawyer* whether on an interim basis under section D of Part 5 or otherwise under section B of Part 5;

.c if the *barrister* or *registered European lawyer* has notified the *Bar Council* or the *Bar Standards Board* that he no longer wishes to have a *practising certificate*; and

.2 may revoke a *practising certificate*:

.a in the circumstances set out in Rule S59; or

.b if the *barrister or registered European lawyer* has given an undertaking to pay the appropriate *practising certificate fee* and fails to comply with that undertaking in accordance with its terms,

but in either case only after:

(i) giving written notice to the relevant *barrister or registered European lawyer* of the grounds on which the *practising certificate* may be revoked; and

(ii) giving the relevant *barrister or registered European lawyer* a reasonable opportunity to make representations.

**rS74** The *Bar Council* (acting by the *Bar Standards Board*):

.1 shall revoke a *litigation extension* if the *barrister* or *registered European lawyer* has notified the *Bar Council* or the *Bar Standards Board* that he no longer wishes to have the *litigation extension*; and

.2 may revoke a *litigation extension*:

.a in the circumstances set out in Rule S59; or

.b if the *barrister or registered European lawyer* has given an undertaking to pay the appropriate *litigation extension fee* and fails to comply with that undertaking in accordance with its terms,

but in either case only after:

(i) giving written notice to the relevant *barrister or registered European lawyer* of the grounds on which the *litigation extension* may be revoked; and

(ii) giving the relevant *barrister or registered European lawyer* a reasonable opportunity to make representations.

## C6.  Applications for review

**rS75**    If you contend that the *Bar Council* (acting by the *Bar Standards Board*) has:

.1    wrongly failed or refused to issue or amend a *practising certificate*; or

.2    wrongly amended or revoked a *practising certificate*; or

.3    wrongly failed or refused to issue a *litigation extension*; or

.4    wrongly revoked a *litigation extension*,

in each case in accordance with this Section 3.C, then you may lodge an application for review with the *Qualifications Committee* using the form supplied for that purpose by the *Bar Standards Board* which can be found here https://www.barstandardsboard.org.uk/qualifying-as-a-barrister/forms-and-guidelines/bar-training-waivers-and-exemption-forms/. For the avoidance of doubt, this Section 3.C6 does not apply to any amendment or revocation of a *practising certificate* or *litigation extension* made by order of a *Disciplinary Tribunal, Interim Suspension or Disqualification Panel, Fitness to Practise Panel*, the *Visitors to the Inns of Court* or the High Court.

**rS76**    The decision of the *Bar Council* (acting by the *Bar Standards Board*) shall take effect notwithstanding any application for review being submitted in accordance with Rule S75. However, the *Bar Council* (acting by the *Bar Standards Board*) may, in its absolute discretion, issue a temporary *practising certificate* or *litigation extension* to a *barrister* or *registered European lawyer* who has lodged an application for review.

**rS77**    If the *Qualifications Committee* finds that the *Bar Council* (acting by the *Bar Standards Board*):

.1    has wrongly failed or refused to issue a *practising certificate*, then the *Bar Council* (acting by the *Bar Standards Board*) must issue such *practising certificate* as ought to have been issued; or

.2    has wrongly failed or refused to amend a *practising certificate*, then the *Bar Council* (acting by the *Bar Standards Board*) must make such amendment to the *practising certificate* as ought to have been made; or

.3    has wrongly amended a *practising certificate*, then the *Bar Council* (acting by the *Bar Standards Board*) must cancel the amendment; or

.4    has wrongly revoked a *practising certificate*, then the *Bar Council* (acting by the *Bar Standards Board*) must re-issue the *practising certificate*; or

.5    has wrongly failed or refused to grant a *litigation extension*, then the *Bar Council* (acting by the *Bar Standards Board*) must grant such *litigation extension* as ought to have been granted; or

.6    has wrongly revoked a *litigation extension*, then the *Bar Council* (acting by the *Bar Standards Board*) must re-grant the *litigation extension*.

# B. BAR TRAINING RULES

## B1. Purpose of the Bar training rules

**oQ1** To ensure that any *person* who qualifies to *practise* as a *barrister* is a fit and proper *person*, and competent to do so.

**R** | **Rules**

**rQ3** To be called to the *Bar* by an *Inn* a *person* must:

  .1 be a member of that *Inn*;

  .2 complete (or be exempted from):

  (a) the Academic Stage, and

  (b) the *Vocational stage*

  of training; and

  .3 fulfil any applicable requirement to attend *qualifying sessions*.

**rQ4** To become qualified to *practise* as a *barrister* a *person* must:

  .1 be called to the *Bar* by an *Inn*;

  .2 complete (or be exempted from) the Professional Stage of training; and

  .3 satisfy such further requirements as are set out in Part 3 of this *Handbook*.

**rQ5** The *Bar Standards Board* may charge such fees as it prescribes for dealing with applications, conducting assessments or examinations and issuing certificates under this Section 4.B.

**rQ6** Any function or power which under this Section 4.B is exercisable by the *Bar Standards Board* may be delegated (and sub-delegated) to any committee, body or *person* to the extent permitted by the standing orders of the *Bar Standards Board*.

## B2.   Admissions to an Inn of Court

### Eligibility for admission

**rQ7**    To be eligible for *admission to an Inn* under this Section 4.B a *person* must:

.1    have the necessary educational qualifications; and

.2    be a fit and proper *person* to become a *practising barrister*.

**rQ8**    A *person* has the necessary educational qualifications to be admitted to an *Inn* if that *person*:

.1    is reading for a qualifying law degree; or

.2    is attending (or has been accepted for and is about to attend) a Conversion Course; or

.3    has completed (or been exempted under Section 4.B7 from) the Academic Stage of training.

**rQ9**    A *person* is a fit and proper *person* to become a *practising barrister* if:

.1    there is no reason to expect that that *person*, if admitted to an *Inn,* will engage in conduct which is dishonest or which otherwise makes that *person* unfit to become a *practising barrister*; and

.2    that *person* does not suffer from serious incapacity due to mental disorder (within the meaning of the Mental Health Act 1983), addiction to alcohol or drugs or any other condition which makes that *person* unfit to become a *practising barrister*.

**rQ10**    In the case of an applicant who is authorised to *practise* by another *Approved Regulator* or who is a *Qualified European Lawyer*, a *certificate of good standing* is to be treated as conclusive evidence that the applicant is a fit and proper *person* to become a practising *barrister*.

**rQ11**    A *person* whose application for *admission to an Inn* has been rejected on the ground that that *person* is not a fit and proper *person* to become a practising *barrister* or who has been expelled from an *Inn* because of a disciplinary offence may not apply for *admission to an Inn* unless a period of at least five years (or such other period as the *Bar Standards Board* may determine in the particular case) has elapsed from the date of such rejection or expulsion.

### Application procedure

**rQ12**    To apply for *admission to an Inn* a *person* ("the applicant") must submit to the Inn:

.1    a duly completed and signed application including an *admission declaration* in the form prescribed by the *Bar Standards Board* from time to time;

.2    two certificates of good character which comply with the requirements in Rule Q13 below or, if the applicant is a *qualified lawyer*, a *certificate of good standing*, which (in either case) was issued within the previous three months; and

.3    the fee prescribed by the Inn.

### Certificates of good character

**rQ13**    A certificate of good character must contain the information specified by the *Bar Standards Board* from time to time and be provided by a professional *person* or *person* of standing in the community who:

.1    has known the applicant for at least one year;

.2    does not have a close family or personal relationship with the applicant; and

.3    has read the *admission declaration* submitted by the applicant under Rule Q12.1.

## Decision to admit or refuse admission

**rQ14**    Before deciding whether to admit the applicant, the *Inn* may make any further enquiries or require the applicant to provide any further information that it considers relevant.

**rQ15**    The *Inn* must admit the applicant if the applicant:

.1    is eligible for *admission to an Inn* and has given the undertaking on the *admission declaration* to commence the *Vocational stage* within five years of *admission to an Inn* and complete that Stage within ten years of admission; and

.2    has complied with Rule Q12,

otherwise the *Inn* must reject the application and inform the applicant of its reasons for doing so.

**rQ16**    If the applicant falls within Rule Q17, the *Inn* must refer the question whether the applicant is a fit and proper *person* to become a *practising barrister* to the Inns' Conduct Committee to decide and must notify the applicant that it has done so.

**rQ17**    An applicant falls within this Rule Q17 if:

.1    the applicant applicant has been convicted of a *Criminal offence* (or is the subject of pending Criminal Proceedings); or

.2    the applicant has been convicted of a disciplinary offence by a professional or regulatory body (or is the subject of pending proceedings for such an offence); or

.3    the applicant has been found guilty of an academic offence by a higher education institution (and has not successfully appealed against that finding); or

.4    the applicant has been the subject of a *Bankruptcy Order* or *director's disqualification* order or has entered into an individual voluntary arrangement with creditors; or

.5    the applicant has previously been refused admission to or expelled from an *Inn*; or

.6    there is any other circumstance which in the opinion of the *Inn* calls into question the applicant's fitness to become a *practising barrister*.

**rQ18**    When the Inns' Conduct Committee is asked to decide whether the applicant is a fit and proper *person* to become a *practising barrister*, it must send a report of its decision and the reasons for the decision to the applicant and to the Inn.

**rQ19**    If the Inns' Conduct Committee decides that the applicant is not a fit and proper *person* to become a *practising barrister* or if the *Inn* rejects an application for admission for any other reason, the applicant may request a review of the decision under Section 4.B10, provided that the request is made in writing to the *Bar Standards Board* within one month of the date when notice of the decision was given.

**rQ20**    If on a review under Section 4.B10 the *Bar Standards Board* is satisfied that the applicant is eligible for *admission to an Inn* and has complied with Rule Q12, the *Inn* must admit the applicant.

## B3.  The Academic Stage

**rQ21**    A *person* completes the Academic Stage of training by:

.1    obtaining a qualifying law degree; or

.2    obtaining a qualifying degree and successfully completing a Conversion Course.

**rQ22**    For the purpose of Rule Q21.1 a qualifying law degree is a qualifying degree approved by the *Bar Standards Board* which includes a course of study of the *foundations of legal knowledge*.

**rQ23**    For the purpose of Rule Q21.2 a qualifying degree is:

.1    a degree of the required standard awarded by a *University* in the United Kingdom following a course of study of the minimum period; or

.2    a degree awarded by a *University* or establishment of equivalent level outside the United Kingdom which the *Bar Standards Board* accepts as equivalent to a degree satisfying the requirements of Rule Q23.1.

and a *person* obtains a qualifying degree on being adjudged to have successfully completed the academic requirements of the degree irrespective of when the degree is actually conferred.

**rQ24**    For the purpose of Rule Q23.1, unless the *Bar Standards Board* on an application showing good grounds permits otherwise, the required standard is first or second class honours.

**rQ25**    A Conversion Course is a course approved by the *Bar Standards Board* which includes study of the *foundations of legal knowledge*.

**rQ26**    For the purpose of Rules Q22 and Q25, *foundations of legal knowledge* means those subjects the study of which is prescribed by the *Bar Standards Board* for the purposes of obtaining a qualifying law degree and for inclusion in any Graduate Conversion Course, and which currently comprise:

.1    Obligations I (Contract)

.2    Obligations II (Tort)

.3    Criminal Law

.4    Public Law

.5    Property Law

.6    Equity & The Law of Trusts

.7    Foundations of EU Law

## B4.   The Vocational Stage

**rQ27**   A *person* starts the *vocational stage* of training on starting to attend at a *Bar Professional Training Course*, and completes the *vocational stage* on being certified by the course provider that he has successfully completed a *Bar Professional Training Course*.

**rQ28**   Before starting the *vocational stage*, a *person* must:

   .1   have completed (or been exempted under Section 4.B7 from) the Academic Stage; and

   .2   have successfully completed the *Bar Course Aptitude Test* which is set by the *Bar Standards Board* from time to time; and

   .3   be a member of an *Inn* of Court.

**rQ29**   A *person* may not start the *vocational stage* more than five years after completing the Academic Stage except with the permission of the *Bar Standards Board* and after complying with any condition which *the Bar Standards Board* may impose.

# B5.  The Professional Stage

**rQ30**  A *person* starts the professional stage of training when he starts *pupillage* in accordance with this Section 4.B5 and completes the professional stage by:

.1  satisfactorily completing 12 months of *pupillage* and such further training as may be required by the *Bar Standards Board*; and

.2  being issued with a *full qualification certificate.*

**rQ31**  Before starting the professional stage, a *person* must have completed (or been exempted under Section 4.B7 from) the *vocational stage.*

**rQ32**  A *person* may not start the Professional Stage more than five years after completing the *vocational stage* except with the permission of the *Bar Standards Board* and after complying with any condition which the *Bar Standards Board* may impose.

## Pupillage

**rQ33**  *Pupillage* is divided into two parts:

.1  a non-practising period of six months; and

.2  a practising period of six months.

**rQ34**  Except with the written permission of the *Bar Standards Board*, the non-practising period of *pupillage* must be done :

.1  in a *Member State* of the European Union; and

.2  in a continuous period of six months.

**rQ35**  Except with the written permission of the *Bar Standards Board*, the practising period of *pupillage* must:

.1  start within 12 months after completion of the non-practising period;

.2  be done in a *Member State*; and

.3  be completed within an overall period of nine months.

**rQ36**  Any period of *pupillage* must provide training which is adequate and which complies with such criteria as may be published by the *Bar Standards Board.*

**rQ37**  Except as provided in Rule Q60, any period of *pupillage* must be done :

.1  in an *approved training organisation*; and

.2  with a *barrister* who is a registered *pupil supervisor.*

**rQ38**  During any period of *pupillage* the *pupil* must;

.1  be diligent in receiving the instruction given; and

.2  observe all legal and professional obligations of confidence.

## Approved training organisations

**rQ39** The *Bar Standards Board* may authorise any organisation as an *approved training organisation* subject to such terms as the *Bar Standards Board* may from time to time determine.

**rQ40** The *Bar Standards Board* may withdraw approval from an *approved training organisation* if it considers after investigation:

.1 that *pupillage* training provided by the organisation is or has been seriously deficient; or

.2 that the organisation has not made proper arrangements for dealing with pupils and *pupillage* in accordance with the Code of Conduct.

**rQ41** The *Bar Standards Board* will give notice in writing:

.1 in the case of a decision to refuse to designate an organisation as an *approved training organisation*, to that organisation; and

.2 in the case of a decision to withdraw approval from an *approved training organisation*, to:

.a that organisation;

.b any *person* who is undertaking or has agreed to undertake a *pupillage* in that organisation; and

.c the *Inn* of which any such *person* is a member.

**rQ42** Any *person* or organisation to whom the *Bar Standards Board* is required to give notice of a decision under Rule Q41 may ask for a review of the decision under Section 4.B10, provided that the request is made in writing to the *Bar Standards Board* within one month of the date when notice of the decision was given.

**rQ43** If the *Bar Standards Board* withdraws approval from an *approved training organisation*, the organisation may not claim repayment of any *pupillage* award or other sum paid to any *pupil* or prospective *pupil*.

## Acting as a pupil supervisor

**rQ44** A *barrister* may act as a *pupil supervisor* if the *barrister*:

.1 is on the register of approved *pupil supervisor*s kept by the *Bar Standards Board*;

.2 has a current practising certificate; and

.3 has regularly practised as a *barrister* during the previous two years.

## Registration as a pupil supervisor

**rQ45** The *Bar Standards Board* may enter a *barrister* on the register of approved *pupil supervisor*s if the *barrister* is approved by an *Inn* of which the *barrister* is a member.

**rQ46** The *Bar Standards Board* may refuse to enter a *barrister* on the register of approved *pupil supervisor*s if the *Bar Standards Board* finds that the *barrister* is unsuitable for any reason to act as a *pupil supervisor*.

**rQ47** If the *Bar Standards Board* refuses to enter a *barrister* on the register of approved *pupil supervisor*s, it will notify the *barrister* and the *Inn* which approved the *barrister* as a *pupil supervisor* of its decision and of the reasons for it.

**rQ48**    An *Inn* must approve a *barrister* as a *pupil supervisor* if:

    .1    the *barrister* has a current *practising certificate*;

    .2    the *Inn* is satisfied that the *barrister* has the necessary experience and is otherwise suitable to act as a *pupil supervisor*; and

    .3    the *barrister* has submitted an application in accordance with Rule Q50.

**rQ49**    To have the necessary experience to act as a *pupil supervisor* a *barrister* should normally:

    .1    have practised in the United Kingdom or another *Member State* as a *barrister* (other than as a *pupil* who has not completed *pupillage* in accordance with this Section 4.B5) or as a *person* authorised to exercise a *right of audience* or to *conduct litigation* by another *Approved Regulator* for a period for at least six years in the previous eight years; and

    .2    for the previous two years have regularly practised as a *barrister* and been entitled to exercise a *right of audience* before every *court* in England and Wales in relation to all proceedings.

## Application procedure to become a pupil supervisor

**rQ50**    A *barrister* who wishes to be entered on the register of approved *pupil supervisor*s must submit to the *Inn* an application in the form currently prescribed by the *Bar Standards Board*. The application must be supported:

    .1    by an independent *person* who is a High Court Judge or Circuit Judge, a Leader of a Circuit, a Deputy High Court Judge, a Recorder, a Queen's Counsel, a Master of the Bench of an Inn, Treasury Counsel or a *person* of comparable standing who is able to comment from *person*al knowledge on the applicant's suitability to act as a *pupil supervisor*; and

    .2    Subject to Rule Q50.3 below,

    .3    in the case of a *self-employed barrister*, by the applicant's Head of *chambers*, or

        .a    in the case of an employed *barrister*, by a more senior lawyer employed in the same organisation and who has direct knowledge of the work of the applicant;

    .4    If the applicant is a Head of *chambers*, or there is no more senior lawyer employed in the same organisation with the required knowledge, or for any other reason the support of the *person* referred to in Rule Q50.2 is not available, by a second *person* falling within Rule Q50.1 above.

## Training of pupil supervisors

**rQ51**    The *Bar Standards Board*, in consultation with the Inns, may and will normally require *pupil supervisor*s to undertake training before they may be entered or after they have been entered on the register of approved *pupil supervisor*s.

## Removal from the register of pupil supervisors

**rQ52**    The *Bar Standards Board* may remove a *barrister*'s name from the register of approved *pupil supervisor*s if the *barrister*:

    .1    ceases to practise as a *barrister* or is *suspended* from *practice* as a *barrister*; or

    .2    requests the *Bar Standards Board* in writing to be removed from the register; or

    .3    fails to complete any training required under Rule Q51; or

.4    is found by the *Bar Standards Board* to be unsuitable for any reason to act as a *pupil supervisor*; or

.5    has not acted as a *pupil supervisor* for the previous five years.

**rQ53**    If the *Bar Standards Board* decides that a *barrister*'s name should be removed from the register of approved *pupil supervisor*s, it will notify the *barrister* and the *Inn* which approved the *barrister* as a *pupil supervisor* of its decision and of the reasons for it.

## Duties of pupil supervisors

**rQ54**    A *pupil supervisor* must when responsible for supervising any pupil:

.1    take all reasonable steps to provide the *pupil* with adequate tuition, supervision and experience;

.2    have regard to any *pupillage* guidelines issued by the *Bar Standards Board* and to the Equality and Diversity Rules of the Code of Conduct; and

.3    ensure that the *pupil* prepares for and attends any further training required by the *Bar Standards Board* such as advocacy training provided by the *pupil*'s Circuit or Inn.

**rQ55**    A *pupil supervisor* may not be responsible for supervising more than one *pupil* at a time except with the approval in writing of the *Bar Standards Board*.

## Complaints about pupil supervisors

**rQ56**    If any complaint or other matter which appears to affect the suitability of a *barrister* to continue to act as a *pupil supervisor* comes to the notice of the *Inn* which approved the *barrister*, the *Inn* must inform the *Bar Standards Board* of the matter.

**rQ57**    If any complaint or other matter which appears to affect the suitability of a *barrister* to continue to act as a *pupil supervisor* comes to the notice of the *Bar Standards Board*, the *Bar Standards Board* will investigate the matter.

**rQ58**    After such an investigation, the *Bar Standards Board* may:

.1    dismiss any complaint; or

.2    take no action; or

.3    if in its opinion the matter is such as to require informal treatment, draw it to the *barrister*'s attention in writing and if thought desirable direct the *barrister* to attend upon a nominated *person* for advice; or

.4    if in its opinion the conduct disclosed shows that the *barrister* is unsuitable to act as a *pupil supervisor*, remove the name of the *barrister* from the register of approved *pupil supervisor*s.

**rQ59**    A *barrister* whose application to be approved as a *pupil supervisor* is rejected or whose name is removed from the register of approved *pupil supervisor*s may ask for a review of the decision under Section 4.B10, provided that the request is made in writing to the *Bar Standards Board* within one month of the date when notice of the decision was given.

## External training

**rQ60**    With the written permission of the *Bar Standards Board*, part or all of the practising period of *pupillage* may be satisfied by training:

.1    with a *solicitor*, judge or other suitably *qualified lawyer* who is not a registered *pupil supervisor*; and/or

.2    in an organisation which is not an *approved training organisation* but which, in the opinion of the *Bar Standards Board*, provides suitable training and experience.

## Advertising

**rQ61**    Subject to Rule C114, all vacancies for *pupillage* must be advertised on a website designated by the *Bar Council* and the following information must be provided:

.1    In respect of *chambers*:

.a    the name and address of *chambers*;

.b    the number of tenants;

.c    a brief statement of the work done by *Chambers*, e.g., "predominantly criminal";

.d    the number of *pupillage* vacancies;

.e    the level of award;

.f    the procedure for applying;

.g    the minimum educational or other qualifications required;

.h    the closing date for applications;

.i    the date by which the decisions will be made;

.2    in respect of entities:

.a    the name and address of the *BSB authorised body*;

.b    the number of *barristers* employed by that entity;

.c    a brief statement of the work done  by the entity, eg, "predominantly criminal";

.d    the number of *pupillage* vacancies;

.e    the level of award;

.f    the procedure for application;

.g    the minimum educational or other qualifications required;

.h    the closing date for  applications;

.i    the date by which the decisions will be made.

## Registration of pupillage

**rQ62**    Before starting any period of *pupillage* (including any period of external training) a *person* must apply to the *Bar Standards Board* for registration of the *pupillage* by submitting an application in the form prescribed by the *Bar Standards Board*.

**rQ63**   The *Bar Standards Board* will register the *pupillage* if it is satisfied that the application has been duly completed and that the *pupillage* complies with this Section 4.B5.

**rQ64**   If a *person* applies to the *Bar Standards Board* for registration of a *pupillage* after the *pupillage* has started, the *pupillage* will be treated as having started on the date the application is received, unless the *Bar Standards Board* permits otherwise.

**rQ65**   If the *Bar Standards Board* refuses to register a *pupillage*, it will inform the *pupil* in writing of its decision and of the reasons for it.

**rQ66**   If the *Bar Standards Board* refuses to register a *pupillage*, the *pupil* may ask for a review of the decision under Section 4.B10, provided that the request is made in writing to the *Bar Standards Board* within one month of the date when notice of the decision was given.

**rQ67**   If any of the information provided in an application for registration of a *pupillage* changes before the *pupillage* has been completed, the *pupil* must promptly notify the *Bar Standards Board* in writing of the change.

## Qualification certificates

**rQ68**   On completion of the non-practising period of *pupillage*, the *Bar Standards Board* will issue the *pupil* with a *provisional qualification certificate* provided that the *pupil* has been called to the *Bar* under Section 4.B9 and the *Bar Standards Board* is satisfied:

   .1   that the *pupil* has satisfactorily completed the non-practising period of *pupillage* and any further training required under Rule Q30.1; and

   .2   that the *pupillage* is registered and complied with this Section 4.B5.

**rQ69**   When the *pupil* completes  the practising period of *pupillage*, the *Bar Standards Board* will issue him with a *full qualification certificate*, if the *pupil* has a *provisional qualification certificate* and the *Bar Standards Board* is satisfied:

   .1   that the *pupil* has satisfactorily completed the practising period of *pupillage* and any further training required under Rule Q30.1; and

   .2   that the *pupillage* is registered, and has complied with this Section 4.B5.

**rQ70**   For the purpose of this Section 4.B5, a *pupil* is to be treated as having satisfactorily completed a period of *pupillage* if the *pupil*:

   .1   has been diligent in receiving the instruction given; and

   .2   has achieved the minimum level of competence required of a *pupil* at the end of the relevant period.

**rQ71**   The *Bar Standards Board* may accept as evidence that a *pupil* has satisfactorily completed any period of *pupillage* a certificate to this effect from the *pupil supervisor* (or the *person* responsible for external training) with whom the *pupil* has completed that period.

**rQ72**   If a *pupil supervisor* is unable or unwilling to provide a certificate that a *pupil* has satisfactorily completed a period of *pupillage*, the *Bar Standards Board* may accept such a certificate signed by the Head of *chambers* or *person* in charge of *pupillage* in the training organisation where the *pupillage* has been done if the certificate contains a satisfactory explanation of why the *pupil supervisor* has not signed it.

**rQ73**   If the *Bar Standards Board* is not satisfied:

.1   that the *pupil* has satisfactorily completed a period of *pupillage*, and/or

.2   that the *pupillage* is registered and complied with this Section 4.B5;

the *Bar Standards Board* may specify further training which the *pupil* must satisfactorily complete before the *Bar Standards Board* will issue the *pupil* with a *provisional qualification certificate* or a *full qualification certificate* (as the case may be).

**rQ74**   If the *Bar Standards Board* refuses to issue a *provisional qualification certificate* or a *full qualification certificate*, the *pupil* may ask for a review of the decision under Section 4.B10, provided that the request is made in writing to the *Bar Standards Board* within one month of the date when notice of the decision was given.

## B6.  Qualifying sessions

**rQ75**    In this Part 4.B6 a qualifying session means an event (or part of an event) of an educational and collegiate nature arranged by or on behalf of an Inn;

**rQ76**    Subject to Rules rQ77 and rQ82 , a *person* who is admitted to an *Inn* must attend 12 *qualifying sessions* during a period of no more than five years ending on the date on which that *person* is called to the Bar.

**rQ77**    An *Inn* may on an application showing such exceptional grounds as satisfy criteria agreed by all four Inns waive or modify the requirement to attend *qualifying sessions*.

**rQ78**    Each *Inn* is responsible, in cooperation with the other Inns, for:

.1    ensuring that suitable *qualifying sessions* are available for its members; and

.2    deciding what requirements must be satisfied for a *person* to be credited with attendance at one or more qualifying session*s*; and

.3    agreeing criteria which specify the grounds on which the requirement to attend qualifying sessions may be waived or modified.

# B7. Exemptions from training requirements

**rQ79**   The *Bar Standards Board* may grant exemptions from part or all of:

    .1    the Academic Stage,

    .2    the *vocational stage*, and/or

    .3    the Professional Stage,

of training.

**rQ80**   In exercising its discretion whether to grant an exemption from part or all of any Stage of training, the *Bar Standards Board* will determine whether the relevant knowledge and experience of the applicant make it unnecessary for the applicant to do such training.

**rQ81**   An exemption from part or all of any Stage of training may be granted unconditionally or subject to conditions, which may include in an appropriate case:

    .1    a requirement to do training instead of the training prescribed by this Section 4.B; and/or

    .2    a condition that the applicant must pass a *Bar* Transfer Test.

**rQ82**   Where the *Bar Standards Board* exempts a *person* from the Vocational or Professional Stage of training, it may also:

    .1    grant exemption in whole or in part from the requirement to attend *qualifying sessions*; and

    .2    specify the period within which any requirement to attend *qualifying sessions* must be fulfilled, which may be a period ending after the *person* concerned has been called to the *Bar* and in the case of a Specially Qualified Applicant is usually a period of three years during which the applicant must attend six *qualifying sessions* unless special circumstances apply.

## Applications

**rQ83**   An application for exemption under this Section must be in such form as may be prescribed by the *Bar Standards Board* and contain or be accompanied by the following:

    .1    details of the applicant's educational and professional qualifications and experience;

    .2    evidence (where applicable) that the applicant is or has been entitled to exercise rights of audience before any court, specifying the rights concerned and the basis of the applicant's entitlement to exercise such rights

    .3    any other representations or evidence on which the applicant wishes to rely in support of the application;

    .4    verified English translations of every document relied on which is not in the English language; and

    .5    the prescribed fee.

**rQ84**   Before deciding whether to grant any exemption under this Section, the *Bar Standards Board* may make any further enquiries or require the applicant to provide any further information that it considers relevant.

**rQ85**   A *person* whose application for exemption is rejected may ask for a review of the decision under Section 4.B10, provided that the request is made in writing to the *Bar Standards Board* within one month of the date when notice of the decision was given.

## Full exemption

**rQ86**   If the *Bar Standards Board* is satisfied that an applicant falls within Rule Q87, the *Bar Standards Board* will:

.1   exempt the applicant from any Stage of training prescribed by this Section 4.B which the applicant has not fulfilled;

.2   issue the applicant with a *full qualification certificate*; and

.3   authorise the applicant to practise as a *barrister* on his being admitted to an *Inn* and called to the *Bar* under Section 4.B9 subject to complying with the Code of Conduct.

**rQ87**   The following categories of *person* fall within this Rule Q87:

.1   a *person* who has been granted rights of audience by an *authorised body* and is entitled to exercise those rights in relation to all proceedings in all courts of England and Wales;

.2   subject to Rule Q88, a *person* who has been granted rights of audience by an *authorised body* and is entitled to exercise those rights in relation to either all proceedings in the High Court or all proceedings in the Crown Court of England and Wales (but not both);

.3   a *barrister* of Northern Ireland who has successfully completed *pupillage* in accordance with the rules of the *Bar* of Northern Ireland;

.4   subject to Rule Q89, a *Qualified European Lawyer.*

**rQ88**   The *Bar Standards Board* may exceptionally require an applicant who falls within Rule Q87.2 to do part or all of the practising six months of *pupillage* if it considers this necessary having regard in particular to the knowledge, professional experience and intended future *practice* of the applicant.

**rQ89**   Subject to Rules Q91 to Q95, the *Bar Standards Board* may require a *Qualified European Lawyer* to pass a *Bar Transfer Test* if the *Bar Standards Board* determines that:

.1   the matters covered by the education and training of the applicant differ substantially from those covered by the Academic, Vocational and Professional Stages of training; and

.2   the knowledge acquired by the applicant in the course of his professional experience does not fully cover this substantial difference.

## Registered European Lawyers

**rQ90**   The Rules governing registration as a *Registered European Lawyer* in Section 3.D of this *Handbook.*

**rQ91**   The *Bar Standards Board* may not require an applicant who is a *Registered European Lawyer* and who falls within Rule Q93 or Q94 to pass a *Bar Transfer Test* unless it considers that the applicant is unfit to *practise* as a *barrister.*

**rQ92**   In considering whether to require an applicant who falls within Rule Q94 to pass a *Bar Transfer Test,* the *Bar Standards Board* must:

.1   take into account the professional activities the applicant has pursued while a *Registered European Lawyer* and any knowledge and professional experience gained of, and any training received in, the law of any part of the United Kingdom and of the rules of professional conduct of the Bar; and

.2   assess and verify at an interview the applicant's effective and regular pursuit of professional activities and capacity to continue the activities pursued.

**rQ93**    To fall within this Rule Q93 an applicant must have:

    .1    for a period of at least three years been a *Registered European Lawyer*; and

    .2    for a period of at least three years effectively and regularly pursued in England and Wales under a Home Professional Title professional activities in the law of England and Wales.

**rQ94**    To fall within this Rule Q94 an applicant must have:

    .1    for a period of at least three years been a *Registered European Lawyer*; and

    .2    for a period of at least three years effectively and regularly pursued in England and Wales professional activities under a Home Professional Title; and

    .3    for a period of less than three years effectively and regularly pursued in England and Wales under a Home Professional Title professional activities in the law of England and Wales.

**rQ95**    For the purpose of this Section 4.B17, activities are to be regarded as effectively and regularly pursued if they are actually exercised without any interruptions other than those resulting from the events of everyday life.

## Partial exemption

**rQ96**    If the *Bar Standards Board* is satisfied that an applicant falls within Rule rQ97, the *Bar Standards Board* will:

    .1    exempt the applicant from the Academic Stage and the *vocational stage* and, if the *Bar Standards Board* thinks fit, from part or all of the Professional Stage of training; and

    .2    if the applicant is exempted from the whole of the non-practising six months of *pupillage*, issue the applicant with a *provisional qualification certificate*.

**rQ97**    The following categories of *person* fall within this Rule Q97:

    .1    a *person* who has been granted rights of audience by another Approved Regulator and is entitled to exercise those rights in relation to any class of proceedings in any of the *Senior Courts* or all proceedings in county courts or magistrates' courts in England and Wales;

    .2    a *Qualified Foreign Lawyer* who has for a period of at least three years regularly exercised full rights of audience in courts which administer law substantially similar to the common law of England and Wales;

    .3    a teacher of the law of England and Wales of experience and academic distinction.

## Temporary call to the Bar of Qualified Foreign Lawyers

**rQ98**    A *Qualified Foreign Lawyer* ("the applicant") who falls within Rule Q97.2 is entitled to be admitted to an *Inn* and called to the *Bar* on a temporary basis for the purpose of appearing as counsel in a particular case before a *court* of England and Wales without being required to satisfy any other requirements of this Section 4.B if the applicant has:

    .1    obtained from the *Bar Standards Board* and submitted to an *Inn* a *Temporary Qualification Certificate* specifying the case for the purposes of which the applicant is authorised to be called to the Bar;

    .2    duly completed and signed a *call declaration* in the form prescribed by the *Bar Standards Board* from time to time; and

    .3    paid the fee prescribed by the Inn.

**rQ99**    The *Bar Standards Board* will issue a Temporary Qualification Certificate if the applicant submits to the *Bar Standards Board*:

    .1    evidence which establishes that the applicant is a *Qualified European Lawyer* or falls within Rule rQ97.2;

    .2    a *certificate of good standing*; and

    .3    evidence which establishes that a Professional *Client* wishes to instruct the applicant to appear as counsel in the case or cases for the purposes of which the applicant seeks temporary *call* to the Bar.

**rQ100**    *Admission to an Inn* and *call* to the *Bar* under Rule rQ98 take effect when the applicant is given notice in writing by the *Inn* that the applicant has been admitted to the *Inn* and called to the *Bar* under Rule rQ98 and automatically cease to have effect on conclusion of the case or cases specified in the applicant's Temporary Qualification Certificate.

## B8.  Conduct of students

**rQ101**  References in this Section to "the Inn" are to any *Inn* of which the *student* concerned is a member.

**rQ102**  A *student* must observe any regulations about to conduct and discipline made by the Inn.

**rQ103**  If a *student*:

.1  becomes the subject of *pending Criminal Proceedings* or is convicted of a *Criminal offence*, or

.2  becomes the subject of pending disciplinary proceedings or is convicted of a disciplinary offence by a professional or regulatory body, or

.3  is the subject of a *Bankruptcy Order* or *directors disqualification order* or enters into an individual voluntary arrangement with creditors, or

.4  is found guilty of an academic offence by a higher education institution (and has not successfully appealed against that finding),

the *student* must immediately notify the *Inn* in writing.

**rQ104**  This Rule Q104 applies where notification is given or a *complaint* or report is made or it appears to an *Inn* from information given in the *student*'s *call declaration* or otherwise that a *student* of the *Inn* has or may have:

.1  made any false statement or acted in breach of any undertaking given in the *student*'s *admission declaration* or *call declaration*; or

.2  while a *student*:

.a  committed any breach of any regulations made by the *Inn* concerning the conduct and discipline of its members; or

.b  been convicted of a *Criminal offence*; or

.c  been convicted of a disciplinary offence by a professional or regulatory body; or

.d  been the subject of a *Bankruptcy Order* or *directors disqualification order* or entered into an individual voluntary arrangement with creditors; or

.e  been found guilty by the course provider of cheating or other misconduct on a *Bar Professional Training Course* (and has not successfully appealed against that finding); or

.f  otherwise been guilty of any conduct discreditable to a member of an Inn.

**rQ105**  Where Rule Q104 applies, the Inn:

.1  may make any enquiries or require the *student* to provide such information as it may think fit; and

.2  must consider whether the matter is a *serious matter*.

**rQ106**  If the *Inn* decides that the matter is not a *serious matter*, the *Inn* may deal with the matter under its internal disciplinary procedure and at the conclusion of that procedure may:

.1  dismiss any complaint; or

.2  decide to take no action; or

    .3    advise the *student* as to future conduct; or

    .4    reprimand the *student*; or

    .5    ban the *student* for a specified period from using some or all of the Inn's facilities.

**rQ107**    A *student* may appeal from a decision of an *Inn* under its internal disciplinary procedure to the Inns' Conduct Committee.

**rQ108**    If at any stage the *Inn* decides that the matter is a *serious matter*, the *Inn* must refer the matter to the Inns' Conduct Committee for determination. After determining the matter, the Inns' Conduct Committee must send a report of its findings and reasons to the *student* and to the Inn.

**rQ109**    If the Inns' Conduct Committee (or the *Bar Standards Board* on a review under Section 4.B10) finds a *serious matter* proved, it may:

    .1    advise the *student* as to future conduct; or

    .2    reprimand the *student*; or

    .3    order that the *student*'s *call* to the *Bar* be postponed for a specfied period; or

    .4    direct that the *student* be expelled from the *Inn* (in which case the *Inn* must expel the *student*).

**rQ110**    If the Inns' Conduct Committee finds a *serious matter* proved, the *student* may ask for a review under Section 4.B10 of the decision of the Inns' Conduct Committee, provided that the request is made in writing to the *Bar Standards Board* within one month of the date when notice of the decision was given.

**rQ111**    Where Rule Q104 applies, the *student* is not entitled to be called to the Bar:

    .1    until the *Inn* has decided that the matter is not a *serious matter*; or

    .2    if the *Inn* decides that the matter is a *serious matter*, until the matter has been determined; or

    .3    if the Inns' Conduct Committee (or the *Bar Standards Board* following a review under Section 4.B10) orders that the *student*'s *call* to the *Bar* be postponed for a specified period, until that period has expired.

# B9.  Call to the Bar

## Requirements for call

**rQ112**    Subject to Rules Q111, Q113 and, Q117 a *person* is entitled to be called to the *Bar* by an *Inn* of which that *person* is a member if that *person* has:

    .1    completed or been exempted from the *vocational stage* of training in accordance with this Section 4.B;

    .2    complied with any applicable requirement to attend *qualifying sessions*;

    .3    submitted to the *Inn* a duly completed and signed a *call declaration* in the form prescribed by the *Bar Standards Board* from time to time; and

    .4    paid the fee prescribed by the Inn.

**rQ113**    Before deciding whether a *person* who has complied with Rule Q112 ("the candidate") is entitled to be called to the Bar, the Inn:

    .1    may make any enquiries or require the candidate to provide any further information that it considers relevant;

    .2    must consider whether Rule rQ104 applies; and

    .3    if Rule rQ104 applies, must give effect to Rule Q111.

**rQ114**    If the *Inn* decides that the candidate is not entitled to be called to the Bar, the *Inn* must inform the candidate of its decision and of the reasons for it.

**rQ115**    If the *Inn* decides that the candidate is not entitled to be called to the Bar, the candidate may request a review of the decision under Section 4.B10, provided that the request is made in writing to the *Bar Standards Board* within one month of the date when notice of the decision was given by the Inn.

**rQ116**    If on a review under Section 4.B10 the *Bar Standards Board* decides that the candidate is entitled to be called to the Bar, the *Inn* must *call* the candidate to the Bar.

**rQ117**    Where it is alleged that the *call declaration* made by a *barrister* on *call* is false in any material respect or that the *barrister* has engaged before *call* in conduct which is dishonest or otherwise discreditable to a *barrister* and which was not, before *call*, fairly disclosed in writing to the Benchers of the *Inn* calling him or where any undertaking given by a *barrister* on *call* to the *Bar* is breached in any material respect that shall be treated as an allegation of a breach of this *Handbook* and will be subject to the provisions of Part 5.

## Call days and procedure

**rQ118**    Calls to the *Bar* will take place on such days as may be authorised from time to time by the Inns' Council.

**rQ119**    A candidate must be called to the *Bar* in *person* unless given written permission by the *Inn* to be absent from the *call* ceremony.

## B10. Review and appeals

**rQ120**    Where provision is made under this Section 4.B for a review by the *Bar Standards Board* of a decision, any request for such a review must be accompanied by:

  .1    a copy of any notice of the decision and the reasons for it received by the *person* or organisation requesting the review ("the applicant");

  .2    where the decision is a decision of an *Inn* or of the Inns' Conduct Committee, copies of all documents submitted or received by the applicant which were before the *Inn* or the Inns' Conduct Committee (as the case may be);

  .3    any further representations and evidence which the applicant wishes the *Bar Standards Board* to take into account; and

  .4    the prescribed fee.

**rQ121**    Where the decision under review is a decision of an *Inn* or of the Inns' Conduct Committee, the *Bar Standards Board* will invite the *Inn* or the Inns' Conduct Committee (as the case may be) to comment on any further representations and evidence which the applicant submits under Rule Q120.3.

**rQ122**    On a review under this Section the *Bar Standards Board*:

  .1    may affirm the decision under review or substitute any other decision which could have been made on the original application;

  .2    may in an appropriate case reimburse the fee paid under Rule Q120.4; and

  .3    will inform the applicant and any other interested *person* of its decision and the reasons for it.

**rQ123**    Where under this Section 4.B provision is made for a review by the *Bar Standards Board* of a decision, no appeal may be made to the High Court unless such a review has taken place.

**rQ124**    Subject to Rule Q123, a *person* or organisation who is adversely affected by a decision of the *Bar Standards Board* may appeal to the High Court against the decision, in accordance with Civil Procedure Rules.

## B11. Powers of the Inns

### Inns' Conduct Committee

**rQ125**    Subject to this Section 4.B, the Inns' Conduct Committee shall have power to carry out the functions specified in the Inns' Conduct Committee Rules.

**rQ126**    The Inns' Conduct Committee Rules must be approved by the *Bar Standards Board* and any amendment to those rules will take effect on:

.1    the date when the amendment is approved by the *Bar Standards Board*; or

.2    such later date as the *Bar Standards Board* appoints.

**rQ127**    The *Bar Standards Board* may:

.1    issue guidance which the Inns' Conduct Committee must follow in carrying out its functions; and

.2    ask for information about the performance of those functions which the Inns' Conduct Committee must provide to the *Bar Standards Board*.

### Other powers

**rQ128**    Subject to the approval of the *Bar Standards Board*, an *Inn* may charge such fees as it prescribes for dealing with applications and calling *person*s to the *Bar* under this Section 4.B.

**rQ129**    Any function or power which under this Section 4.B is exercisable by an *Inn* or by the Inns' Conduct Committee may be delegated (and sub-delegated) to any committee, body or *person* to the extent permitted by the standing orders of the *Inn* or the Inns' Conduct Committee Rules (as the case may be).

# C. THE CPD RULES

## The mandatory continuing professional development requirements

**rQ130**   For the purpose of this Section 4.C:

.1   "calendar year" means a period of one year starting on 1 January in the year in question;

.2   the "mandatory requirements" are those in Rules Q131 to Q136 below.

.3   a "*pupillage* year" is any calendar year in which a *barrister* is at any time a *pupil*.

**rQ131**   Any practising *barrister* who, as at 1 October 2001, had started but not completed the period of three years referred to in the Continuing Education Scheme Rules at Annex Q to the Sixth Edition of the Code of Conduct must complete a minimum of 42 hours of continuing professional development during his first three years of *practice*.

**G**   **Guidance**

### Guidance on Rules Q131

**gQ1**   Rule Q131 is intended to apply only in those limited circumstances where a *barrister* started *practice* before 1 October 2001 but after the New Practitioners Programme ("NPP") first came into force, left *practice* before completing the NPP, but has since returned. Rule Q131 requires them to finish their NPP during whatever is left of their first three years of *practice*.

**rQ132**   Any practising *barrister* who starts *practice* on or after 1 October 2001 must during the first three calendar years in which the *barrister* holds a practising certificate after any *pupillage* year complete a minimum of 45 hours of continuing professional development.

**rQ133**   Subject to Rule Q134, any *barrister*:

.1   must, if he holds a practising certificate or certificates throughout the whole of any calendar year, complete a minimum of 12 hours of continuing professional development during that period; and

.2   must, if he holds a *practising certificate* or certificate for part only of a calendar year, complete one hour of continuing professional development during that calendar year for each month for which he holds a *practising certificate*.

**rQ134**   Rule Q133 does not apply:

.1   in the case of a *barrister* to whom Rule Q131 applies, to any calendar year forming or containing part of the period of 3 years referred to in Rule Q131; or

.2   in the case of a *barrister* to whom Rule Q132 applies, during any *pupillage* year or during the first three calendar years in which the *barrister* holds a *practising certificate*.

| SECTION C: THE CPD RULES |
| --- |
| The mandatory continuing professional development requirements |

**PART 4**

rQ135   Any *practising barrister* must submit details of the continuing professional development he has done to the *Bar Standards Board* in the form prescribed, and at the time specified, by the *Bar Standards Board*.

rQ136   The *Bar Standards Board* may, by resolution, specify the nature, content and format of courses and other activities which may be done by *barristers* (or by any category of *barristers*) in order to satisfy the mandatory requirements.

rQ137   The *Bar Standards Board* may, by resolution and after consultation with the Inns, Circuits and other providers as appropriate, increase the minimum number of hours of continuing professional development which must be completed in order to satisfy any of the mandatory requirements.

# APPENDIX 2
# EXCERPTS FROM THE BAR STANDARDS BOARD CODE GUIDANCE

The Bar Standards Board

# Handbook

**CURRENT GUIDANCE**

## Unregistered Barristers (Barristers without Practising Certificates) – Supplying Legal Services and Holding Out

### 1.    Introduction

The BSB Handbook defines a practising barrister as a barrister who is supplying legal services and holds a practising certificate. There are many barristers who do not have a practising certificate either by choice or because they do not qualify for a practising certificate.

Such barristers are now called "Unregistered Barristers" because they are not on the public register of barristers who have practising certificates. It is important to note that the term "non-practising barrister" which has been used in the past should no longer be used as it can cause confusion since some barristers without practising certificates do provide legal services and are, in effect, practising as lawyers.

Many unregistered barristers will have chosen careers other than the law or may be retired and are therefore not covered by this guidance unless they provide any legal services.

Even though the rules which apply only to practising barristers do not apply to them, all unregistered barristers remain members of the profession and members of their Inn and are expected to conduct themselves in an appropriate manner. In this context, they remain subject to certain Core Duties and Conduct Rules at all times. If they provide legal services, they must comply with all the Core Duties and they have a responsibility not to mislead anyone about their status. These are new requirements introduced by the Handbook. This guidance will assist those barristers to comply with their obligations contained in the BSB Handbook.

### 2.    Who is this guidance for?

This guidance relates to 'unregistered barristers', or barristers without practising certificates, who wish to provide legal services to employers or to the public, whether such barristers are employed or self-employed. It also addresses restrictions on 'holding out' as a barrister in connection with the supply of legal services.

It is now a criminal offence for a barrister without a practising certificate to provide legal services which are Reserved Legal Activities under the Legal Services Act 2007. This guidance provides advice on what legal services may be provided by a barrister without a practising certificate and on the rules which must be followed when doing so.

Core duties 5 and 9 of the BSB Handbook apply to unregistered barristers at all times. The other Core Duties apply when supplying legal services, as do certain other rules (see below).

The Bar Standards Board
# Handbook

The main Outcome this guidance relates to is Outcome C34 in the BSB Handbook -

*Clients who receive legal services from unregistered barristers are aware that such unregistered barristers are not subject to the same regulatory safeguards that would apply if they instructed a practising barrister.*

### 3.    *What are Legal Services and Reserved Legal Activities?*

Rule s6 in the BSB Handbook determines that you must not carry on any reserved legal activity unless you are entitled to do so under the Legal Services Act.

Under the Legal Services Act certain legal services are reserved to those who are authorised to provide them. For barristers, only those who have practising certificates are authorised persons. Such services are known as 'reserved legal activities'[1] *which* are as follows:

- the exercise of a right of audience;
- the conduct of litigation;
- reserved instrument activities;
- probate activities;
- notarial activities[2] and
- the administration of oaths.

As it is now a criminal offence to carry out a reserved legal activity without a practising certificate, it is important that unregistered barristers are clear that they are not permitted to carry out these services. In particular, the administration of oaths, which formerly could be performed by any barrister, is now reserved for those with practising certificates. Advocacy is not a reserved legal activity unless it involves the exercise of a right of audience. Thus, advocacy before an arbitrator or other tribunal where rights of audience are not required is not a reserved legal activity.

If you are also a solicitor, or regulated by another approved regulator you may be authorised to carry out reserved legal activities in that capacity. Guidance for those barristers who are dual qualified can be found at paragraph 8.6 below.

*As an unregistered barrister, you can provide any legal services that are not reserved legal activities. However there are some important rules in the BSB Handbook which you need to follow in doing so.*

---

[1] Section 12 of the Legal Services Act 2007
[2] The Bar Council does not authorise any barrister whether practising or not to perform notarial activities.

---

The Bar Standards Board

# Handbook

Legal services are defined in the definitions section of the Handbook as follows:

"[Legal services] includes legal advice representation and drafting or settling any statement of case witness statement affidavit or other legal document but does not include:

> a) sitting as a judge or arbitrator or acting as a mediator, early neutral evaluation, expert determination and adjudications;
> b) lecturing in or teaching law or writing or editing law books articles or reports;
> c) examining newspapers, periodicals, books, scripts and other publications for libel, breach of copyright, contempt of court and the like;
> d) communicating to or in the press or other media;
> e) giving advice on legal matters free to a friend or relative or acting as unpaid or honorary legal adviser to any charitable benevolent or philanthropic institution;
> f) in relation to a barrister who is a non-executive director of a company or a trustee or governor of a charitable benevolent or philanthropic institution or a trustee of any private trust, giving to the other directors trustees or governors the benefit of his learning and experience on matters of general legal principle applicable to the affairs of the company institution or trust;

### 4. Holding out as a barrister

Rule s8 provides that you must not practise as a barrister unless you have a practising certificate, and rule s9 defines practising as a barrister as including holding yourself out as a barrister while providing legal services. The restriction on 'holding out' prevents barristers who do not have a practising certificate but who are supplying or offering to supply legal services from using the title 'barrister' or otherwise conveying the impression that they are practising as barristers. It is not possible to provide a comprehensive list of the circumstances which might amount to holding out but it is hoped that the following examples will give an idea of what is prohibited.

- Describing oneself as a barrister in any printed material used in connection with the provision of legal services: in particular in advertising or publicity, on a card or letterhead, or on premises

- Describing oneself as a barrister to clients or prospective clients

- Describing oneself to clients or prospective clients as a non-practising barrister or barrister-at-law (titles which have been allowed in the past but not in recent years)

- Indicating to opposing parties or their representatives (e.g. in correspondence) that one is a barrister

- Describing oneself as a barrister or (when supplying services to the public) as "counsel", wearing robes, or sitting in a place reserved for counsel, in court

The Bar Standards Board

# Handbook

- Using other descriptions in connection with supplying, or offering to supply, legal services which imply that the individual is a barrister (e.g. membership of an Inn of Court)

(These examples are not exhaustive.)

The restriction on holding out only applies in the context of legal services. If you have been called to the Bar, there is no restriction on referring to yourself as a barrister if it is not in connection with the supply of legal services.

It should also be noted that for a BVC or BPTC graduate to mention that he/she is a holder of this qualification, is not considered as holding out as a barrister.

**5.    What job title can I hold; what can I/my employer put on a business card/letterhead/website etc.?**

The fundamental principle is that you must not mislead or allow anyone else to mislead any person to whom you or your employer supply or offer to supply *legal services*.

You can use the title "barrister" when **not** providing *legal services*. See paragraph 3 for activities which are not regarded as *legal services* ("non-legal" services).  However, you must be careful not to mislead third parties as to your status as a barrister. This would apply particularly if you were also providing *legal services* to the same people to whom you provide "non-legal" services.

It is important that you/your employer do not use the title barrister, unregistered barrister or non-practising barrister on business cards, promotional material, letterheads, and business names. If you are employed whether by a regulated or unregulated firm, you should make sure that your employer does not use any of these titles in connection with you in its printed material or on its website.

You can use the titles "lawyer" or "legal adviser". If you are self-employed, or work for an unregulated employer, you should not use the title "counsel".  However, if you provide legal services only to your employer you may use titles commonly used in companies, such as legal counsel, general counsel, corporate counsel. You may also use the description "of Counsel" if you work for an employer which is an authorised person under the Legal Services Act.

In a curriculum vitae, you can state that you qualified as a barrister.

You can refer to yourself as a BVC/BPTC graduate.

If you are a QC but do not have a practising certificate, you may continue to use the title but if you are providing *legal services* you must explain that you are not practising as a barrister.

The Bar Standards Board
# Handbook

### 6.  Why do special rules apply to unregistered barristers who supply legal services?

Legal services, other than reserved legal activities, can be supplied by anyone and are not subject to any special statutory regulation. It would therefore be disproportionate to impose regulatory requirements on unregistered barristers who supply such services just because they are barristers, except where there would otherwise be a clear risk to their potential clients. The risk that needs to be managed is that most potential clients are not aware of the different categories of barrister and will tend to assume that the same regulatory requirements and protections apply to all barristers. Barristers with practising certificates are subject to important requirements, such as having insurance and keeping their professional knowledge up-to-date, which do not apply to unregistered barristers. Some of their clients also have the right to complain to the Legal Ombudsman. These are important safeguards for clients, who may assume that they will apply whenever they seek legal services from someone they know or believe to be a barrister. The rules discussed below are intended to manage this risk while still allowing unregistered barristers to provide unreserved legal services.

### 7. What Rules and Duties apply to you as an unregistered barrister providing legal services?

When you are providing legal services all the Core Duties in the BSB Handbook apply to you (see Rules C1.2 and C2.1-2.2).  The Core Duties are:

CD1 - You must observe your duty to the court in the administration of justice
CD2 - You must act in the best interests of each client
CD3 - You must act with honesty and integrity
CD4 - You must maintain your independence
CD5 - You must not behave in a way which is likely to diminish the trust and confidence which the public places in you or in the profession
CD6 - You must keep the affairs of each client confidential
CD7 - You must provide a competent standard of work and service to each client
CD8 - You must not discriminate unlawfully against any person
CD9 - You must be open and co-operative with your regulators
CD10 - You must take reasonable steps to manage your practice, or carry out your role within your practice, competently and in such a way as to achieve compliance with your legal and regulatory obligations

Even when you are not providing legal services, Core Duties 5 and 9 apply to you.

The Conduct rules (and associated guidance) which apply to unregistered barristers at all times are as follows:

- Rule c8 – Your duty not to do anything which could be seen to undermine your honesty, integrity and independence

The Bar Standards Board

# Handbook

- Rule c16 – Your duty to your client is subject to your duty to the court, and your obligations to act with honesty and integrity, and to maintain your independence.
- Rules c64-70 - Duties in relation to provision of information to the BSB and co-operation with the BSB. These duties include the new duty to report serious misconduct by other barristers (see separate guidance).

In addition, the following Conduct Rules and associated guidance apply when providing legal services:

- Rules c4 and c5 – your duty to your client is subject to your duty to the court , and your duty to the court does not require you to breach your duty to keep the affairs of your client confidential
- Rule c19 – not misleading clients
- Rules c144 and 145 – rules relating to information which unregistered barristers must give to inexperienced clients

Rule c19 is a new rule which applies to all barristers. It provides that **you must not mislead** anyone to whom you supply or offer to supply *legal services*. For unregistered barristers this means:

- You must not use the title "barrister" in connection with the supply of or offer to supply *legal services*. This is known as "holding out" and is explained further in section 4. Similarly, you should not use the description "unregistered barrister" when supplying or offering to supply *legal services* except to the very limited extent discussed in paragraph 8 below and subject to explaining what the term means. Barristers who were registered under paragraph 206 of the previous Code may continue to use the title "barrister", but must comply with the terms of rule s15.[3]

- You must not mislead clients or employers about:

    - your status;
    - the extent to which you are regulated;
    - the services you can supply and
    - your insurance cover

In order to comply with the obligation not to mislead clients or employers, you will need to consider what information you should give them about your status as discussed further in paragraph 8 below. In certain circumstances, the Handbook prescribes the information you must give (see below).

---

[3] There are special rules for those barristers registered under paragraph 206 of the 8th edition of the Code of Conduct.

The Bar Standards Board

# Handbook

REGULATING BARRISTERS

Rules c144-145 set out the information which must be provided by unregistered barristers when providing legal services to an inexperienced client (see paragraph 8.4 below)

## 8.    Information to be given by unregistered barristers to employers, clients or prospective clients

This section describes what information you may, or in some cases **must**, give to those with whom you deal. Keep in mind the purpose of giving the information as discussed in paragraph 6 above. Check which of the following applies to you. When you provide the explanation required by rule c144 or suggested by this guidance, the BSB would not normally consider this as constituting holding yourself out as a barrister.

### 8.1 I provide *legal services* only to my employer

You may describe yourself orally as an unregistered barrister or a barrister without a

practising certificate, to your employer, colleagues and any third parties with whom

you deal and you should explain what this means if there is any risk of anyone being

misled. You may also state on a CV that you have been called to the Bar.

### 8.2 I work for a regulated professional body and provide services to clients

This applies to unregistered barristers working for solicitors firms, other bodies which are authorised under the Legal Services Act such as licensed conveyancers, or other regulated professional firms such as accountants or Patent Agents.

You may describe yourself to your employer and colleagues as an unregistered barrister or a barrister without a practising certificate and you should explain what this means if there is any risk of anyone being misled. You should **not** describe yourself as a barrister or unregistered barrister to clients of your employer but if you are asked whether you are a barrister or if it becomes known that you are, you may say that you are an unregistered barrister and explain what this means. You should seek to ensure that any publicity put out by your employer does not describe you as a barrister. You must also comply with any regulatory requirements of the professional body which regulates your employer.

The Bar Standards Board

# Handbook

**8.3 I am self-employed and I provide unreserved *legal services* to experienced business clients**

This applies to those barristers dealing with larger businesses or firms which can be expected to make informed judgments about sourcing legal services.

You may not advertise or refer to yourself as a barrister but in tendering for work you may state to a prospective client that you are an unregistered barrister provided that you explain to the client what this means. If you are in any doubt, a written statement should be provided along the same lines as that detailed in paragraph 8.4 below. Whilst we strongly advise all barristers providing legal services to carry professional indemnity insurance, if you decide not to insure then you should so advise clients or prospective clients.

**8.4 I am self-employed and supply unreserved *legal services* to inexperienced clients, such as individuals, small companies and charities.**

If you supply legal services to inexperienced clients, rule c144 applies to you. Inexperienced clients are defined as including individuals and small organisations which would be entitled under the Legal Ombudsman Scheme Rules to make a complaint to the Legal Ombudsman if you were a practising barrister.[4] As you are not practising as a barrister your clients have no redress under this scheme so you are required to make your status very clear to them. But other clients, for example slightly larger organisations which only occasionally require legal services, may also be inexperienced. If you are in any doubt as to whether your client has sufficient experience to understand the implications of instructing an unregistered barrister instead of a practising barrister, then you should give them the written statement detailed in this paragraph.

Where rule c144 applies, you **must** explain to your client:

- that you are not acting as a barrister
- that you are not subject to certain Conduct Rules applying to practising barristers and the Bar Standards Board cannot consider complaints against you in relation to these rules but only in relation to the rules which do apply to you
- if you are not covered by professional indemnity insurance you must say so

---

[4] They provide that complaints may be made by micro enterprises (headcount below 10 and turnover or balance sheet total of 2 million euros or less), charities with an income of £1million or less and clubs and other organisations with a turnover of £1 million or less). See http://www.legalombudsman.org.uk/.

The Bar Standards Board

# Handbook

REGULATING BARRISTERS

- that your client has no right to complain to the Legal Ombudsman

Your client must also confirm in writing that they have received this explanation.

A suggested form of statement is contained in Annex 1.

These requirements do not apply to legal services provided when working for a Legal Advice Centre[5] as defined in the Code, or if you are authorised to provide reserved legal activities by another Approved Regulator[6] (see paragraph 8.6 below). They do however apply if you were formerly registered under rule 206 of the previous version of the Code. You may also wish to refer to the definition of legal services in paragraph 3 above in deciding whether you are providing legal services.

### 8.5 I am employed by an unregulated organisation which provides unreserved *legal services* to the public

The same requirements apply as if you were self-employed depending on whether the client is an experienced large business or an inexperienced client such as an individual or small business. You should follow the guidance in paragraph 8.3 or 8.4 above as appropriate. It is your responsibility and not your employer's to see that the relevant information is given and you should advise your employer of the rules so that they do not hold you out as a barrister.

Barristers who do not hold practising certificates (including first six pupils) are permitted to provide free legal advice to clients of a legal advice centre, providing they do not hold themselves out as barristers and do not undertake or offer to undertake any reserved legal services.

### 8.6 I am authorised to carry out legal services by another Approved Regulator

Under the LSA, only Approved Regulators can authorise the carrying out of reserved legal activities (see above). The following Approved Regulators can currently authorise the conduct of litigation and/or exercise of rights of audience: the Law Society (acting by the Solicitors Regulation Authority), the Chartered Institute of Legal Executives, the Chartered Institute of Patent Agents and the Institute of Trade Mark Attorneys.

Rule s43 determines that, if you are authorised by another Approved Regulator to carry on a reserved legal activity and currently permitted to practise by that Approved Regulator, you must not practise as a barrister and you are not eligible for a practising certificate. If you are practising as a person authorised by one of the other Approved Regulators, you may hold yourself out as a barrister in addition to

---

[5] Rule c145.3 and section S B9.
[6] Rule c145.4

The Bar Standards Board
# Handbook

your other qualification, provided that you comply with Rule s14. This Rule requires that, in these circumstances, if you hold yourself out as a barrister or a registered European lawyer, when supplying legal services to any person or employer for the first time, you must inform them clearly in writing at the earliest opportunity that you are not practising as a barrister or a registered European lawyer.

## 9.  What are the Rules for Pupils?

In your first six, as you do not have a practising certificate, you cannot supply legal services as a practising barrister but you can accept a noting brief with permission of your pupil supervisor or head of Chambers. You may describe yourself as a pupil barrister in that capacity. If you provide unreserved legal services in any other capacity, for example if providing pro bono advice, you should not describe yourself as a barrister or a pupil barrister and should follow the rules and guidance for unregistered barristers.

In your second six, when you have a provisional practising certificate, you may provide legal services in accordance with Rule S19. You may describe yourself as a pupil barrister and you should ensure that the client understands your status.

## *10.  Further Help and Advice*

*It is recognised that the rules are complex. Further advice and information is available from the BSB on 020 7611 1444. The Bar Council Ethical Queries helpline (020 7611 1307) is also available for questions on professional issues.*

The Bar Standards Board

# Handbook

REGULATING BARRISTERS

Annex 1 – Explanation to clients

**The Code of Conduct**

**Suggested statement to be given in accordance with Rule C144**

**This statement, or an explanation containing the same information on the points shown in bold, must be given to any inexperienced client to whom you offer to provide *legal services* and you must receive written confirmation that they have received it before providing any such services.**

**Your name:**                                                    **Date:**

This statement is to explain my status in offering to provide you with legal services.

Although I am qualified as a barrister, **I am not entitled to practise as a barrister. I do not have a practising certificate** and am not on the register of practising barristers.

Therefore, in providing any legal services to you I am not acting as a barrister and **I am not subject to many of the rules which regulate practising barristers.**

**This limits the services I can provide to you.** I can provide you with legal advice and represent you before certain Tribunals but **I cannot exercise rights of audience in Court**.

I aim to provide you with a good service and if you have any concerns about what I do for you, please let me know and I will try to resolve the problem. But you should know that **you would have only limited rights to complain about me to anyone else.**

 **The Legal Ombudsman, which can adjudicate on complaints about poor service by practising barristers, cannot consider any complaint against me.**

If I cannot resolve your concerns, **you can complain to the Bar Standards Board** and it will investigate whether I have failed to comply with any of the rules which apply to me but it cannot investigate possible breaches of rules which apply only to practising barristers

**I am [am not] covered by professional indemnity insurance.**

Signed:                                                    Date:

I confirm that I have received the above statement from [      ].

Signed:                                                    Date:

The Bar Standards Board
# Handbook

REGULATING BARRISTERS

**January 2014**
**Bar Standards Board**

The Bar Standards Board
# Handbook

BAR
STANDARDS
BOARD

REGULATING BARRISTERS

**CURRENT GUIDANCE**

## The Public Access Scheme Guidance for Barristers

The Bar Standards Board
# Handbook

### Scope of this guidance

1.    A barrister may accept instructions directly from or on behalf of a member of public, also known as a lay client (the "client") (rS24 of the Scope of Practice section of the BSB Handbook). This is known as public access. In carrying out public access work a barrister must comply with the BSB Handbook and in particular the Public Access Rules which are at rC119-rC131 of the Code of Conduct section.

2.    This document gives guidance on the interpretation of the Handbook and good practice. You should have regard to it in considering whether to accept and in carrying out public access instructions in accordance with the rules set out in the Handbook.

### Qualification requirements

3.    Before you may accept public access instructions, you must:

   (1)    Hold a full practising certificate. If you have less than three years' standing you must have a qualified person readily available to you to provide guidance, if necessary (see paragraph 5 below);

   (2)    Have undertaken and satisfactorily completed a Bar Standards Board approved training course. Details of such courses can be obtained from the BSB website;

   (3)    Notify the Bar Council of your intention to undertake such work; and

   (4)    Have insurance cover as required by the Handbook. BMIF cover satisfies this requirement.

### Additional requirements for barristers with less than three years' standing

4.    The prohibition on barristers with less than three years' standing undertaking public access work has been removed. However there are two additional requirements with which a barrister under three years' standing must comply.

5.    You must have a qualified person available to provide guidance. A person shall be a "qualified person" for these purposes if they are public access accredited and have[1]:

   (a) been entitled to practise and have practised as a barrister or have been authorised to practise by another approved regulator for a period (which need not have been as a person authorised by the same approved regulator) of at least six years in the previous eight years;

---

[1] rS22, BSB Handbook

The Bar Standards Board
# Handbook

(b) made such practice their primary occupation for the previous two years; and

(c) been entitled to exercise a right of audience before every Court in relation to all proceedings.

6.    You are also required to:

(a) keep a log of the public access cases you have dealt with and record any issues or problems that have arisen; and

(b) where possible and appropriate, seek feedback from public access clients.

7.    A pro forma for logging cases is attached at Annex A. The purpose of this requirement is twofold:

(a) Its primary purpose is as a tool to assist you to reflect upon and learn from your practice, (in this connection a barrister will need to consider whether seeking feedback from a client involved in an unsuccessful criminal case would be appropriate) and

(b) to assist the Bar Standards Board in assessing whether the removal of the prohibition has introduced any unacceptable risk in to the process. Therefore the BSB will sample a selection of these logs to gauge the impact of the rule change.

**Nature and scope of public access work**

8.    A barrister may accept public access instructions in any area of practice. You are reminded that rC21.8 of the Handbook prohibits you from accepting instructions if you lack sufficient experience or competence to handle the matter. In a public access case you should remember that dealing directly with a client may be more difficult or demanding than acting for a professional client and you must be able to handle those demands.

9.    Public access does not widen the types of work a barrister may do. You are performing the same functions as you would if you were instructed by a solicitor. Examples of the type of work you may do for a public access client are:

- advocacy;

- drafting documents;

- advising in writing or in conference;

The Bar Standards Board

# Handbook

- representation in alternative dispute resolution (ADR) such as mediation or arbitration;

- Negotiating on behalf of your client;

- Investigating and collecting evidence. You should however have regard to the BSB's 'Guidance on Self-Employed Practice', which is published on the BSB's website and provides guidance on investigating or collecting evidence and taking witness statements. In particular, you must not conduct a case in court if you have previously investigated or collected evidence in the case unless you reasonably believe that the investigation and collection of that evidence is unlikely to be challenged;

- Corresponding on behalf of your client. You may send letters on your Chambers' letterhead or faxes or emails. However, you must only conduct correspondence if you are satisfied it is in your client's best interests to do so and you have adequate systems, experience and resources for managing the correspondence (see rC130 and relevant guidance at gC24 and gC71). Bear in mind that solicitors' offices have systems for logging incoming and outgoing correspondence and dealing with urgent letters in the absence of the fee earner which your Chambers may not be able to offer.

**General restrictions**

(A) Restriction on conducting litigation without authorisation

10.     Public access does not put barristers on a par with solicitors. A key difference is that solicitors may conduct litigation on behalf of their client. A barrister in independent practice does not have the right to conduct litigation unless authorised by the BSB to do so. If you conduct litigation without authorisation you are not only breaching the Handbook but also committing a criminal offence under the Legal Services Act 2007.

11.     The Legal Services Act 2007 defines the conduct of litigation as:

a.      the issuing of proceedings before any court in England and Wales;

b.      the commencement, prosecution and defence of such proceedings; and

c.      the performance of any ancillary functions in relation to such proceedings (such as entering appearances to actions).

12.     The BSB takes the view that the following fall within this definition and therefore **you should refuse to do them if you are not authorised to conduct litigation**:

The Bar Standards Board

# Handbook

BAR STANDARDS BOARD

REGULATING BARRISTERS

- issuing proceedings or applications;

- acknowledging service of proceedings;

- giving your address as the address for service;

- filing documents at court or serving documents on another party; and

- issuing notices of appeal.

13.    You may advise your client on how to take any of these steps. For example you may advise on the procedure for lodging an appeal and you may of course draft the grounds of appeal. However the steps in question must be taken by the client as a litigant in person if you are not authorised to do them. Normally public access clients who are litigants in person will be expected to be able to perform the activities usually undertaken by an authorised litigator with little or no prompting. If this is not the case you must consider whether it is proper to act on a public access basis (see paragraphs 21 to 25 below). This consideration is particularly relevant when dealing with vulnerable clients. 'Vulnerable clients' is interpreted widely and may include clients who have English as a second language, who have mental or physical impairments or who are otherwise vulnerable eg because of their age, caring responsibilities or immigration status.

14.    Certain activities at first blush look like they might fall within the definition of conducting litigation but in fact do not. This is generally because it is work that barristers have traditionally done when instructed by solicitors. The following are therefore **permissible if you are not authorised to conduct litigation**:

- Lodging documents for hearings. It is proper for you or your clerk to lodge certain types of documents for hearings, provided that they are ancillary to your role as an advocate. Barristers often draft the case summary, chronology, list of issues or position statement. There is nothing wrong with clerks or barristers lodging these sort of documents.

- Skeleton arguments. Exchanging skeletons with an opponent or sending skeletons and bundles of authorities to the court is allowed. In a criminal case defence barristers often hand a defence case statement to the Crown or the court and this would also be permitted if instructed directly.

- Covering applications to fix trial dates. Clerks regularly fix trial dates to ensure that the date is convenient for counsel instructed. This is permissible whether instructed by a solicitor and therefore also when instructed directly. Clerks making representations to the Masters in relation to hearing dates is

The Bar Standards Board
# Handbook

REGULATING BARRISTERS

permissible for the same reasons.

- Court orders. Liaising with the other side or the court over the preparation of an order is something barristers often do and is allowed. Clerks regularly deal with the sealing of court orders and so this, too, is permitted.

- Discharging a duty or a courtesy to the court. For example a letter or e-mail to a judge explaining an absence from court or providing dates to avoid or corrections to a draft judgment.

- Signing a statement of truth. A statement of truth may be signed by a legal representative, which is defined as including a barrister (Civil Procedure Rules Part 2.3). Therefore you may sign a statement of truth on behalf of your client (*O'Connor v BSB* (2012) Visitors to the Inns of Court, August 17, unrep.). However you should ensure that the provisions of the Civil Procedure Rules are complied with before you do so, in particular Part 22 PD paragraph 3.8.

(B) Code of Conduct restrictions

15.     The following are expressly prohibited by the Code of Conduct:

- Receiving or handling clients' money, except as payment for fees. The prohibition against holding clients' money means that a barrister cannot make disbursements on behalf of a client, for example by paying court fees or witnesses' expenses.(rC73-rC75, BSB Handbook).

- Undertaking the general management, administration or conduct of a client's affairs (rS25, BSB Handbook).

**Public funding (legal aid)**

16.     In each case, before a barrister accepts a public access instruction, it is a Code of Conduct requirement to:

> 'Take such steps as are reasonably necessary to ensure that the client is able to make an informed decision about whether to apply for legal aid or whether to proceed with public access.' (rC120.4, BSB Handbook)

17.     If a client qualifies for legal aid it may be, and often will be, in their best interests to instruct a solicitor on a public funding basis. There may however be some situations where the client will prefer to instruct a barrister on public access – for example if their legal aid contributions would be higher than instructing a barrister

The Bar Standards Board
# Handbook

REGULATING BARRISTERS

without a solicitor, or they want to instruct a more senior barrister, such as a QC, than they would be entitled to on legal aid.

18.    It is important that the client makes an informed choice about public funding. In many cases it will be obvious from the nature of the case, or the nature of the client, that public funding is unlikely to be available. However in other cases you may take the view that it would be in the best interests of the client to explore their eligibility for legal aid. In those cases, you are likely to want to discuss this with them when you first meet and draw their attention to where they can find out more about legal aid and get help to assess their eligibility. Before accepting an instruction you will want to discuss this matter with the client to ensure that they understand the position regarding legal aid, have made an informed decision and that proceeding on a public access basis will be in their best interests.

19.    Information about public funding is available to clients in the guidance for clients, which is available on the BSB's website at:

https://www.barstandardsboard.org.uk/regulatory-requirements/bsb-handbook/code-guidance/

20.    The model client care letter (see paragraph 33 below) explains that a barrister cannot be instructed directly on a legal aid basis, gives details of how the client can find out if they are eligible for public funding and the basis on which you can advise and represent them. Writing to your client in the terms set out in the model client care letter can therefore help to demonstrate that you have covered this matter with them.

### Interests of the client and interests of justice

21.    You cannot accept public access instructions if you form the view that it is either in the best interests of your client or in the interests of justice for the client to instruct a solicitor or other professional client (rC120.3, BSB Handbook). This is a continuing duty which you must keep under review during the course of a case.

22.    This decision is likely to depend both on the complexity of the case, the capability of the client and whether you are authorised to conduct litigation eg a well-resourced client, such as a large corporation, may be able to handle very complex litigation.

23.    In making this assessment you are likely to reach one of three views:

- The level of the case and the likely work involved is within the client's capabilities and there is no obvious reason why a solicitor or other professional client should be instructed.

The Bar Standards Board

# Handbook

- The case is of such complexity or has reached a stage that it is not in the client's interests or the interests of justice to instruct a barrister without a solicitor or other professional client. Having reached such a view you can no longer act on a public access basis. You would be able to act if instructed by a solicitor (or other professional client) and you can make recommendations as to who could act.

- The case may well become complex and may involve work which the client cannot do, but you do not consider that a solicitor or other professional client needs to be instructed yet.

24.    In every case you must make your client aware at the outset that there may be circumstances in which you will have to recommend that a solicitor (or other professional client) is instructed, and that you will have to withdraw if that advice is not heeded. There is a paragraph in the model client care letter (see paragraph 33 below) setting this out.

25.    It is essential that barristers should consider at every point at which they are instructed whether a client needs to instruct a solicitor and to advise as soon as it becomes clear that this is the case. This is of particular importance where limitation periods are involved or where hearings are imminent. Barristers failing to do this may find themselves at risk of actions in negligence, findings of inadequate professional service by the Office of the Legal Ombudsman, or professional misconduct charges by the BSB.

**Relationship with client**

(A) Initial contact

26.    It is likely that initial contact will be by a telephone call or email between the client and yourself or your clerk, or the receipt of written instructions in Chambers. You are required to keep a record of the date that instructions were received, the name of the client, the name of the case and any requirement of the client as to time limits (rC128). As you will also need to send a client care letter you will need the client's address.

27.    You may take the view that a preliminary meeting is required. This may be necessary to comply with the requirements of the Money Laundering Regulations (see paragraphs 72 to 75 below). If so, you should write to the client summarising those regulations and setting out what is required in order to satisfy the identification requirements. A preliminary meeting may be helpful to decide whether you will accept the instructions. It is open to you to accept instructions for the limited purpose of reading papers and advising whether you are able to perform substantive professional work; in such a situation it is open to you to make an

The Bar Standards Board
# Handbook

REGULATING BARRISTERS

arrangement that you are paid a fee for doing so. If you decide to charge for the preliminary meeting, a client care letter should be sent to the client in the usual way, setting out the charge for the advice and any other work done and making it clear that you do not agree to do more in the first instance than assess whether or not you can assist the client. In many cases, you may consider that it is good client care not to charge for a preliminary meeting.

(B) Identifying and representing vulnerable clients

28.    There are a number of factors which may make a client vulnerable and which may have implications for how you manage their case. Some of these factors may be obvious, for example a client may be very young or may not be able to speak English. Issues related to the protected characteristics listed in the Equality Act 2010 which may make a client vulnerable include:

Race
- Clients with English as a second, third or non-existent language.
- Asylum seeking or refugee clients who may have mental health issues such as post-traumatic stress conditions related to treatment (e.g. torture or persecution) in their home country.
- Immigration clients who may have been separated from their families or who are new to the UK, may be unfamiliar with the UK legal system and who may have difficulties carrying out litigation work.

Gender
- Clients with caring responsibilities for young or disabled children, particularly lone parents who may have difficulties in undertaking tasks such as serving documentation at court.
- Clients with caring responsibilities for older dependents, in particular lone carers.
- Lone parents who may have access to less financial resources than other clients.
- Sensitivity of men or women in relation to one to one meetings with the opposite sex - if this is necessary or in relation to questioning/discussion of intimate subjects.

Disability
- Clients with physical impairments which may impact upon their ability to undertake physical aspects of litigation.
- Clients with physical or mental health issues which may impact upon their ability to undertake litigation activities.
- Clients with learning disabilities.
- Clients who are heavily reliant on carers to manage their day to day activities.

The Bar Standards Board
# Handbook

<u>Age</u>
- Very young clients.
- Clients who for reasons relating to their age (particularly older clients) may find the physical aspects of litigation difficult.
- Clients who for reasons relating to their age have difficulties associated with memory loss and/or confusion.

<u>Pregnancy/Maternity</u>
- Heavily pregnant or new mothers who may find the physical aspects of conducting litigation difficult.
- New mothers with post natal health issues affecting physical mobility or mental health (e.g. post natal depression).

<u>Gender re-assignment</u>
- Clients undergoing transition (which may involve frequent visits to hospital or other medical appointments).

<u>Religion or belief</u>
- Clients whose religious beliefs make it difficult for them to undertake litigation activities on particular days or at particular times.

29.     Other relevant factors to consider in relation to the vulnerability of a client include:

- Limited access to financial resources to pay for the cost of litigation activities or additional unforeseen costs.
- Illiteracy or low levels of literacy.
- Vulnerability or trauma arising from the matter at issue (e.g. the matter involves a serious crime such as serious assaults or sexual offences perpetrated against the client).
- Homelessness.
- Drug or alcohol dependency or other addiction issues.

30.     The term 'vulnerable client' should be interpreted widely. You will need to identify any factors that may make a client vulnerable when considering whether or not to take on their case. Having identified any such factors, you will need to consider what additional measures, if any, are necessary to ensure that the client is supported properly and understands fully any information which you communicate to them, so that you may act in their best interests. This may involve ensuring that documentation provided to your client is translated into another language or into plain English. You should also consider whether you can direct the client to any external resources or agencies for further advice and support.

(C) The basis of the agreement and the client care letter

The Bar Standards Board
# Handbook

REGULATING BARRISTERS

31.    The agreement between barrister and client is contractual. This means that:

- the barrister is bound by the agreement and may be liable in contract for failure to perform;
- it should be clear what is to be done under the contract, the charging rate and any other special terms that may be agreed (note your general duties under rC22 in addition to the public access rules);
- the barrister will be able to sue for fees.

32.    There are a number of things a barrister must inform his client about at the outset of the agreement. These are set out in rC125. They include warning a client that you are an independent practitioner and there may be occasions where a clash of professional commitments prevents you from carrying out an instruction.

33.    A model client care letter is on the BSB's website. Provided you have promptly written to your client in the terms of the model letter you will have complied with the notification requirements in rC125. Where the client has previously instructed you in respect of the same matter it may well be unnecessary for you to provide a full client care letter in respect of every new instruction received. Barristers must still ensure that the fundamentals of the client care letter are set out in respect of each new instruction i.e. the work that is to be undertaken, the cost and the payment mechanism. Other matters which you are required to inform your client about, such as the barrister's limitations (if any) with respect to litigation, how to complain and the fact the barrister may have to withdraw can be covered by referring the client to the original client care letter.

34.    It may also be possible in limited circumstances for you to enter into a retainer or novel fee arrangement with a public access client. However, care should be taken to ensure you continue to observe your general Handbook duties around independence and conflict of interest.

(D) Non-discrimination rules

35.    In deciding not to accept an instruction, you should be mindful of rC28 of the Handbook. This states that you must not withhold your services or permit your services to be withheld:

a.    on the ground that that the nature of the case is objectionable to you or to any section of the public;

b.    on the ground that the conduct, opinions or beliefs of the prospective client are unacceptable to you or to any section of the public; or

The Bar Standards Board
# Handbook

     c.     on any ground relating to the source of any financial support which may properly be given to the prospective client for the proceedings in question.

36.     rC12 states that a barrister must not discriminate unlawfully against, victimise or harass any other person on the grounds of race, colour, ethnic or national origin, nationality, citizenship, sex, gender re-assignment, sexual orientation, marital or civil partnership status, disability, age, religion or belief or pregnancy and maternity.

37.     The effect of these rules is that, whilst the 'cab rank' rule does not apply to public access cases, you must not discriminate in the way you accept, refuse or carry out public access instructions. Potential clients may feel aggrieved if a barrister refuses to take on a case and may allege that they did so for improper reasons. It would be prudent for a barrister refusing a case to make a brief note of the reasons for so doing in case this is questioned in future.

(E) Withdrawal from a case

38.     rC25 to rC27 of the Handbook highlight the scenarios where a barrister must or may cease to act and return instructions.

39.     In addition to the usual reasons for withdrawal from a case, barristers are required to cease to act in a public access case where they have formed the view (for instance, as a result of receiving further information about the case) that it is in the interests of the client or in the interests of justice for the client to instruct a solicitor or other professional client.

40.     If, as a result of being told that you cannot continue to act without a solicitor or professional client being instructed, the client instructs a solicitor or other professional client, then you will be able to continue to act. It is open to you, therefore, to give the client the opportunity to instruct a solicitor or other professional client before you finally withdraw from the case.

41.     In a public access case, the issue of withdrawing from a case will only arise once you have accepted the instruction. That will usually be when the client care letter is sent. You will need to take care in deciding whether to withdraw not only because you owe a duty under the Handbook to act in the best interests of your client, but also because you may owe them contractual duties. Unless your decision to withdraw is justified by your obligations under the Handbook you are likely to place yourself in breach of your contract with the client.

42.     It will therefore very rarely be appropriate for you to withdraw where there is simply a difference of opinion between yourself and the client. In particular, the fact that a client legitimately rejects your advice on tactics or a settlement will not of itself justify you in withdrawing from the case; nor does the fact that a client may raise a minor complaint or question about the service provided by you. Where such

The Bar Standards Board
# Handbook

disagreements arise, however, you would be prudent to make full attendance notes of the discussion and have them agreed by the client.

43.    A barrister acting for a client who is a party to proceedings must bear in mind the particular difficulties which the client might encounter if the barrister withdraws. A hearing may be imminent; or the client may experience real difficulty in finding a solicitor willing to take on the case. Where there is doubt, or a difference of opinion as to whether you should withdraw, and withdrawal would or might cause difficulties for the client, it would be prudent for a barrister to contact the Bar Council Public Access enquiries line (0207 611 1472) for guidance.

44.    Where you consider that you are required to withdraw and it appears that, by reason of the proximity of a hearing, a client may have difficulty finding another lawyer to take on the case in the time available, you should provide such assistance as is proper to protect the client's position. This can include:

a.    applying to the court for an adjournment if it is necessary to withdraw during the course of the hearing;

b.    drafting letters for the client to send to the court and the other side seeking an adjournment;

c.    providing supporting letters for the client explaining that, for professional reasons, you have had to withdraw and, so far as this is possible without breaching confidentiality or prejudicing the client's position, explaining the reasons;

d.    where the matter is urgent or it is otherwise appropriate, contacting solicitors or other suitable intermediaries who may be willing to take on the client's case.

## (F) Complaints

45.    The Handbook requires barristers to have in-house procedures for dealing with complaints (rC99-rC109). Such procedures can be a useful source of feedback to Chambers and also a way of retaining client goodwill when mistakes occur. Public access work may result in Chambers receiving a substantially greater number of complaints from clients, which may or may not be legitimate. However, all such complaints should be addressed and acted upon within an appropriate timescale.

46.    You should have regard to the BSB's guidance on complaints handling. In particular, you must:

a.    ensure that the client is told about the procedure in the client care letter;

b.    deal with complaints promptly and according to that procedure as they arise;

The Bar Standards Board
# Handbook

    c.    inform the client that, if they are dissatisfied with the way in which the complaint has been handled, they may refer it to the Legal Ombudsman.

**Fees**

(A) Notifying the client

47.    If you accept public access instructions you must forthwith notify your client in clear and readily understandable terms of the work you have agreed to perform and the fees which you propose to charge or the basis on which your fee will be calculated. You should therefore complete those parts of the model client care letter which deals with these matters.

48.    rC22 and rC88 require barristers to keep adequate records to support fees charged, and to provide such records or details to clients on request. Such records should contain separate items for each piece of paperwork and, where substantial telephone advice is provided, separate items for each piece of such advice. If the client requires further detail and, notably, the exact work done and the cost of it in respect of each item involved this should be provided.

(B) Payment in advance

49.    rC73 prohibits a barrister from handling client money. The associated guidance (gC106-gC107) clarifies that a fixed fee paid in advance is not client money for the purposes of rC73. If you agree with a client, who can reasonably be expected to understand the implications of such an agreement, that (1) your fee for any work will be charged according to the time spent on it, but (2) you will be paid a fixed fee in advance for it, and (3), when the work has been done, you will pay the client any difference between that fixed fee and the fee which has actually been earned, and (4) you will not hold the difference between the fixed fee and the fee which has been earned on trust for the client, that difference will not be client money. Such fees may be considered as client money if you cannot demonstrate that the agreement was made in advance and on clear terms. You should also consider carefully whether such an arrangement is in the client's interest and that the client fully understands the implications.

(C) Withholding paperwork until paid

50.    Barristers may withhold paperwork until fees have been received. We recommend, however, that it should be made clear to the client at the time of instruction that this will be the arrangement. It should be expressly stated in the client care letter. Barristers should note that while they are permitted to withhold the work they have done, they may not be permitted to withhold the client's papers.

The Bar Standards Board

# Handbook

(D) Lien

51.     We are not aware of any authority by which barristers gain a general lien on documents belonging to the client until the fees are paid, although there seems to be nothing in the law to invalidate an express agreement made between a barrister and a client permitting the barrister to exercise such a lien. In the absence of a contractually enforceable lien you should return the papers to your client on request, but first ensure that you have complied with your record keeping obligations (see paragraphs 67 to 71 below).

(E) Disbursements

52.     You may agree with your client that you are entitled to charge disbursements, such as travel and accommodation expenses and photocopying. This can include charging for the work of a clerk, administrative assistant or paralegal. This must be agreed in advance and therefore should be included in the client care letter.

(F) Over-charging and disputes

53.     It is likely that clients will, on occasion, seek to dispute the amount that is charged by a barrister or to claim that they have been overcharged. The scope for such disputes is obviously greatly reduced if there is clarity about the charging arrangements beforehand.

54.     It is obviously appropriate for you to seek to resolve the dispute informally if this is possible. Otherwise two options exist:

    a.     the client can refuse to pay and the dispute may have to be resolved by litigation;

    b.     the client can complain to the Office of the Legal Ombudsman ("LeO"), if they consider that you have provided inadequate professional services. In appropriate cases LeO has the power to fine you and/or order that fees be repaid. Complaints may also be made to the Bar Standards Board where the alleged conduct may amount to a breach of the Handbook.

(G) Conditional Fee Agreements (CFA) and Damages-based Agreements

55.     While in principle there is nothing to prevent barristers undertaking public access work on a Conditional Fee Agreement or a Damages-based Agreement, particular care should be taken with such arrangements. You should consider the level of risk and the likelihood of recovering base costs and the success fee in the case of a Conditional Fee Agreement and the likelihood of recovering the percentage of the claimant's damages in the case of a Damages-based Agreement.

# Handbook

56.     You should also consider the question of payment. Payment in advance or on completion of a particular piece of work would not be possible since, by definition, no fee is payable until success had been achieved. Generally, any money paid in advance would be considered client money and barristers are not permitted to hold this (see paragraph 49 above for circumstances when payment in advance may be possible).  If you require further advice please contact the Bar Council.

**Intermediaries**

57.     You may find yourself asked to perform legal services by a person or organisation that is an intermediary, for the benefit of a named client.  For example, an independent financial adviser may wish to take advice for a client, or arrange to have a document drafted. A son or daughter may want to instruct you on behalf of an elderly parent. A sponsor in this country may wish you to act in an immigration matter for a person who is out of the country. There is no objection in principle to a barrister accepting instructions from such an intermediary, but care must be taken in respect of a number of matters.

58.     You must ensure that the intermediary is not acting, or proposing to act, as a 'litigator'. It is a criminal offence under the Legal Services Act 2007 for an unauthorised person to act as a litigator, and a barrister who facilitated such activity might also be criminally liable.

59.     When specifically providing services to an immigration adviser who is acting as an intermediary, barristers should satisfy themselves that they are not engaging with anyone who is acting outside of the Immigration and Asylum Act 1999 (IAA 1999), as anyone acting in this way would be committing a criminal offence and be liable to face prosecution. Barristers who accept work which is within the scope of the IAA 1999 and do so from an OISC regulated advisor should take steps to ensure they are aware of what that advisor is entitled to do.

60.     You must ensure that both intermediary and client understand the true nature of the arrangement. To this end, you should send a client care letter to both the intermediary and the client. It is assumed that the intermediary will undertake contractual responsibility for your fees. If the intermediary does not wish to do so, you would be entitled to enquire why you should deal with the intermediary at all, rather than directly with the client. Model letters to both intermediary and client are on the BSB's website at:

https://www.barstandardsboard.org.uk/regulatory-requirements/bsb-handbook/code-guidance/

61.     You should bear in mind the possibility that the intermediary may have negotiated a contingent fee arrangement with the client and the potential conflict of interest which could thus arise between the intermediary and the client. Barristers are already familiar with the risks of potential conflicts of interest between solicitors and

The Bar Standards Board
# Handbook

clients where conditional fee agreements have been made. However, in the case of unregulated intermediaries you may feel that there is an even greater need to be alert to the risk that the manner in which information is transmitted to you may have been coloured by the intermediary's own commercial interests.

62.  If you form the view that there is a conflict of interest between client and intermediary, for example, because the intermediary has been negligent, Core Duty 2, rules such as rC15 and rC17 and related guidance require you to consider whether it would be in the client's interest to instruct another professional, and, if you consider it would be, you must both so advise and take steps to ensure that such advice reaches the client. However, it is not your duty to police the relationship between intermediary and client, which is a private matter to them.

63.  Where the intermediary instructs you to perform advocacy services, for example, before a domestic tribunal or in an arbitration, you must take such steps as appear appropriate to ensure that the client does, in fact, wish you to appear for them. In many cases this will involve having a conference with the client. A barrister performing advocacy services should inform the tribunal that they are acting for their client. You have the same obligation to a tribunal to which you send a skeleton argument.

64.  You must have regard to the relevant provisions of the Money Laundering Regulations (see paragraphs 72 to 75 below). Where instructed by an intermediary, you must normally follow the identification procedures in respect of the client. The only exception will be where the intermediary is a regulated professional and informs you by letter or certificate that they are a professional within the regulated sector as defined in Proceeds of Crime Act (POCA) and the Money Laundering Regulations and has carried out identification procedures

65.  If you are approached by an intermediary you remain under the same obligation to satisfy yourself before accepting the case that it is appropriate to do so without a solicitor or other professional client as you would be under if you were approached by the client direct. If you are familiar with the intermediary and the way in which the intermediary operates then this will be a relevant factor, but will not obviate the need for you, in respect of each prospective case, to satisfy yourself that no solicitor is required.

66.  The client care letter to the client should be sent to the client's home or, as appropriate, business address and not to the intermediary's address. The client's address will therefore be one of the pieces of information which you will need before accepting instructions through an intermediary.

67.  It is prohibited for you to pay or receive a referral fee to or from an intermediary, or to any other person for introducing a client or providing you with work. Full guidance on referral fees can be found at:

The Bar Standards Board

# Handbook

BAR
STANDARDS
BOARD

REGULATING BARRISTERS

https://www.barstandardsboard.org.uk/regulatory-requirements/bsb-handbook/code-guidance/

### Administration and record keeping

68.     When taking on public access work, Chambers need to be aware that the expectations of clients are likely to be very different from those of solicitors. They will not necessarily understand that barristers work on a different basis from solicitors and that it will not always be possible to speak directly to the barrister and that there are limits to what can and cannot be done by barristers. This should be made clear at an early stage and may be something that you would want to discuss with a client at a preliminary meeting. Barristers and clerks may need to adopt a flexible approach to dealing directly with the public and keep under review whether Chambers' administration should be adjusted accordingly.

69.     In the absence of a solicitor it will be crucial for you to maintain records about your role in providing advice to the client in case questions or complaints arise afterwards. In particular, if it is not clear from other documentation, you should maintain a record of:

   a.     the initial contact with the client;

   b.     the work you have been asked to do;

   c.     the dates of conferences and notes of advice given;
   d.     records of telephone conversations and advice given;

   e.     significant changes to instructions; and

   f.     hearings attended and advice given.

   These records should be retained for at least seven years.

70.     It is likely that clients will provide you with original documents. It is for each barrister to decide, in consultation with the client, whether they wish to retain those documents or work from copies. It is perfectly appropriate to charge for photocopying the documents but you should make it clear in your client care letter what the charge will be. You may also be asked to store the original documents on behalf of the client, but barristers are strongly discouraged from agreeing to do so unless retention by you is required in order to undertake litigation on behalf of the client (if you have been authorised to do so). The following matters should be kept in mind:

The Bar Standards Board

# Handbook

a. the original documents belong to the client and, unless otherwise agreed (for example because a lien has been agreed), must be returned to the client on demand at any stage;

b. if you agree to store original documents for the client you must keep the documents in a secure place and may be liable in negligence for failing to do so;

c. it will almost always be impractical for you to store original documents for long periods of time unless your Chambers is prepared to guarantee such a service even after you have left Chambers or ceased to practise. If originals are retained you should specify to the client a date by which they must be collected or will be returned.

71. In any case it is prudent to keep papers following the conclusion of the case because there might be an appeal, a complaint or an action for professional negligence. If a solicitor is instructed that obligation generally falls on the solicitor. In a public access case the obligation falls on the barrister. You must keep for a period of seven years the originals, copies or a list of all documents you have received or take reasonable steps to ensure that the client will do so.

72. Electronic storage is permissible if appropriate – you may wish to consult the Bar Council for further information on Information Security.

**Money laundering and proceeds of crime**

73. The Bar Council has produced detailed briefings on the Money Laundering Regulations 2007 and the Proceeds of Crime Act 2002.

74. The Money Laundering Regulations apply to barristers who are asked to advise at the planning or execution stage in transactions which involve either:

a. the buying or selling of real property or business entities;
b. the creation, operation, or management of trusts, companies or similar structures.

75. The requirements upon barristers who conduct relevant business can be summarised as:

- Customer due diligence e.g. (i) identifying the client or beneficial owner prior to the establishment of the business relationship, or the execution of the transaction, (ii) obtaining information about the business relationship or transaction, (iii) monitoring the business relationship on an ongoing basis.

The Bar Standards Board

# Handbook

- Record keeping procedures – records of all relevant transactions and evidence of client identity must be maintained for five years from the date on which the last transaction was completed.

- Procedures to forestall money laundering, and training staff – all barristers and sets of Chambers who undertake work within the ambit of the Regulations should have in place and operate general systems and procedures for ensuring compliance with the Regulations. This includes training staff on the law relating to money laundering/terrorist financing and on how to recognise and deal with transactions and other activities which may be related to money laundering/terrorist financing.

76.    The POCA makes it an offence to enter into or become concerned in an arrangement which you know or suspect facilitates (by whatever means) the acquisition, retention, use or control of criminal property by or on behalf of another person.

**Solicitors and professional clients**

77.    Two main issues arise in respect of solicitors and other professional clients in relation to public access work:

a.    acceptance of work where there is already a solicitor or professional client advising the client; and

b.    the recommendation of solicitors to public access clients.

78.    There is no objection to you accepting instructions from a client where a solicitor is currently instructed in the matter, if the solicitor is aware that the client is doing so. There is no obligation on the solicitor to instruct you directly and, in some cases, solicitors having done the necessary preparatory work will be content for the client then to brief you directly. In such circumstances, however, it is important that you should:

a.    consider whether there is any reason why the solicitor needs to instruct you directly (for example, because the matter is complex or the client cannot properly undertake the litigation component of the case, if you are not authorised to do so);

b.    be satisfied that the solicitor is aware that the client is instructing you.

If you are satisfied that the client does not require a solicitor's involvement, then you may accept the case.

The Bar Standards Board
# Handbook

BAR
STANDARDS
BOARD

REGULATING BARRISTERS

79.    A more difficult question arises where the solicitor does not know that the client is coming to you for advice. In some cases, the client will be seeking advice on the conduct of the solicitor or for a second opinion. Here there is no reason why you should not provide advice. You should not inform the solicitor of this without the client's consent. Where a case is litigious it is advisable for you, if client gives their consent, to liaise with the solicitor as necessary

80.    It is possible that clients will wish to seek counsel's advice directly in respect of matters for which a public funding certificate is already in existence and where the certificate does not extend to counsel's advice. Counsel should be alert to guard against any breach of the rules against "topping up". Where the client has indicated that they already have a solicitor, counsel should seek to establish whether or not a certificate is in existence in respect of such work.

81.    If you decide that a client should instruct a solicitor or professional client, the client may well ask you to recommend a particular individual. You may properly do this (and, if prudent, may well suggest suitable names) provided that:

   a.    you have reasonable grounds to believe that the solicitor or professional client is competent to do the work; and

   b.    you receive no payment for the referral; and

   c.    the solicitor is free to instruct another barrister.

**January 2016**
**Bar Standards Board**

The Bar Standards Board
# Handbook

BAR
STANDARDS
BOARD

REGULATING BARRISTERS

**ANNEX A**

**PRO FORMA FOR USE BY BARRISTERS WITH LESS THAN THREE YEARS' STANDING**

Name of Barrister:............................................

Date of call (month/year)................................

Chambers/entity:.............................................

| | |
|---|---|
| **Basic case details e.g. month and year accepted, when concluded and area of law** | |
| **Case issues e.g. any difficulties in the client undertaking the litigation component, problems/matters that required advice to be sought from a 'qualified** | |

The Bar Standards Board

**Handbook**

BAR
STANDARDS
BOARD

REGULATING BARRISTERS

| | |
|---|---|
| person', matters that required additional research or learning, was it necessary to involve a solicitor or withdraw. | |
| Summary of any complaint raised by the client and, if so, nature of complaint and how resolved | |
| Summary of any other comments or feedback received from the client about the service provided and any steps taken to address feedback | |

BAR
STANDARDS
BOARD

REGULATING BARRISTERS

The Bar Standards Board
# Handbook

The Bar Standards Board

# Handbook

BAR
STANDARDS
BOARD

REGULATING BARRISTERS

**CURRENT GUIDANCE**

## Cab rank rule: professional clients who are authorised persons not authorised by the Solicitors Regulation Authority (SRA)

This guidance applies to:

- Self-employed barristers instructed by a professional client;
- Authorised individuals working in a BSB authorised body; and
- BSB authorised bodies in receipt of instructions that seek the services of a named authorised individual.

### Background

The cab rank rule is set out at rC29 of the BSB Handbook. It states that if you receive instructions from a professional client and the instructions are appropriate taking into account your experience, seniority and/or field or practice, you must (subject to the exceptions in rC30) accept those instructions irrespective of:

- The identity of the client;
- The nature of the case to which the instructions relate;
- Whether the client is paying privately or is publicly funded; and
- Any belief or opinion which you may have formed as to the character, reputation, cause, conduct, guilt or innocence of the client.

rC30.9.c states that you are only obliged to accept instructions where you are being asked to act on **either** the Standard Contractual Terms for the Supply of Legal Services by Barristers to Authorised Persons 2012 (published on the Bar Council's website) **or** if you publish standard terms of work, on those terms.

1

The Bar Standards Board

# Handbook

### Non-solicitor authorised persons

The Bar Council's Standard Terms are currently drafted as if the professional client were an authorised person regulated by the SRA. However, the cab rank rule applies (subject to the various exceptions in rC30) to instructions from any professional client, therefore you may be instructed under the cab rank rule by authorised persons who are regulated by another approved regulator.

The BSB expects all authorised persons to be able to access the cab rank rule on behalf of their clients in the same way. Therefore, if you are instructed by an authorised person who is not regulated by the SRA, you are obliged to act on the same terms. You should therefore apply the Bar Council terms as if:

- The definition of professional client includes that authorised person; and
- Any references to the SRA or its Code are references to that person's approved regulator and its regulatory arrangements.

If you publish your own terms you should consider making similar amendments, where appropriate.

**September 2015**
**Bar Standards Board**

The Bar Standards Board

# Handbook

REGULATING BARRISTERS

## CURRENT GUIDANCE

## First Tier Complaints Handling

1. This guidance supplements Section D1.1 of the Code of Conduct It covers three areas:

    a. the scope of chambers complaints handling

    b. the obligation to notify clients of their right to complain

    c. guidance to chambers in developing chambers complaint procedures

2. References to "client" in this guidance are to the lay client.

### A. Scope of chambers complaints handling

3. Complaints are expressions of dissatisfaction by clients. This guidance draws a distinction between complaints that relate to service, professional negligence and misconduct. A single complaint may have elements of all three and the obligations on chambers are different for each aspect.

### Service complaints

4. The requirements set out in Section D1.1 of the Code of Conduct relate to the handling of service complaints which are within the jurisdiction of the Legal Ombudsman.

5. Chapter 2 of the Legal Ombudsman's scheme rules set out the types of complaint that are within its jurisdiction. These are complaints that relate to an act or omission by an authorised person in relation to services provided to the complainant (directly or indirectly).

6. In addition, the Legal Ombudsman's website sets out a list of the categories of complaint which it investigates. These include the following categories (some of which may also include aspects of negligence or misconduct):

- Costs information deficient
- Costs excessive
- Delay
- Unreasonably refused a service to a complainant
- Persistently or unreasonably offered a service that the complainant does not want
- Failure to advise

The Bar Standards Board
# Handbook

- Failure to comply with agreed remedy
- Failure to follow instructions
- Failure to investigate complaint internally
- Failure to keep complainant informed of progress
- Failure to keep papers safe
- Failure to progress complainant's case
- Failure to release files or papers
- Failure to reply

**Misconduct and Professional Negligence**

7. Chambers may not be best placed to seek to resolve or provide redress for complaints which relate to misconduct or professional negligence and there is no positive obligation to investigate matters of misconduct.

8. However, it is likely that in many cases a complaint which raises issues relating to professional misconduct or professional negligence will also amount to an accusation of the provision of poor service or will include a service element. Where this is the case, the service issues should be dealt with in accordance with Section D1.1 of the Code of Conduct. It is not acceptable for chambers not to investigate elements of a complaint which relate to service because the complaint also amounts to, or includes elements which relate to, misconduct or could potentially give rise to a negligence claim.

9. Complainants should be informed in writing if any aspects of their complaint are deemed to be outside of chambers' complaints handling procedures. This should include information on how to complain to the Legal Ombudsman.

*Barristers are also reminded that they must report promptly to the BSB if they have committed serious misconduct. In addition, subject to their duty to keep the affairs of each client confidential, barristers must report to the BSB if they have reasonable grounds to believe that there has been serious misconduct by another barrister. The relevant provisions of the BSB Handbook are Rules C65 – C69 and Guidance C95 – C102. Guidance C96 in particular provides examples of what serious misconduct includes without being exhaustive. Further guidance on reporting serious misconduct of others is also available on the BSB's website: https://www.barstandardsboard.org.uk/regulatory-requirements/bsb-handbook/code-guidance/*

The Bar Standards Board
# Handbook

**Bar Mutual Indemnity Fund**

10. Where a complaint raises an allegation of negligence it may be appropriate to inform BMIF and to consult them before any proposals for resolution are made to the client.

**Non-client complaints**

11. The Legal Ombudsman will only deal with complaints from consumers of lawyers' services. This means that only complaints from the barrister's clients fall within the Ombudsman's jurisdiction. This does not mean that non-client complaints should not be investigated by Chambers. Some non-client complaints, such as discourtesy, may be capable of resolution by Chambers. However, the BSB recognises that Chambers' ability to resolve many kinds of non-client complaints is limited and that they are more suited to consideration under the disciplinary processes of the Bar Standards Board. Accordingly, if Chambers feel that the issues raised by non-clients cannot be satisfactorily resolved through the Chambers complaints process they should refer the complainant to the Bar Standards Board.

**B. Notifying the client of the right to complain**

**The New Regime**

11. From 6 October 2010, Barristers must notify clients in writing at the time of engagement or if not practicable at the next appropriate opportunity:

> (a) Of their right to make a complaint, how and to whom this can be done, including their right to complain to the Legal Ombudsman at the conclusion of the complaints process, the timeframe for doing so and the full details of how to contact the Legal Ombudsman;

> (b) That the lay client may complain directly to Chambers without going through solicitors

12. At the conclusion of the complaints process, complainants must be informed in writing of their right to complain to the Legal Ombudsman, who from 6 October 2010 has taken on responsibility for dealing with all service complaints against legal professionals, the timeframe for doing so and the full details of how to contact them.

The Bar Standards Board

# Handbook

## Complaints to chambers

13. The Legal Services Board (LSB) have specified a requirement to which the BSB is obliged to give effect under s112(2) of the Legal Services Act 2007. The requirement relates to "first-tier" complaints which, and so far as self-employed barristers are concerned, relate to the procedure whereby a client makes a complaint to Chambers in the first instance.

14. The LSB seeks to ensure consumers have confidence that:

(a) complaint handling procedures provide effective safeguards for them

(b) complaints will be dealt with comprehensively and swiftly, with appropriate redress where necessary.

15. Chambers complaint handling processes must be convenient and easy to use (in particular for those that are vulnerable or have disabilities). They should make provision for complaints to be made by any reasonable means. The way in which complaints are dealt with must be transparent and clear in relation to process, well publicised and free. The process itself should be prompt and fair, with decisions based on a sufficient investigation of the circumstances. Where appropriate, there should be an offer of a suitable remedy.

16. Most consumers will be able to make a complaint to the Legal Ombudsman about the services they received after they have exhausted Chambers complaints processes. Sufficient information must be provided to all clients to identify whether they do have a right to take their complaint to the Legal Ombudsman and to contact the Legal Ombudsman direct to clarify whether they can.

17. Please note that the Legal Ombudsman, the independent complaints body for service complaints about lawyers, has time limits in which a complaint must be raised with them. The time limits are:

a) Six years from the date of the act/omission

b) Three years from the date that the complainant should reasonably have known there were grounds for complaint (if the act/omission took place before the 6 October 2010 or was more than six years ago)

The Bar Standards Board
# Handbook

c) Within six months of the complaint receiving a final response from their lawyer, if that response complies with the requirements in rule 4.4 of the Scheme Rules (which requires the response to include prominently an explanation that the Legal Ombudsman was available if the complainant remained dissatisfied and the provision of full contact details for the Ombudsman and a warning that the complaint must be referred to them within six months

18. The Ombudsman can extend the time limit in exceptional circumstances. Chambers must therefore have regard to that timeframe when deciding whether they are able to investigate your complaint. Chambers will not therefore usually deal with complaints that fall outside of the Legal Ombudsman's time limits.

19. Clients who have, or may have, a right to complain to the legal Ombudsman, must at the conclusion of the complaint process be informed of their right to complain to the Legal Ombudsman, the timeframe for doing so and full details of how to contact the Legal Ombudsman.

20. Where a barrister accepts instructions from a new client, or instructions on a new matter from an existing client, the client must be notified of the right to make a complaint, how and to whom this can be done. It is essential that systems be set up by Chambers to ensure that these requirements are properly complied with. This will be straightforward for public access clients, but because self-employed barristers will usually be instructed by a solicitor or other professional client on behalf of the client, new procedures will need to be put in place for notifying other clients.

**Compliance with requirements to notify clients**

21. The LSB has specified a requirement that the BSB must require all individuals and entities they regulate to notify all clients in writing at the time of engagement, or existing clients at the next appropriate opportunity, of their right to make a complaint, how and to whom this can be done (including their right to complain to the Legal Ombudsman at the conclusion of the complaint process, the timeframe for doing so and full details of how to contact the Legal Ombudsman).

22. The Bar Standards Board is required to enforce the LSB requirement and compliance by Chambers. The BSB will monitor Chambers to ensure that the requirement is being complied with.

The Bar Standards Board

# Handbook

23. Significant concerns have been expressed by barristers in a variety of fields of practice that a requirement to notify clients directly of their right to complain would be difficult or impossible to comply with. The BSB are fully aware of these concerns and have discussed them with the LSB. The guidance below is set out to assist barristers and Chambers in setting up systems to effect compliance with the requirement of the LSB in a way that is neither disproportionate nor onerous.

24. Where the barrister is aware of the contact details for the client, the obligation can be satisfied by a letter or e-mail sent directly to the client (which may be sent by someone else on his behalf) providing the required information.

25. If the information has not been provided beforehand in writing, it may be provided on the first occasion that the barrister meets the client at court, or in conference.

26. Subject to the points made below, it is not acceptable for barristers simply to make the information available to solicitors. Nor is it sufficient that the information is available on Chambers' website. There is a positive obligation on the barrister to provide it to the client.

27. An unequivocal agreement by the professional client to pass on chambers' complaint information to the client, either in a particular case, or in relation to each case in which a member of chambers is instructed by that professional client, will serve to discharge the obligation to provide the client with the information. However, there must be a positive agreement on the part of the professional client: silence is not sufficient. Where Chambers receive high volume instructions from a particular professional client it will not be necessary to obtain written confirmation in relation to each instruction. In those circumstances, positive written confirmation should be obtained at regular and reasonable intervals from the professional client that complaints information continues to be passed on to lay clients.

**Client information sheets**

28. Some barristers may be unhappy at the prospect that the first thing they do when they meet the client is to advise the client how to make a complaint. A "client information sheet" is one way in which the information may be communicated to the client. The information sheet giving details about the barrister as well as information on how to complain could be given to the client by the barrister. An example of a client information sheet is annexed. Whilst the information sheet carries the necessary information, it also carries helpful information for the client about the barrister and should not give rise to any negative

The Bar STANDARDS Board

# Handbook

impression. The client information sheet may be sent or handed out to the client; it may also be provided by the clerk or receptionist when the client arrives for a conference.

## Compliance

29. Whilst these requirements came into force on 6 October 2010, since 2008 Section D1.1 of the Code of Conduct has required barristers or a member of staff when first instructed to notify clients of their Chambers Complaints Procedure. The principal difference was that the requirement in force since 2008 permitted compliance by requesting in writing the solicitor or intermediary to pass the information on to the client. These requirements since 2008 have not given rise to concerns on the part of the profession.

30. It is recognized that there will be circumstances in which, in individual cases, it is impractical to comply strictly with the requirements. What is important is that Chambers set up systems, and establish procedures, to effect compliance with these requirements consistent with this guidance. The precise solutions will differ according to different fields of practice. If this has been done responsibly, then the BSB will in their monitoring visits regard sympathetically particular and specific problems and difficulties which occur or are likely to occur in individual cases.

## Cases where the procedure cannot be followed

31. Where the barrister has the contact details of the client, or when the barrister meets the client in the course of the matter, compliance should not in general present a problem.

32. However, there will be areas of practice, and particular cases, where it is not possible or practical for the barrister to satisfy the notification requirement in this way. For example, the barrister may not have the contact details of the client, cannot readily obtain them, and does not anticipate meeting the client in the course of being instructed or at least not for some time.

33. Some common sense is required in setting up procedures so as to fulfil the notification requirements. For example, where a barrister acts for government departments or public bodies it should be possible to agree a standing arrangement with treasury solicitors or other inhouse lawyers whereby details of the complaints system is provided to the professional client to be passed on to the client body. Most barristers will be able to think of examples within their own field of practice where procedures can be responsibly adopted so as to fulfil the notification requirement.

The Bar Standards Board
# Handbook

REGULATING BARRISTERS

34. In some cases there will be no realistic alternative to compliance by providing the requisite information to the solicitor or other professional client with instructions to provide that information to the client on behalf of the barrister, even when the solicitor has not expressly agreed to do so. But this course should only be adopted when other better means of compliance are not practical.

## C. Chambers complaints procedure: guidance

35. This guidance is provided to Chambers to assist them to develop a complaints procedure which is compliant with the mandatory requirements set out at Section D1.1 of the Code of Conduct. Chambers are not obliged to follow the guidance absolutely. If Chambers decide not to adopt the model procedure provided at Appendix 1 below, they should have regard to this guidance when devising their own complaints handling arrangements.

36. All barristers must be familiar with the requirements of Section D1.1 of the Code of Conduct.

37. Those barristers who are responsible for dealing with complaints should ensure that they and any staff who deal with complaints are adequately trained. The Bar Standards Board will audit and monitor Chambers complaints handling, including the sufficiency of training.

38. This annex sets out the contents of an effective procedure. Model complaints procedures are at Appendix 1 (multi member sets of Chambers) and Appendix 2 (sole practitioners). Chambers will need to insert names/positions etc into the sections in square brackets. Chambers must ensure that their website and brochure carries information about the Chambers' Complaints Procedure.

39. Chambers are not obliged to adopt the model complaints procedures provided below. The model procedures set out good practice arrangements for handling complaints but the BSB is aware that there are alternative methods that may be just as effective. Chambers have discretion to either devise their own procedure or to amend the model procedure to best fit their own administrative arrangements or the particular circumstances of a complaint. The only requirements are that Chambers adopts a complaints procedure that includes the mandatory requirements laid down in the complaints protocol set out at Section D1.1 of the Code of Conduct.

The Bar Standards Board
# Handbook

40. Possible alternatives to the arrangements in the model procedure have been provided where appropriate. These alternatives are not exhaustive but are used to highlight that other procedures may be more suitable for Chambers depending on their size, practice type or administrative set up.

**Chambers complaints procedure: First Stage**

41. Where a client is dissatisfied with some aspect of the service provided by a barrister or by Chambers he should be invited to telephone an individual nominated under the Chambers Complaints Procedure to deal with complaints. For example, the Chambers Director, Practice Manager or Head of Chambers. In order to ensure consistency of approach, this individual should be the first point of contact for all complaints. The client should also be told that if he prefers he may make the complaint in writing and the Chambers Complaint Procedure should be sent to him unless it has already been provided.

42. Where a complaint is made by telephone, a note of the complaint should be made. It should record:

- The name and address of the complainant;
- The date of the complaint;
- Against whom the complaint is made;
- The detail of the complaint; and
- What the complainant believes should be done about the complaint.

43. In many cases the complaint will be resolved over the telephone during the first call. When that occurs the individual nominated to deal with complaints should record the outcome on the note of complaint. The client should be asked whether he is content with the outcome and informed of the Legal Ombudsman's complaints procedure. If he is, that fact will be recorded. The complaints procedure should suggest that the client may wish to make his own note. If the client is not content he should be invited to put the complaint in writing so that it may be investigated formally. At that stage he should be sent a copy of the Chambers' Complaints Procedure unless it has already been provided: The client should also be informed of the Legal Ombudsman's complaints procedure.

**Chambers complaint procedure: Second Stage**

44. It is recommended that Chambers set up a complaints panel made up of experienced practitioners from different practice areas and a senior member of staff. A head of panel

The Bar Standards Board

# Handbook

should be appointed. There should be a nominated deputy. All complaints (other than those resolved at stage one) should be put before the head of the panel or, in his absence, the deputy. The role of the panel is to appoint from its members an independent person to investigate a complaint and to ensure that all complaints are handled consistently and in accordance with the Chambers complaints procedure.

45. It may not be appropriate or possible for a small set of Chambers to convene a complaints panel. Chambers are encouraged to set up a complaints panel where possible or otherwise nominate an individual or individuals to investigate the complaint.

46. Sole practitioners may not feel able to investigate independently a complaint raised against them and should therefore offer mediation or arbitration if a complaint remains unresolved. A suggested approach to mediation/arbitration is set out in the model procedure for sole practitioners at Appendix 2 below.

47. A complaint received in writing should, where possible, be acknowledged within two days of receipt and, in any event, promptly. Within 14 days of that acknowledgment the head of the panel (where one has been set up) (or his deputy) should appoint a member of the panel to investigate the complaint. Where the complaint is against a member of staff the person appointed normally will be the senior staff member. Where the complaint is against the senior staff member the head of the panel should appoint another member of the panel to investigate. Where the complaint is against the head of the panel, the Head of Chambers should investigate or, in his discretion, appoint a member of the panel to investigate. Where the Head of Chambers is the head of the panel, the deputy head of the panel should be the appointed person. No barrister should investigate a complaint of which he is the subject. Where no panel has been established, Chambers should ensure that the individual or individuals nominated to investigate the complaint is impartial.

48. The appointed person/nominated individual should write to the client as soon as he is appointed. He should inform him that he is to investigate the complaint and that he will report back to the client within 14 days. If it becomes plain that a response cannot be sent within 14 days a realistic time frame should be set and the client informed accordingly.

49. The appointed person/nominated individual should investigate the complaint. He should speak to the barrister/member of staff complained against, and any other people he identifies as having something to contribute. He should review all relevant documents. If necessary he should revert to the client for further information and clarification.

The Bar Standards Board
# Handbook

50. The appointed person/nominated individual should prepare a report to the client (with a copy to the barrister/member of staff complained against). The report should set out all the matters referred to at paragraph 42 above, the nature and scope of the investigations carried out in respect of each complaint, his conclusions and the basis for his conclusions. The report should be drafted using clear and concise language. Where a complaint is found to be justified, the report should provide proposals for resolution (e.g. reduction in fees, apology, compensation).

51. The report should be sent to the client within 14 days of the appointed person's appointment (or such longer period as has been communicated to the client in advance - see paragraph 48). A copy of the report should be provided to the barrister/member of staff complained against.

**Charging for complaints**

52. Chambers should not charge clients for dealing with their complaint. To do so brings the Bar into disrepute and could amount to professional misconduct.

**Confidentiality**

53. All conversations and documents shall be confidential and disclosed only to the extent necessary. They may be disclosed only to the client, the person complained about, the Head of Chambers, the head of the complaints panel or relevant senior member of the panel, the nominated individual, the management committee (for carrying out the task at paragraph 50) and any other individual with whom enquiries need to be made for the purpose of the investigation.

**Record Keeping**

54. Where the procedure ends after the first stage the person responsible for recording the outcome on the note of complaint should ensure that the note of complaint is placed on the Chambers complaints file.

55. Where the procedure ends after the second stage the head of the panel/nominated individual should ensure that the following documents are placed on the Chambers complaints file:

• Note/letter of complaint; (see paragraph 41);

The Bar Standards Board
# Handbook

BAR
STANDARDS
BOARD

REGULATING BARRISTERS

• Appointed person's/nominated individual's report; (see paragraph 50).

**Review, Monitoring and Audit**

56. The Chambers complaints file should be inspected regularly by the management committee. Papers should be anonymised where necessary. The person responsible for the administration of the system should report at least annually to such appropriate committee of Chambers on the number of complaints received and the subject area of the complaints. In such a report all the details should be anonymised, but should be reviewed for trends and possible training issues.

57. The Bar Standards Board will audit and monitor Chambers complaints handling, including, where appropriate, the sufficiency of training. All barristers must comply promptly with requests for information from the committees of the Bar Standards Board dealing with monitoring and auditing.

**First issued: March 2008**

**Last Updated: January 2014**

The Bar Standards Board
# Handbook

BAR
STANDARDS
BOARD

REGULATING BARRISTERS

**Appendix 1**

The model procedures for Chambers and for Sole Practitioners are based on the suggested arrangements for handling complaints set out in the above guidance. Chambers or sole practitioners may decide to adopt the model procedure but are free to develop their own procedure or set of rules for dealing with complaints. Chambers' must ensure that any procedure they develop is compliant with the mandatory requirements set out at Section D1.1 of the Code of Conduct

**Model Chambers Complaints Procedure for multi member sets**

1. Our aim is to give you a good service at all times. However if you have a complaint you are invited to let us know as soon as possible. It is not necessary to involve solicitors in order to make your complaint but you are free to do so should you wish.

2. Please note that the Legal Ombudsman, the independent complaints body for service complaints about lawyers, has time limits in which a complaint must be raised with them. The time limits are:

a) Six years from the date of the act/omission

b) Three years from the date that the complainant should reasonably have known there were grounds for complaint (if the act/omission took place before the 6 October 2010 or was more than six years ago)

c) Within six months of the complaint receiving a final response from their lawyer, if that response complies with the requirements in rule 4.4 of the Scheme Rules (which requires the response to include prominently an explanation that the Legal Ombudsman was available if the complainant remained dissatisfied and the provision of full contact details for the Ombudsman and a warning that the complaint must be referred to them within six months

3. The Ombudsman can extend the time limit in exceptional circumstances. Chambers must therefore have regard to that timeframe when deciding whether they are able to investigate your complaint. Chambers will not therefore usually deal with complaints that fall outside of the Legal Ombudsman's time limits.

The Bar Standards Board
# Handbook

4. The Ombudsman will also only deal with complaints from consumers. This means that only complaints from the barrister's client are within their jurisdiction. Non-clients who are not satisfied with the outcome of the Chambers' investigation should contact the Bar Standards Board rather than the Legal Ombudsman.

5. It should be noted that it may not always be possible to investigate a complaint brought by a non-client. This is because the ability of Chambers to satisfactorily investigate and resolve such matters is limited and complaints of this nature are often better suited to the disciplinary processes maintained by the Bar Standards Board. Therefore, Chambers will make an initial assessment of the complaint and if they feel that the issues raised cannot be satisfactorily resolved through the Chambers complaints process they will refer you to the Bar Standards Board.

**Complaints Made by Telephone**

6. You may wish to make a complaint in writing and, if so, please follow the procedure in paragraph 7 below. However, if you would rather speak on the telephone about your complaint then please telephone the individual nominated under the Chambers Complaints Procedure to deal with complaints - NAME or (if the complaint is about a member of staff) the [senior member of staff-NAME]. If the complaint is about the [senior member of staff] telephone [the Head of Chambers - NAME or other member of Chambers appointed by head]. The person you contact will make a note of the details of your complaint and what you would like to have done about it. He will discuss your concerns with you and aim to resolve them. If the matter is resolved he will record the outcome, check that you are satisfied with the outcome and record that you are satisfied. You may also wish to record the outcome of the telephone discussion in writing.

7. If your complaint is not resolved on the telephone you will be invited to write to us about it so it can be investigated formally.

**Complaints made in Writing**

8. Please give the following details:

    • Your name and address;
    • Which member(s) of Chambers you are complaining about;
    • The detail of the complaint; and
    • What you would like done about it.

The Bar Standards Board

# Handbook

9. Please address your letter to [name of preferred recipient and Chambers' address]. We will, where possible, acknowledge receipt of your complaint within two days and provide you with details of how your complaint will be dealt with.

10. Our Chambers has a panel headed by [name] and made up of experienced members of Chambers and a senior member of staff, which considers any written complaint. Within 14 days of your letter being received the head of the panel or his deputy in his absence will appoint a member of the panel to investigate it. If your complaint is against the head of the panel, the next most senior member of the panel will investigate it. In any case, the person appointed will be someone other than the person you are complaining about.

11. The person appointed to investigate will write to you as soon as possible to let you know he has been appointed and that he will reply to your complaint within 14 days. If he finds later that he is not going to be able to reply within 14 days he will set a new date for his reply and inform you. His reply will set out:

   • The nature and scope of his investigation;
   • His conclusion on each complaint and the basis for his conclusion; and
   • If he finds that you are justified in your complaint, his proposals for resolving the complaint.

## Confidentiality

12. All conversations and documents relating to the complaint will be treated as confidential and will be disclosed only to the extent that is necessary. Disclosure will be to the head of Chambers, members of our management committee and to anyone involved in the complaint and its investigation. Such people will include the barrister member or staff who you have complained about, the head or relevant senior member of the panel and the person who investigates the complaint. The Bar Standards Board is entitled to inspect the documents and seek information about the complaint when discharging its auditing and monitoring functions.

## Our Policy

13. As part of our commitment to client care we make a written record of any complaint and retain all documents and correspondence generated by the complaint for a period of six years. Our management committee inspects an anonymised record regularly with a view to improving services.

The Bar Standards Board

# Handbook

BAR
STANDARDS
BOARD

REGULATING BARRISTERS

**Complaints to the Legal Ombudsman**

14. If you are unhappy with the outcome of our investigation and you fall within their jurisdiction you may take up your complaint with the Legal Ombudsman, the independent complaints body for complaints about lawyers, at the conclusion of our consideration of your complaint. The Ombudsman is not able to consider your complaint until it has first been investigated by Chambers. Please note the timeframe for referral of complaints to the Ombudsman as set out at paragraph 2 above.

You can write to them at:

Legal Ombudsman
PO Box 6806,
Wolverhampton
WV1 9WJ

Telephone number: 0300 555 0333
Email: enquiries@legalombudsman.org.uk

15. If you are not the barrister's client and are unhappy with the outcome of our investigation then please contact the Bar Standards Board at:

Bar Standards Board
Professional Conduct Department
289-293 High Holborn
London
WC1V 7JZ

Telephone number: 0207 6111 444
Website : www.barstandardsboard.org.uk

## The Bar Standards Board

# Handbook

BAR
STANDARDS
BOARD

REGULATING BARRISTERS

**Appendix 2**

**Model Complaints Procedure - Sole Practitioners**

1. My aim is to give all my clients a good service at all times. However if you have a complaint please let me know as soon as possible, by telephone or in writing. I will treat your complaint as confidential although I may discuss it with other barristers or officials from the Bar Standards Board for their advice. I will not reveal your name to others unless I am setting up mediation or arbitration. I will deal with your complaint promptly.

2. Please note that the Legal Ombudsman, the independent complaints body for service complaints about lawyers, has time limits in which a complaint must be raised with them. The time limits are:

   a) Six years from the date of the act/omission

   b) Three years from the date that the complainant should reasonably have known there were grounds for complaint (if the act/omission took place before the 6 October 2010 or was more than six years ago)

   c) Within six months of the complaint receiving a final response from their lawyer, if that response complies with the requirements in rule 4.4 of the Scheme Rules (which requires the response to include prominently an explanation that the Legal Ombudsman was available if the complainant remained dissatisfied and the provision of full contact details for the Ombudsman and a warning that the complaint must be referred to them within six months

3. The Ombudsman can extend the time limit in exceptional circumstances. Chambers must therefore have regard to that timeframe when deciding whether they are able to investigate your complaint. Chambers will not therefore usually deal with complaints that fall outside of the Legal Ombudsman's time limits.

4. The Ombudsman will also only deal with complaints from consumers. This means that only complaints from the barrister's client are within their jurisdiction. Non-clients who are not satisfied with the outcome of the investigation should contact the Bar Standards Board rather than the Legal Ombudsman.

The Bar Standards Board

# Handbook

5. It should be noted that it may not always be possible to investigate a complaint brought by a non-client. This is because my ability to satisfactorily investigate and resolve such matters is limited and complaints of this nature are often better suited to the disciplinary processes maintained by the Bar Standards Board. Therefore, I will make an initial assessment of the complaint and if I feel that the issues raised cannot be satisfactorily resolved through my complaints process I will refer you to the Bar Standards Board.

**Complaints made by telephone**

6. If you wish to make a complaint by telephone, I will make a note of the details of your complaint and what you would like done about it. I will endeavour to resolve matters with you on the telephone. If after discussion you are satisfied with the outcome I will make a note of the outcome and the fact that you are satisfied. If you are not satisfied you may wish to make a written complaint.

**Complaints made in writing**

7. If you wish to make a written complaint please give me the following details:-

- Your name, telephone number an address;
- The detail of your complaint; and
- What you would like done about it.

**Procedure for dealing with your complaint**

8. There are a number of ways in which your complaint may be dealt with:

(a) Discussion over the telephone;
(b) Dealt with by correspondence;
(c) Discussion at a meeting between us;
(d) The appointment of a mediator who will try to facilitate the resolution of your complaint;
(e) The appointment of an arbitrator whose decision we both agree shall be binding.

9. If we decide to appoint an arbitrator we both would need to agree how the arbitrator should approach his/her task and the limit of the compensation that can be awarded. The Bar Sole Practitioners Group (BSPG) or local Circuit will be approached and a barrister will be appointed to arbitrate. We will decide together whether it will be the BSPG or the local

# Handbook

Circuit who should be approached. However neither of us may veto the person chosen. It is expected that the BSPG and the Circuit will chose someone who has considerable experience in the area that is the subject matter of the dispute.

10. Upon receipt of a written complaint I will

(a) Reply in writing, normally within 48 hours, to acknowledge the complaint and inform you how I shall be dealing with it.

(b) Reply within 14 days responding in full to your complaint. I will offer you the opportunity to meet with you if that is appropriate. If I find later that I am not going to be able to reply within 14 days I will set a new date for my reply and inform you. My reply will set out:

• The nature and scope of my investigation;

• My conclusion on each complaint and the basis for my conclusion; and

• If I find that you are justified in your complaint, my proposals for resolving the complaint.

11. If you indicate that you are not happy with my written response you may ask for mediation or arbitration or, if you fall within their jurisdiction, you may make a formal complaint to the Legal Ombudsman, the independent complaints handling body for complaints about lawyers. Please note the timeframe for referral of complaints to the Ombudsman as set out at paragraph 2 above.

They can be contacted at:

Legal Ombudsman
PO Box 6806,
Wolverhampton
WV1 9WJ

Telephone number: 0300 555 0333
Email: enquiries@legalombudsman.org.uk

The Bar Standards Board
# Handbook

BAR
STANDARDS
BOARD

REGULATING BARRISTERS

12. If you are not my client and are unhappy with the outcome of our investigation then please contact the Bar Standards Board at:

Bar Standards Board
Professional Conduct Department
289-293 High Holborn
London
WC1V 7JZ

Telephone number: 0207 6111 444

Website: www.barstandardsboard.org.uk

13. I will maintain confidentiality at all times and discuss your complaint only to the extent that is necessary for its resolution and to comply with requests for information from the Bar Standards Board discharging its auditing and monitoring functions.

14. I will retain all correspondence and other documents generated in the course of your complaint for a period of six years and I will review complaints at least once a year to ensure that I maintain good standards of service.

**APPENDIX 3**

Example client information leaflet

Barrister XXXXX

Client Information Leaflet

About XXXX

I am a barrister at xxxx Chambers in xxxx

Include a statement about yourself and your experience eg

I specialise in xxxxxx

How I will work for you

The Bar Standards Board
# Handbook

BAR
STANDARDS
BOARD

REGULATING BARRISTERS

My work for you may involve giving advice, writing legal documents, or representing you in a court, tribunal or meeting.

As your barrister, I will work closely with your solicitor. But my duty is to you. I will do whatever I legally can to protect and advance your interests. However, my overriding duty is to the court so I cannot knowingly or recklessly mislead the court.

I will keep what you tell me confidential if that is what you want. But I cannot tell a court (or anyone else) anything that I know is not true.

I will do whatever I can to help you through the legal process. Please tell me or your solicitor about any concerns you have. And do ask all the questions you want to ask.

Feedback and complaints

I value all feedback. Please do let me know, at any time, what you think.

If anything is wrong, I would always want to know and to put it right. Please tell me, or your solicitor, straight away.

You can also contact the Legal Ombudsman (Tel: 0300 555 0333), enquiries@legalombudsman.org.uk

More information

You can find out more about me and my chambers on Chambers website at XXXX

**January 2014**
**Bar Standards Board**

The Bar Standards Board

# Handbook

BAR
STANDARDS
BOARD

REGULATING BARRISTERS

**CURRENT GUIDANCE**

## Guidance on Referral and Marketing Arrangements for Barristers Permitted by the BSB

### Referral fees

The BSB will consider a number of features when determining whether a payment to a third party making a referral, acting as an introducer or providing administrative and marketing services constitutes a prohibited referral fee. A payment for these purposes includes not only a financial payment but also any benefits in kind such as the provision of services or facilities for no cost or at a reduced rate.

Features which will indicate that the payment is a prohibited referral fee:

1. The payment is made in circumstances which amount to bribery under the Bribery Act 2010
2. The payment is made in connection with personal injury work and is prohibited by the Legal Aid, Sentencing and Punishment of Offenders Act 2012

Features which are likely to indicate that the payment is a prohibited referral fee:

1. The payment is made to a professional person acting for the lay client who has a duty to act in the best interests of that client when making a referral
2. The payment to an introducer is linked to specific referrals
3. The payment to an introducer for services provided by the barrister is not a set fee but is linked to the number of referrals
4. In a publicly funded case, the fee paid to an instructed barrister is less than the Legal Aid Agency fee for those advocacy services
5. The payment is a condition of receiving a referral
6. A payment for marketing or related services is higher than market rates

Features which may suggest that the payment is not a referral fee:

1. The payment is made to an employee or agent of the barrister making the payment, e.g. a clerk or an outsourced clerking service, in return for the services they provide to the barrister and not for onward payment to any person who refers work to the barrister
2. The payment is made to a marketing or advertising agency and the amount does not depend on whether any instructions are received or on the value of any instructions received
3. The payment is made to an introducer who is not an authorised person or other professional person for the purpose of being included in a list of providers of legal services and the amount is not dependent on the number of referrals received from that introducer

The Bar Standards Board

# Handbook

In considering whether to take enforcement action in cases where payments have been made which may amount to referral fees, the BSB will take a purposive approach and will consider the underlying nature and purpose of the arrangements and whether or not they were in the best interests of clients, either by helping them to access legal services not otherwise readily accessible by them or by providing some benefit to them which is directly attributable to the payment made.  For example, where a professional person is under a duty to act in their client's best interests when making a referral, receipt of any payment from barristers seeking to be instructed by that professional person's client creates a risk to their independence and integrity in discharging that duty to the client, without any concomitant benefit to the client in improving their access to justice.  Where, on the other hand, the payment is made by the barrister to a third party whose business is to make information about choices of barrister more readily accessible by clients so that they can make an informed choice of barrister, that is in principle capable of promoting access to justice by clients.

Where on the face of it a payment appears to be related to referrals (for example where the payment varies according to whether work is received) the barrister will need to demonstrate that the payment is genuinely made in return for a service other than in return for the decision by the person who instructs the barrister to instruct that barrister.  Where a payment has been made other than to an agent or employee of the barrister (such as a clerk), the BSB will also consider whether the client has been informed of the fee and had an opportunity to challenge it.

**The following are examples of cases in which a payment is not likely to be a prohibited referral fee**

Example 1 (outsourced clerking arrangements)

A barrister or Chambers arranges to outsource its administrative and clerking arrangements. The barrister or Chambers pay fixed fees on a contractual basis to a company providing these arrangements, which may also include marketing and advertising services. The outsourcing company acts as a barrister's agent and liaises with solicitors and other professional clients, including over billing and fees. The role of the outsourcing company, in respect of referrals of work, is to market the services of the barristers who retain them to those who are looking to instruct them, in the same way that in-house clerks would do.  By competing with others to secure the work from referrers they contribute to a competitive, efficient and informed market place.  The outsourcing company does not purport to make recommendations that are independent of the barristers who retain it and does not assume a duty to advise the client in the client's best interest as to selection of a barrister, so as to owe any duty to the client that would conflict with the duty they owe to those whom they represent.  Rather, the outsourcing company represents the barristers.  It is the barrister who has a duty to the client not to take on work that is outside his competence or which he does not have time to carry out.

Example  2 (marketing services)

Members of a Chambers appoint a marketing or advertising business to promote their services.  Clients who contact chambers in answer to the advert are asked to identify this at the point of instruction in order to measure the effectiveness of the advertising campaign. Members pay a fee for these services which is reviewed quarterly based on the number of

The Bar Standards Board

# Handbook

BAR
STANDARDS
BOARD

REGULATING BARRISTERS

instructions identified as being referable to the marketing campaign or adverts. The marketing techniques used do not mislead clients into believing they are receiving independent advice as to their choice of barrister and are clearly identifiable as advertising. The members are able to demonstrate that the payment was genuinely made for the purpose of receiving the marketing services. (See general guidance above.)

Example 3 (barrister owned referral company)

Members of a Chambers establish, own and manage a limited company in order to advertise and market their services more effectively. The company provides no legal services itself but operates a website or 'shop front' which advertises to potential clients how to instruct barristers on a direct access basis. It is comparable in nature to other limited companies owned by barristers in Chambers which provide administrative and accommodation services to them. Members of the public get in touch by telephone, email or by visiting in person. Clients who are introduced in this way then instruct individual barristers in Chambers via the clerks in the traditional way, paying fees directly to them. Members of Chambers pay regular fixed fees to the company which reflect the costs of the advertising services provided and are not linked to individual referrals. The company acts as agent for Members of Chambers, not as agent for potential clients. The role of the company is analogous to that in example 1 and the analysis is therefore the same.

Example 4 (third party introducer)

A company sets up a service which introduces direct access clients to barristers. The introducer operates a commercial website and a call centre for consumers to phone and outline their legal problems. The introducer provides no legal advice or services itself and is not an authorised body under the LSA 2007. It trades on its offer to put consumers in touch with individual self-employed barristers who have the relevant expertise to meet their needs and who are able to be instructed on a direct access basis. The introducer introduces potential clients to barristers who are on a national panel, pre-selected by the introducer. The introducer undertakes the costs of advertising, operating the website and call centre, setting up the panels and vetting potential clients and recoups these costs from its fees. Barristers on the panel may also be charged a one off or annual fixed fee to the agency but this does not vary depending on the number of referrals received.

Example 5 (third party introducer)

The facts are as in example 4 but the introducer's fee does vary with the number of referrals received. However, the barrister is able to demonstrate (see general guidance above) that the introducer makes its own independent judgment as to which barrister best meets the client's needs for the given case and advises the client accordingly, and that the percentage the introducer receives is the same regardless of which of the barristers on its panel is instructed, rather than it auctioning cases to the highest bidder. The fact that payment varies with success in attracting instructions is then a fair commercial reflection of the value of the service provided to the barrister in vetting the barrister and maintaining the barrister on the

panel and does not adversely affect the client's interests. (Note, however, that quite independently of whether or not the arrangements involve any referral fee, barristers need to ensure they do not enter into any terms with an introducer that would interfere with their ability act independently and in their client's best interests.)

Example 6 (membership subscriptions)

Barristers pay individual membership subscriptions to a body which maintains a panel of accredited barristers from which it proposes barristers to those who contact the body requiring those with particular expertise (for example an alternative dispute resolution (ADR) body, which appoints or recommends persons to provide mediation, arbitration or adjudication services from a list of barristers who pay to maintain their membership of the ADR body). The membership subscriptions paid by barristers are on an annual or regular, fixed basis and are not per referral made or otherwise linked to the number of referrals.

Example 7 (membership subscription)

If the facts are as in example 6 but, instead, fees were paid to the ADR body as a percentage of the fees received for acting, it would be necessary to consider whether the situation was truly analogous to example 1 or example 5, in which case it would not be a referral fee.
By way of contrast, an arrangement such as that in examples 6 or 7 is likely to be a referral fee where the facts are such that clients are likely to be under a mistaken impression that the introducer or ADR body was acting independently in selecting the barrister, when in reality their recommendation was procured by the highest bid, for example, because the percentage to be paid is not fixed in advance or the same for all.

**January 2014**
**Bar Standards Board**

## The Bar Standards Board
# Handbook

BAR
STANDARDS
BOARD

REGULATING BARRISTERS

**CURRENT GUIDANCE**

## Confidentiality Guidance

**Maintaining confidentiality**

Concern has been expressed that the profession is not taking its responsibilities to protect confidential client data and confidential financial data of members of Chambers sufficiently seriously. Examples have been given that client papers and Chambers' data are not being disposed of securely and are simply being discarded in waste paper baskets within Chambers.

The Bar Standards Board would like to remind barristers that all client communications are privileged and that such communications, client information and Chambers confidential data (financial or otherwise) must be stored, handled and disposed of securely.

Attention in particular is drawn to Core Duty 6, Rule C5 and Rule C15.5 of the BSB Handbook, which require barristers to preserve the confidentiality of the client's affairs. Any barrister who does not adhere to this by, for example, allowing other people to see confidential material, losing portable devices on which unprotected information is stored, or not disposing of client papers securely could face disciplinary action by the Bar Standards Board.

Barristers are data controllers under the Data Protection Act and must comply with the requirements of the Act in handling data to which that Act applies.

Barristers are responsible for the conduct of those who undertake work on their behalf and are advised to ensure that clerks and other Chambers' staff are aware of the need to handle and dispose of confidential material securely. Chambers must have appropriate systems for looking after confidential information.

In making arrangements to look after the information entrusted to them, barristers should seek to reduce the risk of casual or deliberate unauthorised access to it. Consideration needs to be given to information kept in electronic form as well as on paper. The arrangements should cover:

- The handling and storage of confidential information. Papers should not be left where others can read them, and computers should be placed so that they cannot be overlooked, especially when working in public places. When not being used, papers should be stored in a way which minimises the risk of unauthorised access. Computers should be password protected.
- Suitable arrangements should be made for distributing papers and sending

The Bar Standards Board

# Handbook

REGULATING BARRISTERS

faxes and emails.
- Particular care should be taken when using removable devices such as laptops, removable discs, CDs, USB memory sticks and PDAs. Such devices should be used to store only information needed for immediate business purposes, not for permanent storage. Information on them should be at least password protected and preferably encrypted. Great care should be taken in looking after the devices themselves to ensure that they are not lost or stolen.
- When no longer required, all confidential material must be disposed of securely, for example by returning it to the client or professional client, shredding paper, permanently erasing information no longer required and securely disposing of any electronic devices which hold confidential information.

Additional safeguards will need to be put in place for particularly sensitive information, or for cases in which Counsel from the same Chambers are appearing on opposing sides.

**January 2014**
**Bar Standards Board**

The Bar Standards Board
# Handbook

**CURRENT GUIDANCE**

## Guidance on Self-Employed Practice

### Investigating or collecting evidence and taking witness statements

1. There is no longer a rule which prohibits a self-employed barrister from investigating or collecting evidence generally or therefore from taking statements from potential witnesses (which is treated for these purposes as investigating or collecting evidence). In this context, taking witness statements means interviewing the potential witness with a view to preparing a statement or taking a proof of evidence. A barrister has always been entitled to settle a witness statement taken by another person, and this is not investigating or collecting evidence. However, Rule C21.10 of the BSB Handbook states 'you must not accept instructions to act in a particular matter if there is a real prospect that you are not going to be able to maintain your independence'. Guidance C73 then states that the rule 'is an aspect of your broader obligation to maintain your independence (Core Duty 4). Your ability to perform your duty to the court (Core Duty 1) and act in the best interests of your client (Core Duty 2) may be put at risk if you act in circumstances where your independence is compromised. Examples of when you may not be able to maintain your independence include appearing as an advocate in a matter in which you are likely to be called as a witness (unless the matter on which you are likely to be called as a witness is peripheral or minor in the context of the litigation as a whole and is unlikely to lead to your involvement in the matter being challenged at a later date)'.

2. It follows that if the nature of the evidence or the circumstances in which it was investigated or collected are such that there is likely to be an issue about that in court, where the barrister might be needed to give evidence, the barrister can properly be involved in the preparations for a case but cannot accept a brief to conduct the case in court, even as the junior member of a team of barristers. Only if the barrister reasonably believes that the investigation and collection of that evidence (as distinct from the evidence itself) is unlikely to be challenged can the barrister properly conduct the case in court. (The above is intended to apply to the case where a barrister properly accepts a brief and then, as part of his conduct of the case at court, has urgently to take a statement from his client or a potential witness. It applies where a barrister has investigated or collected evidence before arriving at court at the start of the case).

3. The Bar Standards Board considers that it is a key function of a junior member of a team of Counsel that s/he should be in a position to conduct the case in court if and when

The Bar Standards Board

# Handbook

required, and that it is unacceptable to have briefed as junior counsel in a case someone who may not be in a position to take on the full advocacy role in that case should it become necessary. The risks to the client's interests and to the due administration of justice generally are too great to allow a barrister to conduct a case in court, even as a junior in a team of barristers, if there is a real risk that the circumstances of the taking of the evidence that barrister has collected will be challenged in the case. If a junior member of the team is called upon to conduct the case and the circumstances of his investigation and collection of evidence is an issue in the case, the barrister might have to stand down, damaging the client's interests (the client having then been deprived of each member of his/her chosen team) and the due administration of justice (through the inconvenience and delay in the conduct of the case).

4. When investigating or collecting evidence, barristers should bear carefully in mind the dangers of unconsciously affecting or contaminating the evidence that a witness is able to give. Barristers should also be aware of the risks as a result of becoming involved in investigating or collecting evidence, and take these risks into account when deciding:-

a. whether to undertake such work in the first place; and

b. if they have done, whether or not they can properly accept a brief at a subsequent trial.

5. The BSB Handbook places the onus squarely on the barrister who has investigated or collected evidence prior to accepting a brief to consider and reach a reasonable conclusion whether or not his/her involvement is likely to be challenged.

6. In assessing whether to accept a brief in these circumstances, the barrister should be mindful of the risk where s/he has been involved in the collection or investigation of evidence. The barrister's duty is to reach a reasonable decision on the risk involved before accepting a brief. The brief can only properly be accepted if it is reasonable for the barrister to conclude that the circumstances of his investigation or collection of evidence are unlikely to be challenged. If the barrister's decision is not a reasonable one, and the trial is subsequently adjourned as a result of the barrister withdrawing from the case, the barrister risks being exposed to an order for wasted costs as well as enforcement action being taken against them for a breach of the BSB Handbook.

7. Even where a brief is properly accepted, the question of whether the barrister should continue to act is a matter that s/he must keep under review during the case in light of any later developments. However, Guidance C73 states 'if you are planning to withdraw from a

## The Bar Standards Board
# Handbook

case because it appears that you are likely to be a witness on a material question of fact, you should only withdraw if you can do so without jeopardising the client's interests'.

### Attendance at police stations

8. Previous rules prevented barristers from attending on clients at police stations. That absolute bar has now been removed. However, barristers should pay attention to Guidance C39 of the BSB Handbook, which states 'you should not attend a police station to advise a suspect or interviewee as to the handling and conduct of police interviews unless you have complied with such training requirements as may be imposed by the Bar Standards Board in respect of such work'. Similarly, Rule C120.1 states 'before accepting any public access instructions from or on behalf of a public access client, a barrister must be properly qualified by having been issued with a full practising certificate, by having satisfactorily completed the appropriate public access training, and by registering with the Bar Council as a public access practitioner'.

9. Barristers undertaking publicly funded police station work under a criminal contract must comply with the training requirements specified by the Legal Aid Agency. Barristers undertaking privately funded police station work must complete the Police Station Qualification ("PSQ") and (if they do not hold higher rights of audience) the Magistrates Court Qualification. If a barrister who wishes to undertake privately funded police station work considers they hold relevant previous experience that would exempt them from completing the PSQ, they should contact the Regulatory Policy Department at the Bar Standards Board with full details of their previous experience.

10. Barristers should also pay particular attention to the BSB Handbook provisions set out in paragraph 1 of this guidance: Core Duties 1, 2 and 4, Rule C21.10 and Guidance C73.

11. A particular difficulty facing a barrister who attends at a police station to advise suspects and interviewees or to take part in identification procedures is that the barrister may have to advise the client whether or not to answer police questions or to volunteer a statement, or may see or hear something that is material to the evidence that will be presented in court. The client's decision whether or not to answer questions, and if so which, is very likely to be a significant matter in any subsequent court hearing. So might compliance with PACE Codes of interviews or identification procedures that the barrister sees or hears. If these are significant evidential matters at trial, the barrister in question may find him or herself in serious professional difficulties if acting as advocate in the case.

# Handbook

12. Advising a suspect at the police station or attending on his behalf at an interview or identification procedure always gives rise to the risk that you may become a witness at the trial or at a Newton hearing or pre-trial admissibility hearing. The fact of advising a suspect or being present in those circumstances does not in itself prevent you from appearing as an advocate for that defendant in all circumstances. If the defendant you have advised is going to enter a guilty plea which you know to be acceptable to the Crown, or has given a full comment interview which remains as his account, then the degree of risk may be relatively low. But if the defendant declined, on your advice or not, to answer all or any questions in interview (whether or not there was a prepared statement) then the risk of becoming a witness will, inevitably, be too great to allow you to deal with the case at trial or at a Newton hearing or pre-trial admissibility hearing. This guidance applies equally whether you were to appear as an advocate alone or being led or leading (see paragraph 3 above).

13. Given the possibility that you may be required to give evidence of events at the police station, you should keep detailed, contemporaneous notes of those events.

14. Attending at police stations is subject to the cab rank rule (Rule C29). However, the BSB Handbook states that the cab rank rule does not apply if:

• 'You are not authorised and/or otherwise accredited to perform the work required by the relevant instruction' (Rule C21.7), i.e. you have not complied with the Bar Standards Board's training requirements in respect of attending at police stations (see paragraph 8 above);

• 'There is a real prospect that you are not going to be able to maintain your independence' (Rule C21.10);

• 'Accepting the instructions would require you…to do something other than in the course of [your] ordinary working time' (Rule C30.2).

In addition, Guidance C89 states that 'you would not be required to accept instructions to…attend a police station in circumstances where you do not normally undertake such work'.

**Bar Standards Board**

**Last reviewed: March 2015**

The Bar Standards Board

# Handbook

BAR
STANDARDS
BOARD

REGULATING BARRISTERS

## CURRENT GUIDANCE

## Reporting Serious Misconduct of Others

### Introduction

1. This guidance provides further explanation about your duty to report the serious misconduct of other barristers or registered European lawyers. You should read it in conjunction with Rules C66 to C69 and Guidance C95 to C101 in the BSB Handbook.

2. Rule C66 states that, subject to your duty to keep the affairs of each client confidential and subject also to Rules C67 and C68, you must report to the Bar Standards Board if you have reasonable grounds to believe that there has been serious misconduct by a barrister or a registered European lawyer.

3. The BSB intends this rule to achieve the following outcomes:

    - oC2:1 BSB regulated persons are effectively regulated;
    - oC22: The public have confidence in the proper regulation of persons regulated by the BSB;
    - oC23: The BSB has the information that it needs in order to be able to assess risks and regulate effectively and in accordance with the regulatory objectives.

4. The duty to report serious misconduct was introduced as a rule in the new BSB Handbook, effective from 6 January 2014. This duty is, however, consistent with previous BSB guidance and best practice. It is strongly in the public interest that the BSB is made aware of any serious misconduct. The duty is also consistent with parallel obligations for professionals in other sectors.

5. The BSB recognises that the application of this rule may be particularly difficult in some circumstances. If you require further guidance you may wish to contact the Bar Council's

The Bar Standards Board

# Handbook

BAR
STANDARDS
BOARD

REGULATING BARRISTERS

Ethical Queries Helpline on 020 7611 1307, or at http://www.barcouncil.org.uk/for-the-bar/introduction-to-member-services/ethical-enquiries-line/. This service is confidential and is provided by individuals on an approved list who are not subject to the duty to report serious misconduct of which they become aware as a result of dealing with enquiries on the helpline.

**What should you report?**

6.  You are obliged to report to the BSB instances of serious misconduct by other barristers or registered European lawyers. Whether or not misconduct is *serious* misconduct is a matter of judgement, which will depend on the particular circumstances. It will ultimately be for the BSB to decide whether enforcement or other regulatory action is necessary in the public interest. If, having considered the factors and circumstances discussed below, you remain unsure whether or not the behaviour in question amounts to serious misconduct, you should err on the side of caution and make a report to the BSB.

7.  You should refer to the list at Guidance C96 for examples of serious misconduct; however, you should be aware that this is not a closed list and that breaches of other provisions may also amount to serious misconduct. Whether serious misconduct has occurred may be a question of the degree to which one or more of the obligations in the Handbook has been breached. Guidance C96 lists the following examples of serious misconduct:

    1.  dishonesty (CD3);
    2.  assault or harassment (CD3 and/or CD5 and/or CD8);
    3.  seeking to gain access without consent to *instructions* or other confidential information relating to the opposing party's case (CD3 and/or CD5);
    4.  seeking to gain access without consent to confidential information relating to another member of *chambers*, member of staff or *pupil* (CD3 and/or CD5);

The Bar Standards Board
# Handbook

5.  encouraging a witness to give evidence which is untruthful or misleading (CD1 and/or CD3);

6.  knowingly or recklessly misleading, or attempting to mislead, the *court* or an opponent (CD1 and/or CD3);

7.  being drunk or under the influence of drugs in *court* (CD2 and/or CD7);

8.  failure by a *barrister* to report promptly to the *Bar Standards Board* pursuant to rC66 (duty to report serious misconduct by others);

9.  a breach by a *barrister* of rC70 below [refers to allowing the BSB access to your practice for inspection purposes];

10. professional conduct that poses a serious risk to the public (see paragraph 16 below).

**When discrimination becomes serious misconduct**

8.  Depending on the severity and impact of the discriminatory behaviour, discrimination can constitute serious misconduct.

9.  You should be aware of the seven different types of discrimination under the Equality Act 2010.

10. These are:

    *   Direct discrimination – where someone is treated less favourably than another person because of a protected characteristic[1].

    *   Associative discrimination – this is direct discrimination against someone because they are associated with another person who possesses a protected characteristic.

---

[1] The Equality Act 2010 introduced the term 'protected characteristics' to refer to groups that are protected under the Act. These are: age, disability, gender reassignment, marriage and civil partnership, pregnancy and maternity, race, religion and belief, sex, and sexual orientation.

The Bar Standards Board
# Handbook

REGULATING BARRISTERS

- Discrimination by perception – this is direct discrimination against someone because others think that they possess a particular protected characteristic. They do not necessarily have to possess the characteristic.
- Indirect discrimination – this can occur when a rule or policy that applies to everyone disadvantages a person with a particular protected characteristic.
- Harassment – this is behaviour that is deemed to be offensive by the recipient. Recipients can now complain about behaviour that they find offensive even if it is not directed at them.
- Victimisation – this occurs when someone is treated badly because they have made or supported a complaint or grievance under this legislation.

**Harassment and victimisation**

11. The Bar functions on a system based on trust and confidence between colleagues, and individual barristers depend to a large extent on the reputation they hold amongst their colleagues. In this context it is understandable that some barristers may be concerned about the personal impact of reporting serious misconduct. This is especially the case where the nature of the misconduct itself relates to harassment or victimisation.

12. Harassment is defined in the Equality Act 2010 as:

- Unwanted conduct that has the purpose or effect of creating an intimidating, hostile, degrading, humiliating or offensive environment for the complainant, or violating the complainant's dignity.
- Unwanted conduct of a sexual nature (sexual harassment).
- Treating a person less favourably than another person because they have either submitted to, or did not submit to, sexual harassment or harassment related to sex or gender reassignment.

The Bar Standards Board
# Handbook

13. Rule C69 creates an obligation on all barristers not to victimise anyone for making in good faith a report of serious misconduct. This means that barristers must not treat any individual less favourably because they have made such a report to the BSB. This rule is intended to expressly protect you where you make a report of serious misconduct. It is of vital importance to the intended outcomes of Rule C66, discussed above, that individuals are not discouraged from reporting serious misconduct by the risk of suffering victimisation as a result of doing so.

14. You should also take account of the fact that pupil barristers and barristers of fewer years' standing may be particularly vulnerable due to their relatively junior status within a practice and their relative dependence on more senior barristers for work, guidance and support. Pupils or new entrants to the profession may worry that by reporting to the BSB they will subsequently be treated less favourably or otherwise subjected to unwanted conduct, or that their career may be impacted negatively (whether or not such concerns are well founded in particular instances).

15. If you are a pupil barrister, or relatively new entrant to the profession, who has become aware of behaviour potentially amounting to serious misconduct, you may wish first to discuss your concerns with relevant colleagues, with your supervisor, the head of chambers or head of legal practice. You may wish to establish whether any other person is aware of the misconduct in question and/or whether that individual is willing to report the misconduct, or has already done so. You do not need to make a report yourself if you reasonably believe that another person has already done so. Alternatively, you can contact the Bar Council's Ethical Enquiries Helpline for further assistance.

16. If the matter relates to conduct which affects you personally, or relates to sexual or other harassment, you still remain under an obligation to report serious misconduct to the BSB. However, the BSB will treat any report of discrimination, harassment (whether of a sexual nature or otherwise), or victimisation as sensitively as possible and will not act without first consulting with any alleged victim. Given the sensitivity of this issue, the

The Bar Standards Board
# Handbook

REGULATING BARRISTERS

BSB would not ordinarily expect to take disciplinary action for failing to comply with the duty to report if you believe you are a victim of the misconduct in question. Nevertheless, you should consider the risk that if the matter is not reported, you or others may suffer from similar treatment in the future.

17. In addition to this guidance, barristers should take full account of the equalities obligations in the Handbook and should refer to the equality and diversity good practice guidelines wherever relevant.

18. If you are in doubt as to whether or not particular behaviour amounts to serious misconduct you should consider discussing this with the Bar Council's Ethical Enquiries Helpline (see above). It is important to be aware that by reporting what you believe may be serious misconduct simply puts the BSB in a position to decide what action, if any, to take by making a fair assessment as to whether or not serious misconduct (or any misconduct) has in fact occurred. Action will only be taken in relation to the barrister or lawyer concerned where this is appropriate, proportionate and in accordance with the BSB's policies.

**How should you report?**

19. You should report serious misconduct to the BSB's Professional Conduct Department by completing the 'Reporting Serious Misconduct Form', which is available on the 'Concerns about a barrister' page of the BSB's website: https://www.barstandardsboard.org.uk/complaints-and-professional-conduct/concerns-about-a-barrister/

When you have completed this Form (either by hand or electronically) please send it, along with any supporting documents:

• By e-mail to: AssessmentComplaints@BarStandardsBoard.org.uk; or,

The Bar Standards Board
# Handbook

BAR
STANDARDS
BOARD

REGULATING BARRISTERS

- By post to: Assessment Team, Professional Conduct Department, Bar Standards Board, 289-293 High Holborn, London. WC1V 7HZ.

  Please note, you do not need to use the Form when making a report of serious misconduct; however, any report should include the information covered by the Form.

20. If you would like advice on the reporting process or if you have any access requirements, please contact our Information Line on 020 7611 1445.

21. You should make a report to the BSB as soon as reasonably practicable. You will receive an acknowledgement of receipt of the report, including an explanation of how the BSB will handle the information we receive. The BSB will decide whether the information should form the basis of a complaint against the barrister – if so, the complaint will be made in the name of the BSB, not the barrister who reported the alleged breach. The Professional Conduct Department may also refer the matter to the BSB's Supervision Department as an alternative to raising a formal complaint.

22. Please note that, while the BSB would not normally stay in contact with you once you have made a report and it has been acknowledged, the BSB may request your assistance in supplying further information if it is necessary to carry out a proper assessment of the information or an investigation. All reports made to the BSB will be treated sensitively. If you wish to provide information confidentially, we may be able to take reasonable steps to protect your identity. However, depending on the facts of the case, it may be difficult to take enforcement action without identifying you.

**When should you report?**

23. Your duty to report serious misconduct is intended to help ensure that the BSB has the information that it needs in order to be able to assess risks and regulate effectively and in accordance with the regulatory objectives. With this practical purpose in mind, you are

The Bar Standards Board
# Handbook

not expected to report unnecessarily or simply as a matter of form. Rule C68 removes the duty to report where:

- the relevant facts are already in the public domain; and/or
- you reasonably consider that those facts will have come to the BSB's attention; and/or
- the relevant person has already reported the misconduct to the BSB.

24. Rule C68 exempts you from the duty to report if you are aware that the relevant person who committed the serious misconduct has already reported it to the BSB. In other cases, if you are aware that another relevant person, such as the head of chambers, head of legal practice, or a person or committee within a practice which has responsibility for the administration of that practice or for investigating the matter in the first instance, has made a report, then you do not need to do so yourself. However, if you are aware for any reason that the relevant person or committee has failed to report the matter to the BSB, or if there is another reason for not doing so, you should be prepared to report the matter yourself. Guidance C96 lists failure by a barrister to report such matters promptly to the BSB as an example of potential serious misconduct.

25. You should also apply your professional judgement to whether there has been serious misconduct. Guidance C97 sets out some matters you should consider before reporting. These are:

- whether the individual's *instructions* or other confidential matters might have a bearing on the assessment of their conduct;
- whether the person concerned has been offered an opportunity to explain their conduct, and if not, why not;
- any explanation which has been or could be offered for that person's conduct;
- whether the matter has been raised, or will be raised, in the litigation in which it occurred, and if not, why not.

The Bar Standards Board

# Handbook

26. Depending on the nature of the misconduct, you may also wish to take further circumstances into account. In particular, you should consider whether there is a risk that the misconduct will continue or be repeated if no action is taken. For example, if the individual's behaviour relates to discrimination, harassment, victimisation, there may be a further risk of discrimination, harassment or victimisation occurring in the future (see below).

27. Having taken into account these and any other relevant circumstances, you should then go on to consider whether you have reasonable grounds to believe the individual has committed serious misconduct. You should report misconduct where you have material before you which as it stands establishes a reasonably credible instance of serious misconduct. Issues of competence will not normally constitute serious misconduct unless so serious that it poses a serious risk to the public or would diminish the trust and confidence which the public places in the profession.

28. Rule C67 states that you must never make, or threaten to make, a report of serious misconduct without a genuine and reasonably held belief that the obligation to report applies. For example, you should not report serious misconduct merely speculatively, out of malice, or to use the reporting of misconduct, or the threat of it, as a 'litigation tactic'. You should only make a report with regard to the outcomes which the rule is intended to achieve, described above.

**Barristers acting in a judicial capacity**

29. Serious misconduct before the court will usually be apparent to the judge, and in such cases, the judge hearing the matter may bring the serious misconduct in question to the attention of the BSB. If you are a barrister acting in a judicial capacity, your conduct duties as a judge take precedence over your professional duties as a barrister. The BSB would not expect to take enforcement action against a barrister acting in a judicial

The Bar Standards Board
# Handbook

capacity. Whilst the obligation to report does not impact on a barrister sitting in a judicial capacity, nothing in this guidance should be taken as preventing barristers from reporting to the regulator serious misconduct observed by a barrister, when sitting, in the normal way.

30. Rules E23 – E25 cover the BSB approach to complaints against a regulated person acting in judicial or quasi-judicial capacity. Rule E25 precludes the BSB from exercising enforcement powers in respect of such a regulated person. Any complaint about the conduct of a barrister acting in a judicial capacity made to the BSB will be referred to the Judicial Conduct Investigations Office (http://judicialconduct.judiciary.gov.uk/).

**Bar Standards Board**

**6 January 2014**

**Updated August 2015**

The Bar Standards Board

# Handbook

## Media Comment Guidance

### Introduction

1. Prior to the introduction of the BSB Handbook, the old Code of Conduct was updated in April 2013 to remove the prohibiton on media comment.

2. The Bar Standards Board believes that, consistent with the rights of freedom of expression that are enjoyed by all, the starting point is that barristers are free to make comments to or in the media (this includes both conventional media - speaking to newspapers or broadcasters - and new media - social media, blogs and websites). However, because of the special position they occupy, certain rules will continue to limit the circumstances in which it will be appropriate for barristers to comment on cases in which they have been instructed and what they can properly say.

3. The purpose of this guidance is to clarify the remaining ethical obligations in relation to media comment and to suggest some of the issues that the barrister should bear in mind whilst exercising professional judgment about whether and how to comment. This will require an assessment of many factors, including the nature and type of proceedings, the stage they have reached, the need to ensure that media comment does not prejudice the administration of justice and the nature of the comment that is proposed to be made. More generally, barristers need to consider carefully whether commenting on individual cases in which they have acted would be appropriate and whether the proposed comment would require any individual client's consent. Ill-judged comments on an individual case may cause unintended harm to the interests of the client. The rule change does not, of course, oblige the barrister to make comments. Indeed, many barristers will decline to do so on the basis that they lack experience in speaking to the press and/or commenting in other media.

### Ethical obligations

4. The ethical obligations that apply in relation to your professional practice generally continue to apply in relation to media comment. In particular, barristers should be aware of the following:

> a. **Client's best interests**: Core Duty 2 and Rules C15.1-.2 of the BSB Handbook require a barrister to promote fearlessly and by all proper and lawful means the lay client's best interests and to do so without regard to his or her own interests.

The Bar Standards Board
# Handbook

b. **Independence**: Core Duties 3 and 4 provide that you must not permit your absolute independence, integrity and freedom from external pressures to be compromised.

c. **Trust and confidence**: Core Duty 5 provides that you must not behave in a way which is likely to diminish the trust and confidence which the public places in you or the profession.

d. **Confidentiality**: Core Duty 6 and Rule C15.5 require you to preserve the confidentiality of your lay client's affairs and you must not undermine this unless permitted to do so by law or with the express consent of the lay client.

## Legal issues

5. Media comment which causes a substantial risk of serious prejudice of current or pending proceedings may lead to proceedings for contempt of court.

6. Barristers should also be aware of the risk of personal liability for claims in defamation or malicious falsehood against the barrister, or even against the client (if the barrister is speaking on the client's behalf). Barristers' professional indemnity insurance does not usually cover liability for such claims.

# INDEX

## A

**abuse of role in court** 86–7
  insults 10–11, 86
  making allegations 11, 86–8
  personal opinions 12
  putting your case 11
**administration**
  of chambers 38, 126–8
  of legal practice 38, 126–8
**advertising**
  pupillage vacancies 187
  soliciting work 17, 92
**association with others** 37–8, 123–4
**authorisation** 47, 154–6
**authorised body**
  definition 45, 47
  scope of practice 161–2

## B

**Bar Professional Training Course
  (BPTC)** 3–5
**Bar Standards Board** 1
  authorised body 45, 47, 161–2
  authorised individuals 37
  authorised person 37
  Code of Conduct *see* **Code of
    conduct**
  duty to *see* **duty to Bar Standards
    Board**
  Legal Ombudsman 34, 117, 256
  QASA *see* **Quality Assurance
    Scheme for Advocates**
  regulated person 3
**Bar Standards Board Handbook** 2
  'cab rank' rule 239–40
  Code of Conduct text 80–201
  complaints handling 241–62
  confidentiality 266–7
  public access work 215–37
  referrals and marketing 262–5
  unregistered barristers 203–13
**Bar Training Rules** 52, 178–99
  academic stage 181
  admission to Inns of Court *see* **Inns
    of Court**
  call to the Bar *see* **call to the Bar**
  conduct of students 52–3, 195–6
  exemptions 191–4
  professional stage 183–9
  pupillage *see* **pupillage**
  purpose 178

qualifying sessions 190
  students *see* **students**
  vocational stage 182
**barristers**
  duty to court *see* **duty to court**
  employed 48, 163, 164–5
  immigration advisors and 41
  licensed access work 40–1, 143–4
  personal opinions 12
  public access work 39–40, 140–2,
    215–37
  self-employed *see* **self-employed
    barristers**
  training *see* **Bar Training Rules;
    pupillage**
  unregistered 3, 44–5, 146–7,
    203–13

## C

**'cab rank' rule** 105–7
  BSB guidance 239–40
  declining instructions 22
  diary clash 28
  disapplying 28–9
  discrimination and 26–8
  fees and 28–9
  professional negligence liability 28
**call to the Bar**
  call days and procedure 197
  postponed 53
  requirement to call 197
  review and appeals 198
  temporary call of foreign
    lawyers 193–4
**chambers**
  administration of 38, 126–8
  complaints procedure *see*
    **complaints**
  pupillage funding 138–9
**clerk's fees** 16
**client money** 119–21
  definition of 35–6
  fixed fee 36–7
  key principle 35
  third party services 37, 119
**clients**
  duty to *see* **duty to client**
  inexperienced 44–5
  without solicitor
    licensed access work 40–1, 143–4
    public access work 39–40, 140–2,
      215–37

**Code of Conduct** 2–3, 65–7
  Bar Professional Training Course
    (BPTC) 3–5
  conflicting duties 68–71
  core duties *see* **core duties**
  outcomes focus 2
  text 80–201
  tripartite reference system 2–3
  underpinning values 67–71
**competent standard of work or
    service** 20–1, 94–7
**complaints** 42–3
  Bar Standards Board 33–4, 241–62
  documents and record keeping 132
  Legal Ombudsman 34, 117, 256
  provision of information 131–2
  response to 132
  self-employed barristers 131–2
**confidentiality**
  BSB guidance 266–7
  declining instructions 22
  duty to client 21–2
  legal professional privilege 57, 60
  misleading the court 8–10, 21,
    97–8
  non-disclosure
    of criminal record 10
    of document 9
    of guilt 9
  'normal circumstances' 22
  public funding 22
  waived 22
  *see also* **Proceeds of Crime Act 2002**
**conflicts of interest** 19–20, 22
**continuing professional
    development rules** 53, 200–1
**core duties** 2, 3, 83
  BSB regulated person 3
  guidance 2, 83
  non-discrimination 16–17, 92
  outcomes 2
  regulations 2
  rules 2
**court, duty to** *see* **duty to court**
**criminal record**
  non-disclosure of 10
**cross-border activities** 148–9
  correspondence between
    lawyers 149
  disputes 149
  fee-sharing with non-lawyers 148
  incompatible occupations 148
  responsibility for fees 149